ADVANCE PRAISE FOR *Friends With Benefits*

"If you're ready to get off the sidelines and get serious about social media marketing, you must read this book first. *Friends With Benefits* is tactical, practical, and above all, useful."
—LEE LEFEVER, COMMON CRAFT

"This book is invaluable and there's nothing like it out there in terms of a realistic portrayal of what works and what doesn't."
—CHRIS ABRAHAM, MARKETING CONVERSATION

"[*Friends With Benefits*] offers some great tips for even the most experienced marketers out there."
—ALYSSA GREGORY, SITEPOINT

"*Friends With Benefits* is a must-read for social media marketers and those new to the field."
—MONIQUE TROTTIER, SO MISGUIDED

"For experienced marketers looking to keep up on their own industries as well as learn the intricate details of social media, I recommend adding this book to your reading list."
—ERIC TSAI, DESIGNDAMAGE

"[*Friends With Benefits* is] very clear, easy to read, and non-threatening."
—MARK DYKEMAN, BROADCASTING BRAIN

"Finally! Here's the book you should buy for your clueless friends (you might learn something too)."
—SETH GODIN, AUTHOR OF *Tribes*

"[*Friends With Benefits*] would make a good resource to pass on to a client or executive you are working with who needs to learn the value and basic practicalities of social media marketing."
—NANCY NALLY, WEBWORKERDAILY

Friends With Benefits

A Social Media Marketing Handbook

by Darren Barefoot *and* Julie Szabo

no starch
press

13 12 11 10 09   1 2 3 4 5 6 7 8 9

ISBN-10: 1-59327-199-9
ISBN-13: 978-1-59327-199-2

Publisher: William Pollock
Production Editor: Philip Dangler
Cover Design: Octopod Studios
Developmental Editor: Tyler Ortman
Technical Reviewer: Kate Trgovac
Copyeditor: LeeAnn Pickrell
Compositor: Riley Hoffman
Proofreader: Emily Quill
Indexer: Karin Arrigoni

For information on book distributors or translations, please contact No Starch Press, Inc. directly:

No Starch Press, Inc.
555 De Haro Street, Suite 250, San Francisco, CA 94107
phone: 415.863.9900; fax: 415.863.9950; info@nostarch.com; www.nostarch.com

Library of Congress Cataloging-in-Publication Data:
Barefoot, Darren Kyle, 1974-
 Friends with benefits : a social media marketing handbook / Darren Barefoot and Julie Lynn Szabo.
-- 1st ed.
    p. cm.
 Includes index.
 ISBN-13: 978-1-59327-199-2
 ISBN-10: 1-59327-199-9
 1. Internet marketing. 2. Online social networks. I. Szabo, Julie Lynn, 1975- II. Title.
 HF5415.1265B3334 2009
 658.8'72--dc22
                         2009032426

For our mothers, who made us writers.

BRIEF CONTENTS

Foreword by Shel Israel xvii

Acknowledgments xxi

Introduction: A Window into the World of
Social Media Marketing xxiii

Chapter 1: What Is Social Media? 1

Chapter 2: Get Social Media Ready. 21

Chapter 3: Flagging a Ride: Finding the Right Bloggers
and Communities 47

Chapter 4: Netiquette: Miss Manners for the Web 63

Chapter 5: Stick Out Your Thumb: Devising Your Pitch 79

Chapter 6: Measuring Success: How to Monitor the Web 99

Chapter 7: Is Social Media Marketing Risky Business? 115

Chapter 8: Damage Control in the Digital Age 131

Chapter 9: Does MySpace Still Matter? 155

Chapter 10: Understanding Facebook 171

Chapter 11: Video Marketing with YouTube and
Other Video Sharing Sites 195

Chapter 12: The Twitter Revolution 219

Chapter 13: The Power of Crowds: Understanding and
Participating in Online Communities 239

Afterword 261

Recommended Reading. 263

Index. 265

CONTENTS IN DETAIL

Foreword by Shel Israel xvii

Acknowledgments xxi

**Introduction: A Window into the World of
Social Media Marketing**. xxiii
How to Learn the Lingo xxiv
Who Is This Book For? xxv
This Book Isn't for You If... xxv
Getting Around: What You'll Learn. xxvi

Chapter 1: What Is Social Media? 1
The Rise of the Social Network 3
Five Fundamentals of Social Media 4
    It's About Democracy: A Communication Revolution 4
    It's About Community: We Are Family 7

It's About Collaboration: Two Heads (or Millions)
    Really Are Better Than One 7
It's About Scope: The Infinite Internet 10
It's About Authenticity: A Cult of Honesty. 10
Social Media Channels: What Are They and
    How Can You Use Them? 11
What Is Social Media Marketing? 13
    Why Should You Embrace Social Media Marketing? 14
    How Does Social Media Fit with Your Marketing Goals? . .15
Now for Some Sober Second Thoughts 16
Hitting the Trail: What You'll Need to Get Started 18
    Time, Time, and More Time .18
    Boss Buy-In 18
    The Buddy System 19
    The Best Books and Blogs 19
Surfing the Wave of Change 19

Chapter 2: Get Social Media Ready. 21
RSS 101 22
    RSS Feeds and Readers. 24
    Mainlining Data. 26
Entering the Blogosphere: The Basics of Launching a
    Corporate Blog 28
    How Do You Start? 29
    Should You Build Your Own Blogging Software? 30
    Who Should Blog? 30
    Why Should You Write a Blog? 31
    What Should You Write About? 33
    How Often Should You Blog? .33
    How Will You Manage All the Feedback? 34
    Where Should the Blog Live? .34
    A Few Blogging Don'ts. 35
Prepping Your Website for Social Media Outreach 37
    Link Me Up 38
    The Social Media Resource Page. 39
The Social Media News Release. 43

Chapter 3: Flagging a Ride: Finding the Right Bloggers and Communities 47

Three Buckets of Blogs 48
Size Matters, and Yes, It Is a Popularity Contest 49
Learn to Read the Road Signs 50
    Finding Blogs with Google. .51
    Metrics: Making a List, Checking It Twice 52
    Google PageRank and Trends. 53
    Technorati, BlogPulse, IceRocket . . . the List Goes On . . .55
    Alexa, Compete, and Quantcast. 56
    Count RSS Subscribers. 57
    Be a Bit Skeptical 58
Don't Overlook Anecdotal Evidence 58
    Blogrolls: Who Is Your BFF? 58
    A Little Help from Your Friends. 59
Trust Your Instincts. 60

Chapter 4: Netiquette: Miss Manners for the Web 63

Lesson #1: Listen First. 64
Lesson #2: Take Baby Steps 65
Lesson #3: Make Friends. 67
Lesson #4: Lay Your Cards on the Table 67
Lesson #5: Bloggers Aren't Journalists 69
Lesson #6: Your Reputation Precedes You 70
Lesson #7: Don't Be a Social Media Spammer 71
Lesson #8: Don't Fib 72
Who Are These New Influencers, Anyway? 74
    Margaret Mason, Shopping Diva at Mighty Goods 74
    Muhammad Saleem on Getting Dugg 75
    For Marshall Kirkpatrick, It's Just the Facts, Ma'am 76
Etiquette Cheat Sheet 77

Chapter 5: Stick Out Your Thumb: Devising Your Pitch. 79

Drums or Smoke Signals: Which Channel to Choose? 82
Pitch Tactics We've Tried. 85
    An "Illuminating" Email Pitch. 85
    Other Ways to Woo 86

Other Blogger Outreach Campaigns We Like 91
It's Not Always About the Pitch: Finding Other
        Creative Ways to Get Noticed 93
What Not to Do 94
Don't Bribe the Border Guard 96
Rules for Following Up 97

Chapter 6: Measuring Success: How to Monitor the Web. . . .99
What Does Success Look Like? 100
Be Realistic. Be Humble. 105
Tricks of the Trade: Tools for Measuring Success 105
    Web Analytics: Your Foreign Language Phrase Book 105
    Google Alerts: An Oldie but a Goodie 106
    Web Monitoring 2.0 106
    The One-Stop Web Monitoring Shop 109
Talking Back: How to Respond to Posts 111
If You Don't Measure, You Can't Manage 113

Chapter 7: Is Social Media Marketing Risky Business? 115
Risk #1: Your Campaign Doesn't Get off the Ground 116
    Secrets to Building Long-Term Relationships 117
    You're Just an Average Joe 118
Risk #2: Blogger Backlash 118
Risk #3: The Crowd Talks Back. 120
Risk #4: You Get Rejected. 121
Risk #5: Your Initiative Dies on the Vine 122
Risk #6: Ignoring Other Marketing Channels 124
Risk #7: Too Much Success, Too Soon. 125
Risk #8: Not Being Proactive. 126
Risk #9: You Will Be Measured 128
Risk #10: Someone Gets Cold Feet 128
Proceed with Caution, Not Cowardice 129

Chapter 8: Damage Control in the Digital Age. 131
A Crisis Management Primer 132
Can Social Media Make Your Crisis Worse?. 133
    The Internet Insta-Crisis. 133

The Predictable Pile-On 134
The Internet Never Forgets, Remember?. 135
Do You Really Have a Crisis on Your Hands? 136
What Is Social Media's Role in Crisis Communications? 139
Rules for Making Social Media Work for You in a Crisis 140
    Rule #1: Don't Hide. 140
    Rule #2: Use Your Blog as a Crisis Management Tool. . . .142
    Rule #3: Monitor the Web Closely. 142
    Rule #4: Clean Up Your Mess with the Right Channels . .144
    Rule #5: Consider "Search" in Your Crisis Strategy. 145
    Rule #6: Outfit Your Website for a Crisis 146
Social Media Pitfalls and How to Avoid Them. 148
    Get Yourself a Lightweight Blogging Policy 148
    What Does a Blogging Policy Look Like? 149
    Test-Run Your Campaign. 151
    Own Your Social Media Campaign Assets 152

Chapter 9: Does MySpace Still Matter?. 155
MySpace 101. 156
    Demographics: Who Goes There? 158
    How Does MySpace Work? 159
    From Social Platform to Social Phenomenon 160
Marketing with MySpace 161
MySpace Marketing Success Stories. 162
    Roller Warehouse 162
    Weird Al Yankovic: "White and Nerdy" on MySpace 164
    Obama Takes the White House with the Help of
        Social Networks 164
    Catering to the MySpace Crowd 165
    Banging the Drums with MySpace. 166
    Tatango and MySpace's Network Effect 168
Tips and Tricks for MySpace Marketers. 169
What's Next for MySpace?. 170

Chapter 10: Understanding Facebook. 171
Profiles and the Network Effect. 173
Anatomy of a Facebook Profile 174

The Basics 177
    Events 178
    Groups and Pages: Which to Use? 178
    Market Passively. 182
    Case Study: Chicken, Biscuits, and Facebook. 182
An Appetite for Fun 183
    Don't Be Apprehensive. 184
    Working with Facebook App Developers 186
    Advertising on Facebook 187
    Case Study: Sharpening Perception with Mystery and
        Social Networks 188
    Case Study: Self-Propelled Video on Facebook. 191
The Future of Facebook and the Facebook of the Future 193

**Chapter 11: Video Marketing with YouTube and
Other Video Sharing Sites** 195
Why Make YouTube a Marketing Channel? 197
Setting Your Expectations and Measuring Results 198
What Makes a Popular YouTube Video? 200
Funny Beats Pretty 205
The Wisdom of Stealth Videos 206
Your Latest Picture 208
Marketing with YouTube Videos 209
    Set the Stage. 210
    Pick the Right Title 211
    Describe and Lead with a Link. 211
    Categorize and Tag Responsibly 212
    Play Nice with Others 212
    Join Groups 212
    Curate with Playlists. 213
    Include Videos in Pitches. 214
    Feature Videos in Other Communication Channels. 214
    Annotate Your Videos. 214
Case Study: Elastic Path Makes E-commerce Platforms
        Fun—No, Really. 215
YouTube Killed the Video Star 217

Chapter 12: The Twitter Revolution .219

From Broadcast to Conversation 220
Getting Started with Twitter 222
    Know Your DMs from Your Hash Tags 224
    Tweeting Beyond the Browser 226
Tweeting for Fun and Profit 227
Case Study: Insta-Fundraising with Twitter 231
Ten Ways to Be a Jerk on Twitter 233
Beyond the Twitterdome 237

**Chapter 13: The Power of Crowds: Understanding and
Participating in Online Communities** 239

Social News and the Wisdom of Crowds 240
    Why Marketers Should Care About Social News 241
    Using Social News to Build Buzz 242
Social Bookmarking and Crowdsourced Curation 245
    A Social Bookmarking Primer .245
    How Marketers Can Benefit from Social Bookmarking . .249
Should You Build Your Own Social Network? 251
What About Wikipedia? 254
Photo Sharing with Flickr 257
Stand Out in Your Crowd 259

Afterword 261

Recommended Reading 263
Books 263
Blogs and Websites 264

Index 265

If you want to know why your business needs to understand, embrace, and participate in social media, do not start by reading this book. Instead, if you have kids, go down the hall and watch them for a while. If you don't have kids of your own, spend some time with a friend's kids.

Watch them playing, communicating, and learning. Notice how much of their lives—for better or worse—are being spent online. Watch what influences them. If they are old enough, you may notice that what they buy, watch, listen to, or read is largely affected by peers they meet online, not by ads on any form of paper.

Watching children is the best possible way to see the future. In a few short years, they will be graduating from college, entering the marketplace, and replacing my generation and the habits we have formed. At their desks—if they still have desks—they will be using the tools they grew up with.

I grew up at a time when business tools included rotary dial telephones, carbon paper, manual typewriters with correction tape, and #2 erasable pencils. We listened to AM radio in our cars and we paid attention to billboards when we drove past them.

All that stuff is now so terribly retro; so yesterday; so quaint and obsolete.

What does all that have to do with this book and the wisdom and information that Julie Szabo and Darren Barefoot have jammed into it? For that matter, what does all that have to do with you and your business and social media?

The answer to both these questions is the same: almost everything. Your children and my grandkids are the future. The habits they are forming now will remain with them and shape everyone's future; they have moved online, and the online world is social.

When these kids enter the workplace, social media tools will be as familiar to them as my #2 pencil was when I took notes in elementary school. When they are assigned projects at work, they will be using the social media tools they know and grew up with.

When they do research for purchasing or voting, for movies or music, restaurants or jobs, chances are overwhelming that they will be using online interactive resources.

And Julie Szabo and Darren Barefoot have put together in this book a simple, straightforward, professional, and comprehensive compendium of the tools, tactics, etiquette, and benefits of social media. Not only that, they've made it a good read.

Friends With Benefits reminds me of a compendium of my youth: *The Boy Scout's Handbook*. First published in 1911, it is now approximately in its 19 zillionth edition. In its almost 100 years in print, the contents have changed dramatically, but each edition covers a whole lot of ground on a whole lot of timely subjects for the period and the youth each edition is intended to serve.

Yet despite all the changes in subject matter, certain aspects have remained the same. *The Boy Scout's Handbook* still teaches preparedness, it still teaches ethical behavior, and it still teaches you how to do a whole lot of neat stuff.

Friends With Benefits delivers the same: preparedness, ethical behavior, and useful how-to stuff on a whole lot of subjects related to social media in business. Both books also serve as survival handbooks for their times and places. In business today, you need to adapt and understand social media if you want your business to survive these rapidly changing, rapidly evolving times.

Friends With Benefits, like the scouting handbook, will probably need to be updated from time to time as the tools of social media evolve. But it will also remain constant in giving you a sense of the big picture, of a world that has moved from one-way messages to conversations. It will show you the benefits of listening and responding over treating customers like targets.

It is a manual for surviving a fundamental change in business and having fun while you're doing it. Enjoy reading it. And enjoy following its map into a new age that I call the Conversational Era.

Shel Israel
San Carlos, CA
October 2009

ACKNOWLEDGMENTS

First, we're deeply indebted to our families. We stand on the generous, broad shoulders of our parents, grandparents, and siblings. They've always supported our sundry writerly pursuits and passed on invaluable wisdom that we apply every day.

Many thanks to Bill and the rest of the team at No Starch for leading us, gently but firmly, through the process of writing our first hardcopy book. Tyler, our editor, demonstrated remarkable patience in accommodating our endless questions and inquiries. Likewise, we're indebted to Kate Trgovac's tireless and exacting work as this book's technical reviewer.

Thanks also to Shel, for writing the excellent foreword to this book. We've admired his work since the early days of blogging, so we're honored to have him contribute. We're also grateful for the proof-reading help of Lesley McKnight and the Trinity Western University English department.

We'd be remiss in not recognizing the dozens of clients of Capulet Communications, our company, who acted as guinea pigs for the lessons we learned and wrote about in this book. We're very grateful for the trust they've placed in us over the years. We also appreciate the many experts and gurus we interviewed. Without their contributions, this book wouldn't exist.

This book has its origins in an earlier ebook entitled *Getting to First Base*. We're digital nomads in training, and so we wrote that ebook and this book at improvised desks and café tables on three continents. We're grateful to many patient restaurateurs and house managers who put up with our lingering cups of coffee and odd requests. Among our favorites were Rangers, a bar in the tiny Maltese village of Gharb (try the funghi pizza); Punta Laurel, some thatched huts above a reef on the Caribbean coast of Panama; and Long Beach Lodge on BC's beautiful coast.

INTRODUCTION:
A WINDOW INTO THE WORLD OF SOCIAL
MEDIA MARKETING

Before you leave on a trip or move to a new country, you make all kinds of preparations. You purchase plane tickets, make a packing list, and exchange your dollars for Euros. But the most important pre-trip purchase is always a guidebook. Sometimes it's a small guide to a city or a detailed map; other times it's a 10-pound tome that you regret buying the moment you put it in your crammed daypack. We love to travel and appreciate good travel advice, which is why we're so pleased to be your guides in the new frontier of social media marketing.

Friends With Benefits is a guidebook to understanding and interpreting the culture and language—spoken and unspoken—of social media creators. Like exploring a new country, learning how to communicate with the locals respectfully and honestly is a big part of running successful social media marketing initiatives.

We're like tour guides in other ways, too. We can help lessen social media culture shock. We'll help you translate foreign phrases into concepts and ideas you can easily understand. We'll introduce you to the nuances, idioms, and cultural niceties of the Web. We'll show you how to avoid embarrassing faux pas and charm the people you most want to impress. We want to see you explore the social media landscape on your own, and we hope that this book will help you get there and enjoy the sights and sounds once you arrive.

So why would you want us as your social media guides? For starters, we live and work in the Web 2.0 world. Darren began writing his personal blog in 2001. He still blogs several times a week and darrenbarefoot.com ranks as one of Canada's most popular blogs. Julie ran her first blogger outreach campaign in 2004, when most marketers thought a blog was endangered wetland. We co-founded Canada's first blogging and personal publishing conference, Northern Voice, in 2004. Most important, we believe in the power of social media marketing.

This book contains plenty of our personal anecdotes, hard-won wisdom, and stories of the successes and failures we've had when marketing to online influencers. We're not holding anything back. We've distilled our web marketing experience and extracted the best ideas and lessons. Plus, we've stolen (an old tech writing boss called it *distealing*) the most useful wisdom we've come across in our combined 15 years in the industry and included many of those stories as well.

How to Learn the Lingo

At the start of 2008, we lived in Morocco for three months. Acclimating to warm January days and the smell of fresh mint in the air was easy. But running day-to-day errands in a foreign language was a real challenge and often led to some unwelcome outcomes.

More than once these pesco-vegetarians inadvertently ordered beef or lamb tagine. But, with a little help from a phrase book, tips from friendly neighbors, and a strong dose of courage, we learned how to barter like locals by the end of our trip. We even mastered a few Arabic phrases.

The Web has its own language too. That's why we've tried to define many of the social media terms and idioms you may not know. You'll be fluent in no time!

NOTE   *Throughout this book, we use synonyms for the mélange of people who are social media creators and* new *influencers. We often call them bloggers, which can mean podcasters, video bloggers, Facebook alpha users, and Twitter addicts. If all that's Greek to you, don't worry. By the end of the book, you'll know your souvlaki from your Oedipus.*

Who Is This Book For?

This book is for marketers. But of course, everyone is a marketer these days, so it's really for anyone with customers to please.

You may be an account manager at a PR agency, the CEO of a technology startup, or a project manager at an environmental agency. You might be a coordinator inside a 20-person marketing department or a product marketer at a 5-person startup. Heck, you might even be an author. Whether you're a straight-up marketer, a fundraiser, or a small business owner, this book is chock full of ideas, case studies, and tips you can use to promote your organization online.

This Book Isn't for You If...

We're loath to say it, but there are a few groups who probably won't reap much benefit from this guidebook. This book isn't for you if:

- You don't know the Internet from a Christmas cactus. This is not an introduction to the Web, and you'll be lost by the end of this chapter. If you're looking for a more general overview of the Web, we recommend *Blogging for Dummies*.

- You're a senior executive vice president at a Fortune 500 company and you're looking to make a six-figure technology investment. This book is about spending time, not money.

- You're already swimming in the social media Kool-Aid. If you've been a blogger for five years and have more than 500 Facebook friends, you're going to enjoy limited returns. There are a number of case studies and anecdotes that will be new to you, but the rest will probably be old hat.

- Your target market is under the age of sixteen. This book is about marketing to adults—teens and tweens live in a different world. That's another book completely. We've included some recommended reading at the end of the book for marketing to the adolescent crowd.

- You just want to sell widgets. We can help you get your message out and build relationships with online influencers, but we're marketers, not sales folks. We learned everything we know about closing a deal from *Glengarry Glen Ross*.

Getting Around: What You'll Learn

Each chapter of this book tackles a different facet of social media marketing, so you don't have to read this book cover-to-cover to step up your web marketing game. But if you do, here are some of the lessons you'll learn along the way:

How to find your way around the social media landscape
You'll learn the difference between an online community, a platform, and a channel, and will get some solid pointers on how to interact with people in these spaces. You'll learn how to identify the players and online influencers, and how to avoid negative dealings with the natives.

How to launch a social media relations campaign
We'll talk you through the basics of running a social media relations campaign—from choosing the right bloggers to outlining the best methods for contacting these busy, influential folks.

How to make your website social media ready

You'll learn how to make it as easy as possible for content creators—bloggers, podcasters, videocasters, and web journalists—to write about your product on their websites. In just a few hours, you'll be able to make your old-school brochure site social media ready.

Ideas and inspiration for original approaches in your own campaigns

We provide plenty of real-world examples of the kinds of social media relations campaigns that succeed, as well as typical points of failure.

How to avoid the risks and pitfalls of social media marketing

You'll learn how to steer clear of newbie mistakes that could put your online reputation—or your company's good name—at risk.

By the end of this book, you'll know *RSS* from *tweets* and *astroturfing* from *analytics*. But first, on to Chapter 1, where we examine the principles of social media and how they affect marketers and other web citizens.

1

Picture Derek, a computer nerd in the mid-1980s. He's pecking away on his Apple IIe and surfing the precursor to the Internet. He's using a 1200-baud modem over his phone line to connect to a *bulletin board system* (*BBS*), a hobbyist-run mini-network. Derek occasionally posts a message. But he mostly spends time downloading cracked software and erotic pictures at an excruciatingly slow three kilobytes per second.

One *is* the loneliest number. Right?

Now for the real picture. The early BBSs were actually very social. They were often *hyperlocal*—specific to a particular offline neighborhood or community—and offered a way to exchange messages and a full menu of text-based online games and computer programs. Users logged on, left each other messages, and played games.[*] A precursor to craigslist, BBSs were fertile ground for making real-world CD, book, and magazine trades. We've miscast Derek as a loner, when in fact he's using these nascent networks to engage with other modem-enabled humans. He's part of the world's earliest online social network. He may even be using this network to meet girls and fall in love. In 2008, the *Chicago Tribune* reported the 25th anniversary of Chris Dunn and Pam Jensen, a couple who first met on a CompuServe chat program that linked computer users nationwide.[†] After a few months of online flirting, Dunn flew across the country to spend the weekend with Jensen. They married a year later and are still together today. Here's the important point: The connections we make with other people online are *real*.

Over the next decade, the conversations that happened on BBSs and Usenet expanded onto the World Wide Web proper, and BBSs began to die off in favor of chat rooms and Internet forums. Then came the late 1990s, the warm glow of the dot-com boom, and the idea that anyone could create and publish a web page. Companies like GeoCities and desktop programs like Microsoft FrontPage made it possible for ordinary humans to build websites about anything and everything. By today's standards, these page designs looked like something your schnauzer coughed up, but the content was what mattered. The Internet was no longer the domain of academics, scientists, and computer geeks. Ordinary people were, with their animated GIFs and pink-on-black text, demonstrating that the Web was becoming a true town square. HTTP-colon-double-slash (*http://*) signified a new kind of democracy.

---

[*] Jason Scott's website *http://www.textfiles.com/* celebrates the early years of online interaction with a collection of nostalgic short stories about life before the World Wide Web, all submitted by BBS users.
[†] Heidi Stevens, "Chicago Couple Blazed the Trail for Internet Love," *Chicago Tribune*, May 18, 2008.

The Rise of the Social Network

Blogs emerged out of the online diaries of the mid-1990s. In 1999, the first commercial blogging services—Blogger and LiveJournal—were launched. Blogs started making serious inroads in 2002 and rapidly rose in popularity over the next few years.

At the heart of the blog explosion was the convergence of a number of technical phenomena. Simplified web publishing tools were a real trigger. Writing a blog became as easy as composing and sending an email message. Similarly, mass adoption of affordable broadband Internet access at home made creating and managing websites easier than ever. Astonishingly, home broadband adoption grew by 40 percent from March 2005 to March 2006, twice the growth rate of the year before.[*] At the same time, consumer electronics, including PCs and laptops, fell in price, making home computing a reality for the first time for many North American families.

While technology may have sparked the blog revolution, technology has never been *the* driving force behind online social interaction. From BBSs to chat rooms, forums, and blogs, human nature is at the heart of creating and building online communities. From the very beginning of computer networking, the Web has been a place for social interaction. That's why we call it *social* media.

Blogs, social networks like Facebook, and microblogging platforms like Twitter are simply technologies that foster communication, sharing, and collaboration. These social media tools fit into a bucket of technologies sometimes called *Web 2.0*, a term you may have come across in your travels. Although online interaction is nothing new, these highly networked technologies make massive, global online communication accessible to anyone with an Internet connection. Even more profound, they add a participatory element to online communications. Blogs and social networks invite participation. With the click of a button, they turn audiences into creators and strangers into friends. Far from being a loner in his basement, Derek was at the forefront of a communication revolution.

---

[*] John B. Horrigan, "Home Broadband Adoption 2006," Pew Internet & American Life Project, May 28, 2006, *http://www.pewinternet.org/Reports/2006/Home-Broadband-Adoption-2006.aspx*.

The Shift to a Conversational Web

Here's another way to think about social media and Web 2.0, compared with the "read-only" Web that came before it:

Web 1.0 was about . . .	Web 2.0 is about . . .
Reading	Writing
Advertising	Word of mouth
Lectures	Conversations
Websites	Web services
Professionals	Amateurs
Companies	Communities
Owning	Sharing

Five Fundamentals of Social Media

We've discussed how technology enabled today's online communications revolution, but more importantly, the philosophy behind Web 2.0 has driven that technological innovation. The fundamental notion of the Web as a social space for interaction and connection shapes technology and is what gives us blogs, Facebook, MySpace, and YouTube. To learn how to use these tools, it is helpful to understand why they were designed in the first place. These five fundamental tenets shape the culture, customs, and technologies of today's social web.

It's About Democracy: A Communication Revolution

To get a broader understanding of how social media fosters richer, more collaborative communication, let's look at how it differs from traditional media. Admittedly, as the two forms blend and merge, this comparison becomes less explicit. Newspapers now pay more attention to their web presence, and you can see YouTube videos on the nightly news. Still, the differences help to illustrate the core values of social media.

Here's a snapshot of the mainstream media in 1998. Some of the nation's most celebrated papers of the day are the *New York Times*, the *Wall Street Journal*, and the *Los Angeles Times*. Nielsen

Media Research ratings for July 1998 put *60 Minutes* at the top of primetime TV and have *NBC Nightly News* and *ABC World News Tonight* battling it out for the nightly news top spot. TV news is delivered by anchors we know and trust—Peter Jennings on ABC, Dan Rather on CBS, and Tom Brokaw at NBC. Millions of readers and viewers consume news from these sources, and individuals have little or no input into what news is reported or how stories are covered. The only audience feedback mechanism is the letter to the editor, which is often shortened or edited by the newspaper. The balance of power isn't just attitudinal; it's financial. The cost of broadcast and print communication that reaches a global audience makes news-making unthinkable for all but the biggest networks and corporations.

Flash forward a decade to 2008. The prevalence of broadband Internet access and social media technologies are disrupting the broadcast or *one-to-many* media model. Thanks to webzines, blogs, podcasts, and YouTube, media consumers are talking back to media creators or becoming media creators themselves—all for the low price of a broadband connection. The Internet has become a public venue where the audience responds to news reports, suggests stories to cover, and even reports on stories. The media is well on its way to being democratized. As NYU professor Clay Shirky says, "The future presented by the Internet is the mass amateurization of publishing and a switch from 'Why publish this?' to 'Why not?'"[*]

Reporting the nightly news is no longer a file-and-forget exercise in serial publishing but has evolved into a developing discussion. The simplest example of this conversation is the ubiquitous *comments* form that follows nearly every blog post on the Web. Even staunch, mainstream media corporations—the ones with all the power a decade ago—are giving up some control, adding comments forms to articles published on their websites. The mainstream media even send out calls for amateur videos of news events to show during broadcasts.

The rise of citizen journalism is a poignant example of how the model is changing. Now the audience takes an active role in

---

[*] Clay Shirky, *Here Comes Everybody: The Power of Organizing Without Organizations*, New York, NY: Penguin Group (2008), p. 60.

collecting, analyzing, reporting, and spreading news and information. Citizen journalism goes by many names: user-generated content, open source journalism, citizen media, participatory journalism, and crowd-powered news. Importantly, citizen journalists are not trained professionals. Anyone can write about an event in her community and post it to her blog. You might upload digital photos of a news event to Flickr, send your own video clip to the nightly news, or simply post it on YouTube. And voilà, you're a citizen journalist.

Citizen journalism on the Web is most often expressed in one of the following ways:

Participatory news sites like OhmyNews and NowPublic These networks publish news submitted by citizen reporters from all around the world, and the sites are really taking off. In its first year, NowPublic published reports from thousands of citizen journalists in over 140 countries. Though some contributors may be professional writers, none of the reporters are paid for their submissions.

Collaborative and contributory news sites like Digg, reddit, and Newsvine On these sites you can read stories submitted by both established media organizations and by individual contributors. Unlike newspapers or television news, the front page stories are determined by the site's own community. The community votes stories to the top of the page or buries them where they'll get far fewer views.

Blogs and forums Many bloggers do their own sleuthing and publish news stories to their personal sites, group sites, or forums. The political forum FreeRepublic.com blew the whistle on Dan Rather by correctly suggesting the documents used in his 2004 *60 Minutes* report about former President Bush's military record were bogus.

Independent news and information websites like the Huffington Post and the Drudge Report These independent news sites look a lot like traditional media, but they aren't part of a media conglomerate, so they have more freedom to cover news stories and voice opinions than CNN or FOX News.

For marketers and PR professionals who rely on the media to get their messages out to audiences, understanding the shift toward citizen journalism, collaborative communications, and the growing power of alternative online media sources can affect how they shape their media strategy, who they contact, and how they interact with these new influencers.

It's About Community: We Are Family

The notion of community was largely absent from traditional media. The one-to-many model didn't invite discussion, nor did it give individuals the ability to open significant discourse on topics outside of the mainstream media's radar. Social media tools enable like-minded people—be they bird watchers, Québécois undertakers, or Vietnam veterans—to find each other. This is a key benefit of social media marketing. Niche communities exist for all kinds of interests. The low cost and simplicity of setting up a website or running a blog or online community mean that Birkenstock fanatics, figure-skating fans, Nikon D70 users, and high-jump enthusiasts can all have their own online real estate. The Web slices our interests—and target demographics—more thinly than newspapers, trade journals, or radio shows have ever been able to do before.

It's About Collaboration: Two Heads (or Millions) Really Are Better Than One

The technology of the last decade has transformed the Web into the ultimate collaboration platform. You can find evidence everywhere: mashups (which remix songs, video, and text from a variety of sources), social bookmarking, wikis, and social networking. Collaboration has become a Web 2.0 cornerstone, in part because it endorses the many-to-many model valued so highly by the content creators who live there. Working together online has done a lot to break down the Web's reputation as a hostile, unfriendly, and unsympathetic place. Collaboration assumes trust and good faith, and the Web is chock full of examples where people bring the very best of themselves to a project, whether raising money online to help fight cancer or making research available for free to anyone who needs it. Here are some web collaborations of varying scope and importance that illustrate how social media tools can encourage online cooperation and goodwill.

Crowdsourcing History

At the beginning of 2008, the Library of Congress launched a remarkable social media pilot project. As a way to make sure that Americans (and the rest of the world) have free access to the Library's extensive photographic and image archives and as a way to gather detailed information about each image, the Library began publishing its photographs and other visual materials to Flickr—a website that hosts images and enables others to categorize and comment on images. The Library started with 3000 images for which no copyright restrictions were known to exist. Then it asked the Flickr community to tag, comment on, and make notes on the images—the idea being that the average Joe could add missing caption information, such as where the photo was taken or who is pictured in it. After all, we can recognize our hometown or a snapshot of our own grandparents more easily than a state-paid librarian can. Since the project began in early 2008, the Library of Congress has collected some fascinating facts from the public. Within 24 hours of launch, the public collectively commented on 500 pictures and tagged 4000 of them.[*] By getting *our* help identifying image data, the Library may be able to enhance the quality of bibliographic records for their images.

The Group Giving Explosion

Collaboration is the catalyst for an explosion in online philanthropy. Kiva is a microlending website that connects entrepreneurs (farmers, street vendors, shop owners, and so forth) with lenders (individuals, not banks or lending agents) who agree to loan these entrepreneurs funds. People lend money collaboratively, and each small contribution compounds, grows, and finances entrepreneurial projects for those who otherwise would never get the chance to fight their way out of poverty or get their business off the ground. In just four years, Kiva has assisted more than 230,000 borrowers and provided a total

---

[*] Library of Congress Flickr blog, Flickr.com, January 17, 2008, *http://blog.flickr.net/en/2008/01/17/wow/*.

of about $95 million in loans.* The genius of Kiva is that the giver has a personal stake in the entrepreneur's future. As a lender, you can watch your small contribution change a life from the comfort of your desk.

Collaborative giving is nothing new, of course. Individuals have been contributing to charities like United Way and The Salvation Army for decades. But the economics of online payment technologies make micropayments of a few dollars feasible. Plus, Internet charities have the potential to attract the attention of millions of givers at very little cost—no direct mail campaigns, telethons, celebrity spokespeople, or print advertising is required.

Collaboration on Steroids

Wikipedia is one of the largest collaborations in human history; the site currently has more than 75,000 active contributors and attracts more than 65 million visitors monthly.† Wikipedia is a free, online encyclopedia built collaboratively using wiki software. A *wiki* is a web page that anyone can access and modify. You may have used wikis at work; many corporations employ them as a communications platform for their employees. In Wikipedia's case, anyone can create, expand, or modify an article on any conceivable topic. Wikipedia relies on the "wisdom of crowds" to achieve accuracy. The more people who read Wikipedia articles and tweak them for accuracy, the more accurate the articles become. Though Wikipedia might sound like a free-for-all, strict rules are in place. For example, if you add information to an article, you must provide solid reference material to back up your contribution. If you don't provide a reliable reference or if you insert personal opinion, your content will be deleted. To reduce factual errors, the Wikipedia community grants individuals editorial responsibilities like reviewing articles or keeping an eye on current edits. To become an editorial administrator, "applicants" for the job must first be approved by peers—currently a 75 to 80 percent peer approval rating is required, based on level of experience, trust, and activity on the site. Wikipedia is one of the top 10 most visited websites on the Internet.

---

* Kiva Facts and Statistics, Kiva.org, *http://kiva.org/about/facts/*.
† Wikipedia.com, *http://en.wikipedia.org/wiki/Wikipedia:About*.

It's About Scope: The Infinite Internet

Piggybacking on the notion of democracy, anyone (who has access to an Internet connection) is invited to participate in online collaboration. Sure, the Web has cliques, closed communities, and cold shoulders just like the real world, but for the most part you are welcome to join. Most social media tools are free—Google Reader, Facebook, MySpace, Twitter—reducing the barrier to entry and encouraging participation and sharing. As a marketer, scope is key. Newspapers have column inches, and television has the 42-minute hour. The Internet, occasionally to our dismay, seems infinite. Not only is the number of blogs and communities to tap into growing, the cost of being online is steadily decreasing. In a 2008 study, the Pew Research Center said broadband bills were 4 percent lower than they were at the end of 2005.[*] Plus, more of us are going online. In the United States today, about 63 percent of all adults have a high-speed Internet connection in their home.[†] That's up from 47 percent in 2007. That means more of your customers are online, and you've got more avenues for making contact than ever before.

It's About Authenticity: A Cult of Honesty

Social media has had a remarkable democratizing effect on creativity. Tools like blogs and photo and video sharing sites inspire us to create and share in ways we never could before. The Internet's ubiquity, the low cost of social media tools, and their ease of use has resulted in a perfect brew for sharing content and ideas. With the culture of sharing comes two key concepts we always cite when discussing social media and specifically blogs: *authenticity* and *transparency*. A cult of honesty has developed in tandem with technical innovation, likely spurred by a desire for genuine connection with like-minded individuals.

Authenticity and transparency are admirable virtues, and the real-time, improvisational nature of social media tools tends to inspire honest, forthright communication. That said, you can't always

[*] John B. Horrigan, "Home Broadband 2008," Pew Internet & American Life Project, July 2, 2008, *http://www.pewinternet.org/Reports/2008/Home-Broadband-2008.aspx.*

[†] John B. Horrigan, "Home Broadband Adoption 2009," Pew Internet & American Life Project, June 17, 2009, *http://www.pewinternet.org/Reports/2009/10-Home-Broadband-Adoption-2009.aspx.*

judge a book by its cover or a blog by its banner. We've seen plenty of social media that hasn't been straight up. Consider lonelygirl15, the teen tell-all video diary that became a YouTube phenomenon in the summer of 2006. lonelygirl15, or Bree, spoke directly to a camera about typical topics of teen angst: strict parents, boys, best friend troubles, and so on. Almost immediately, lonelygirl15 became a raging hit on YouTube with more than one million views in the first three months.[*] Then, in September 2006, Matt Foremski exposed lonelygirl15 in a *Silicon Valley Watcher* article.[†] She was, in fact, a 19-year-old actress raised in New Zealand and living in Los Angeles, not a 16-year-old videoblogger pouring her heart out to like-minded teens on the Web. The same day that Foremski broke the story, Virginia Heffernan and Tom Zeller at the *New York Times* confirmed in their article, "'Lonely Girl' (and Friends) Just Wanted Movie Deal," that lonelygirl15 was indeed devised as an early, serialized version of what its creators hoped would eventually become a movie. If you skim the 145 comments on Heffernan's follow-up article, "Applause for lonelygirl15, and DVD Extras," you'll see that some fans clearly did not appreciate being duped: "I don't think I'd ever go to see one of their films, this isn't a 'new art form.' This is deception, manipulation, and bad acting from the get go," says commenter G. North.

Social Media Channels: What Are They and How Can You Use Them?

Now, let's get practical. To understand social media and generate ideas about how to use today's Web effectively, you need to know what the different social media tools are and when to use them. We use the term *channel* to describe the growing number of communication tools, technologies, and platforms on the Web. A channel is a delivery mechanism, and many social media channels exist for a variety of categories. Popular categories for content shared and distributed online include photos, text, videos, documents, music, and events. Social media channels make sharing this kind of

---

[*] Jonathan Richards, "Worldwide Fame for a Lonely Girl," *The Times*, August 19, 2006.

[†] Matt Foremski and Tom Foremski, "SVW Exclusive: The identity of LonelyGirl15," *Silicon Valley Watcher*, September 12, 2006.

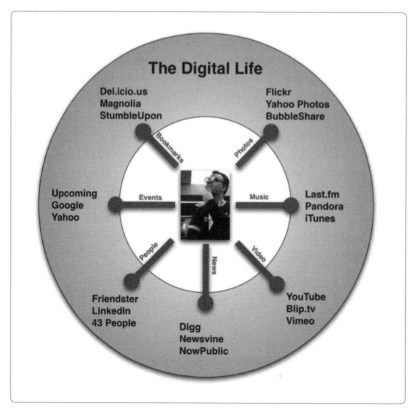

Photo by Rachael Ashe

These are some of the popular social media channels back in simpler times (2006).

information easy. For example, Flickr is the most popular channel for photo sharing; YouTube is the big channel for video sharing; and, of course, Facebook is the ultimate channel for social sharing. But other channels may be new to you: Google Docs is a favorite for collaborating on documents; Upcoming.org is ideal for posting event details; and Delicious is a website for sharing web bookmarks with friends and strangers. The number and variety of social media channels is growing rapidly. A few years ago, we created this diagram to illustrate the popular social media channels of the day.

A lot has happened and a plethora of tools have emerged since we created our humble diagram in 2006. Thanks to PR guru Brian Solis, we've now got another, more extensive view of today's social media channels called the *Conversation Prism*. This illustration provides a snapshot of some of the most popular ways to communicate via

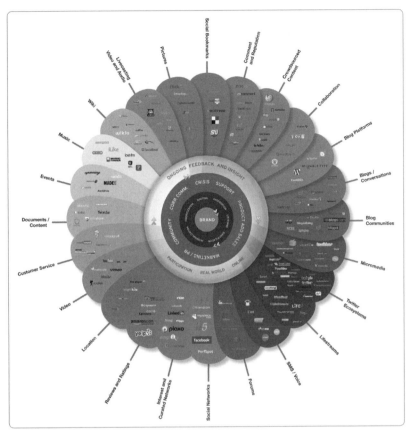

Today, the social media channel landscape is considerably more complex, and it's still growing. The Conversation Prism diagram was created by PR guru Brian Solis.

social media. You'll find the Conversation Prism helpful when you're creating your social media marketing campaigns and deciding which channels to utilize. If you're having trouble getting traction on blogs, return to the prism for inspiration and try a campaign on Facebook, or drive traffic to your website from StumbleUpon or reddit.

What Is Social Media Marketing?

Simply put, *social media marketing* is using social media channels to promote your company and its products. This type of marketing should be a subset of your online marketing activities, complementing traditional web-based promotional strategies like email newsletters and online advertising campaigns. Social media marketing qualifies as a form of *viral* or word-of-mouth marketing. Viral marketing relies on you telling your friends about media, products, or services you love (or loathe). Here's the difference: When you tell your sister about a great new sushi joint, only she hears about it. She may tell her boyfriend or a neighbor, but the news moves slowly. If you have a restaurant review podcast with 500 listeners, however, your review travels a lot farther and a lot faster, and that little Japanese place could be packed by Friday night.

Why Should You Embrace Social Media Marketing?

One reason we love travel is that it puts life into perspective. If you don't know how the rest of the world lives and what opportunities await you in new frontiers, how can you make wise choices? Work is similar to travel. But you don't have to go all the way to South America to stretch your boundaries. If you're already taking advantage of trade shows, media relations, direct mail, and telemarketing, then try a new marketing tactic. And if all our philosophical rhetoric doesn't convince you, then maybe these numbers will:

- More people, particularly young people, are spending less time watching television and listening to the radio and more time online, according to a survey of consumer digital media and entertainment habits run in 2007 by IBM.[*] The survey has TV and personal Internet usage almost tied in a heated battle. Sixty-six percent of respondents reported viewing one to four hours of TV per day, whereas 60 percent reported the same for Internet usage.

- Offline advertising has traditionally been expensive and difficult to measure. Thanks to the hard numbers that web analytics programs like Google Analytics offer up, measuring the success of social media marketing campaigns is a science, not an art. Similarly, the plethora of free tools associated with social media can significantly cut down on high-priced artwork and design that go into offline ad campaigns.

---

[*] "IBM Consumer Survey Shows Decline of TV as Primary Media Device," IBM, August 22, 2007, *http://www-03.ibm.com/press/us/en/pressrelease/22206.wss.*

- Finally, the days of the brochure site are long gone. Markets are conversations, haven't you heard? Conversation is happening, whether you like it or not. The blogosphere, at best estimate, has at least 200 million blogs. Facebook currently has more than 300 million active users (people who have accessed their Facebook account within the last 30 days). Flickr, the popular photo sharing site, published its 3 billionth photograph earlier this year. The marketing dollars are going to social media. A study by Pollara Strategic Insights indicated that one in two Canadian business leaders will spend as much or more on social media in 2009 than they did in 2008, despite an economic downturn.[*]

How Does Social Media Fit with Your Marketing Goals?

You're a marketer, so you know that having clear goals and tracking campaign outcomes is critical. What are your social media marketing goals, or what should they be? Why would you want to trek through the swampy and sometimes treacherous social media marketing landscape when you're comfortable on the paved, tree-lined streets of lead generation, webinars, and media relations? The answer is—drum roll please—*increased online visibility*. A stronger web presence should be the primary goal of every social media marketing campaign. But what are the metrics of a "stronger web presence"? What does "increased online visibility" really mean? Following are the concrete outcomes that should persuade you to get off the familiar paved road:

- More visitors to your website

- More incoming links to your website

- More RSS subscribers

- More views of your content on video and photo sharing sites like YouTube and Flickr

---

[*] Pollara Strategic Insights Survey (commissioned by Veritas Communications), com.motion, December 10, 2008, *http://www.com.motionpoll.ca/release_2008.pdf.*

- More references to your company, products, and services on blogs, podcasts, Twitter, and social networking sites like MySpace and Facebook

- More followers for your Twitter account

- Better search engine optimization and an improved Google ranking

- More genuine interactions with your customers

Sales, obviously, is another popular metric. But converting site visitors and social media consumers into customers is beyond the scope of this book. Many excellent resources are available that explain how to write compelling sales copy and guide a visitor through a website in a way that helps to seal the deal. See "Recommended Reading" on page 263 for some suggested reading on web sales.

Now for Some Sober Second Thoughts

Now you're convinced that social media marketing is for you. That's great; we're glad you're inspired! Before you jump into the social media sphere, however, consider the answers to the following questions to make sure that a social media marketing program is right for your organization:

Where are your peeps?

Are your customers online? One of the reasons social media marketing has taken off so quickly in the high-tech space is that many technology products can be purchased online and immediately downloaded. The Internet is an ideal marketing medium for companies selling products on the Web. If you've got a website with a shopping cart or reservation system, then social media marketing should definitely be on your to-do list. Similarly, if your audience uses the Web for research, social media can be very helpful indeed. The good news is that you don't have to have killer search engine rankings to get in on the action. For example, a free listing in Google's Local Business Center ensures that your business address, phone number, and website pop up when customers search Google Maps for your business or businesses in your area. Customers can even review your business inside Google Maps. Making sure customers can find your brick-and-mortar store with ease—alongside a handful of positive online reviews—is a persuasive way to get them in the door.

On the other hand, if you're a corner store with a very niche market (say, the people who live within a five-block radius), then you may find limited returns from social media marketing. Remember, social media marketing is ultimately about building your reputation online and bringing more people to your website to buy your product, sign your petition, and so forth. If your website doesn't play a key role in your sales and marketing efforts, then think twice before starting down this path.

What are your competitors doing?

Pay attention to what your competitors are doing. If they're all attending the same trade shows, you should be there too. If they're blogging on their corporate blogs and commenting in the comment threads of the right industry websites, then you should be doing the same. Gauging your competitors' online activities is a litmus test for the value of social media marketing in your industry. If your competitors are already reaping the benefits, don't wait another quarter to get in the game. If they're lagging behind, this could be your chance to become an industry leader.

Do you have the resources?

Getting a social media marketing program off the ground takes significant time and effort. You need to dedicate time every day to monitoring the Web, participating in ongoing discussions, posting to your blog, and developing new campaign ideas. If you're a one-person marketing department and already feel overworked and resentful of the time you spend online answering email and doing web research, then social media marketing may just be too stressful. If this is the case, perhaps you should reevaluate your marketing activities to determine where you get the best return on your efforts. In our experience, social media marketing can often replace lower-value marketing activities that don't produce consistently good results.

Hitting the Trail: What You'll Need to Get Started

If we didn't just scare you off, then keep reading, because your first step to social media immersion starts here. This section details the big-ticket items you'll need to get your campaign off the ground.

Time, Time, and More Time

Setting up and running social media marketing can be significantly less expensive than ad buys, traditional PR, and big trade shows. But if time is money, then social media marketing is going to cost you. Time is a commodity that none of us seems to have enough of, and social media marketing campaigns don't run themselves. For social media marketing to pay off you need to get your hands dirty. You'll need to monitor the Web daily for mentions of your brand. You'll need to dedicate time to commenting on related blog posts. And you'll need to contact online influencers on a one-to-one basis. For social media marketing to succeed, we suggest you dedicate around 25 percent of your marketing time to making it work. In our experience, anything less just won't garner results.

Boss Buy-In

Is dedicating a quarter of your time to social media marketing going to fly with the boss? Depending on the size of your organization, selling a marketing program in-house can be the hardest part of getting social media marketing initiatives off the ground. This reluctance is understandable. After all, legal doesn't want to expose the company to risk, and the marketing VP doesn't want to invite criticism. But hiding under the covers and hoping social media will go away isn't going to work.

If you need to convince your boss, start by highlighting these measurable outcomes:

- More website visitors
- More incoming links
- Better search engine optimization
- Better customer interactions and engagement

And if that doesn't work, use old-school peer pressure. If your competitors are active online, try this tactic. Go to Google and in the search field type `link:http://www.yoururl.com`. On the right side of the screen, you'll see the number of incoming links Google finds for your home page. Now do the same with three of your largest competitors. How do you rank against them? Who's got the biggest web presence? Hopefully the numbers are convincing enough to get your boss on board, at least for a pilot program.

The Buddy System

Your boss gives you the nod. Now you need to motivate your colleagues. After all, they're probably going to be doing their fair share of the work. Start by finding out who already has a blog, who is active on Facebook, and who spends the lunch hour mesmerized by YouTube videos. You may be surprised to discover how many of your coworkers are already well versed in social media tools and are chomping at the bit to bring their social interests inline with their work.

The Best Books and Blogs

Now you need to learn everything you can about social media. Read this book. Then read the books listed in "Recommended Reading" on page 263. Attend conferences on social media; they're being held all over the world. If you're a newbie, never fear. We'll get you set up on Facebook so you can get the hang of how social networking works. We'll explain how to sign up for a Google Reader account and subscribe to your favorite websites' RSS feeds. The first step in figuring out how to make social media work for your company is to get a handle on how it can work for you. Try it all and see what sticks. You may have the same experience with social media that we had in France years ago with escargot. We ate snails on a dare. Now we order the slimy little fellas every time they're on the menu.

Surfing the Wave of Change

Before moving on to the next chapter, where you'll learn the inner workings of social media tools, we want to impress this upon you: Social media moves at lightning speed—the popular tools, the lingo, the stars, everything. The best way to keep up with it all is to watch for what the geeks are excited about. By "geeks," we mean the tech community. The technology community seems to have a crystal ball into the future of the Web. Tech blogs like Boing Boing were some of the first to gain serious traffic. Techies were early RSS adopters, and now Twitter and FriendFeed are their darlings. You'll be in the know if you keep an eye on the technology section of Digg or Slashdot, though be prepared for a huge wave of information from these sources. If you're after the latest social media news with a marketing slant, you can't go wrong by subscribing to Steve Rubel's blog (*http://www.steverubel.com/*). You're not done learning about this topic when you finish reading this book—you've got to continue reading if you want to keep up with the digital Joneses. Now you can pull out the map and get started.

But first you need to ensure that your own living room is in order. The next chapter explains how to get social media ready, offering some basic tips on the social web and helping ensure that your website is prepared for the additional attention and interaction you're likely to receive.

2

GET SOCIAL MEDIA READY

Now that you understand a bit more about the social and technological drivers behind today's communication revolution, you're poised to get social media ready. That means becoming skilled in the new technologies and tools that enable mass social communication online. First, we'll walk you through the basics of content syndication and demonstrate how to manage the torrent of content generated by blogs and other social media tools. We'll cover some dos and don'ts of using a blog as a communications channel, and we'll offer pointers on launching your corporate blog. Finally, we'll help you prepare for social media marketing activities to come. We'll show you how to make your company's website social media ready as a precursor to blogger outreach, Facebook marketing, and other online marketing activities. Let's get started.

RSS 101

> I've been looking at the future of information, and part of it is spelled *R-S-S*.
> —Dan Gillmor, *Computerworld*, 2003

Much of the Web's new interconnectivity is enabled by a simple technology that's essential to the social web: RSS. *RSS* is an acronym for *Really Simple Syndication* or *Rich Site Summary*. Neither of these terms is particularly helpful in understanding what RSS means, so we'll try to do better.

To understand RSS, let's get personal. If you're not already an RSS user, how many different websites do you visit on a daily or weekly basis? Let's say each week you visit CNN, ESPN, your friend's blog, your other friend's blog, your stock portfolio, a weather website, and five celebrity gossip blogs.

Each time you visit these websites, you have to:

1. Scan the site.
2. Remember what you've already read.
3. Disregard what doesn't interest you.
4. Click links to the remaining stories and read them.

If you follow those steps for just 10 different sites, you've wasted time and brain power. You probably read a lot of headlines and articles twice and miss some news you would have liked to have read. This is the traditional *hunter-gatherer* model of consuming information on the Web. You find the news and sort through it for the stuff you like but haven't read. Syndication is the *pizza delivery* model of reading news. Instead of seeking out the information you want, you get tailor-made information dispatched to your computer or mobile device.

Hunter-Gatherer Model

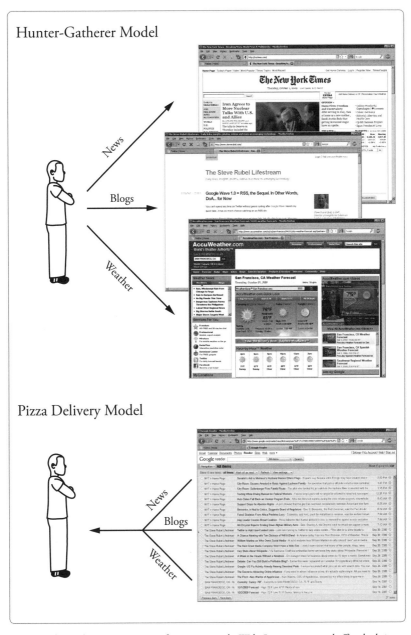

Pizza Delivery Model

RSS transforms the way we access information on the Web. It saves time and effort by bringing information directly to you.

RSS Feeds and Readers

Nearly every blog, and most other news-oriented websites, publish an RSS feed. An *RSS feed* is a computer-readable summary of a website's recent activity (usually the most recently published blog posts, articles, images, or comments). Modern web browsers can automatically detect whether a website offers one or more RSS feeds. If a website is RSS-enabled, the familiar RSS icon will show up in your browser's address bar or toolbar. This icon is also available elsewhere on the web page, often in a sidebar or footer.

An RSS icon like this appears on almost all blogs and most news websites, and also appears in your browser's address bar.

Click this icon to *subscribe* to the RSS feed (also called a *news feed*) for that site. Subscribing to a feed is almost always free. A subscription just means you want to be notified when the site publishes new information you're interested in. Like a pizza delivery guy bringing you dinner, RSS actually pushes the blog posts, articles, and images to you. As you can imagine, consuming information on the Web this way is quite efficient. Because the news comes to you, weeks can often pass between visits to the actual websites you're reading.

You use a web-based or desktop *RSS reader* (also called a *news reader* or *RSS aggregator*) to automatically monitor the sites and receive news from them. As you subscribe to feeds, you're building a kind of customized newspaper just for yourself. RSS readers are a little like Microsoft Outlook or another email application. In fact, some RSS readers integrate directly into Outlook, enabling you to cluster your information inputs into one desktop program. Your subscribed feeds are typically listed on the left-hand side, and you click a feed to view the newest content for a particular site. RSS reader applications remember what you've already looked at, so you almost never see old information. Many RSS readers enable you to flag items for later reference or email a particular item to a friend.

Most sites publish complete feeds, which means you can read the entire content *chunk*—the blog post, article, video, photo, and so forth—in the reader. Some sites only publish excerpt feeds, which show only the news item's title and first few sentences. Owners of

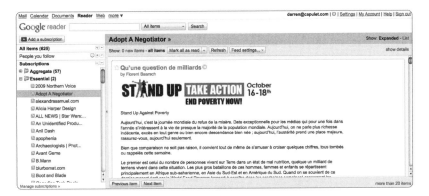

Google Reader is a popular web-based RSS reader.

these sites often want you to click through to the website itself because they rely on advertising for revenue, and those ads often don't appear in your RSS feed. While subscribing to RSS feeds, you may come across a technology called *Atom*. Atom, a competing technology that offers precisely the same service, is simply another flavor of RSS. You can subscribe to or publish an Atom feed and the result is the same as with RSS. More importantly, all RSS readers handle both technologies.

Popular RSS Readers

RSS readers come in two flavors: web-based and desktop. Web-based readers are specialized websites that enable you to read RSS feeds wherever you are. Desktop readers run on your computer like Microsoft Outlook but offer you the advantage of reading RSS feeds while you're offline. Some readers combine both types of functionality.

The following are some of the most popular RSS readers:

- Google Reader (*http://www.google.com/reader/*)

- Bloglines (*http://www.bloglines.com/*)

- NewsGator (*http://www.newsgator.com/*)

- Netvibes (*http://www.netvibes.com/*)

Additionally, current versions of Internet Explorer and Firefox include RSS reading functionality.

Mainlining Data

RSS is about much more than simply subscribing to itemized feeds from your favorite websites. You can also mainline data from all sorts of useful sources. You can subscribe to:

- Weather updates
- Traffic notifications for your drive home
- Flight delays
- Search results that alert you when someone mentions you or your brand
- New real estate listings on your block
- Notifications about when your UPS or Amazon package ships

Now that you understand how RSS can help, recognizing how critical it is to the plumbing of Web 2.0 and social media technologies is important. Nearly every social media website produces a variety of RSS feeds. On YouTube, for example, you can subscribe to:

- Every new video added on the site
- The top-rated videos across the whole site
- The videos voted most favorite across the whole site
- All of the videos from a particular user
- All of the videos tagged with a particular term

But don't forget the computer-readable part of our definition of RSS. Other web services can use RSS feeds, too. For example, the website Popurls.com (shown on the next page) displays RSS feeds from many social media sites like YouTube, Flickr, and Digg. The site is arranged to display the recent most popular items from each site, providing an excellent one-stop shop that answers the question, "What does the social web care about right now?" This type of site wouldn't be possible—or would be much more difficult to build— without RSS. The process of using RSS to gather data from diverse sources is often called *aggregation*. A service called FriendFeed, currently popular with geeks and techies, lets you easily aggregate many

RSS feeds that focus on a particular person, brand, or topic. Many FriendFeed users create *lifestreams* to share with others. A lifestream is a firehose of RSS-powered information from a person's blog, their bookmarks, their Twitter feed, and other channels to which friends and admirers can subscribe.

Popurls.com aggregates RSS feeds from top social media sites, showing you what's most popular on the Web, right now.

A common response to RSS is, "That's way too much information! How will I cope?" Never fear. Plenty of strategies can help you sort through the RSS feeds. First, RSS feeds are getting smarter. As we mentioned, you can subscribe to increasingly granular feeds of information. Instead of subscribing to a celebrity gossip blog, you might just subscribe to blog posts that are tagged with the term *Taylor Swift* or *red carpet*. Instead of subscribing to all the new rental listings for Manhattan, you can choose to be notified only about one-bedroom lofts in SoHo (we don't know how you're going to afford that loft, but that's a topic for another book).

An increasing array of tools also enable you to filter and remix RSS feeds manually. NBA.com offers a wide range of RSS feeds, including one for each basketball team. If you're a fan of both the

Knicks and the Nets (which is unlikely!), you can subscribe to both feeds. Alternately, you could filter NBA.com's video feed so you receive only the highlights of games featuring either the Knicks or the Nets.

NOTE   *As we write this book, the most popular tool for creating these RSS mashups is called Yahoo! Pipes, which provides a relatively easy-to-use graphic interface for manipulating feeds. Read more about Yahoo! Pipes in Chapter 6.*

Humans are another handy technology for filtering RSS. We often subscribe to topical blogs because we trust and rely on the blogger to write about that topic's most important or useful news. We also find human filters in the crowdsourcing corners of the Web. You've probably seen the "most emailed" or "most commented upon" lists of stories on popular mainstream news sites. This list reflects the hundreds or thousands of users who "voted" for a story by sending it to someone else. A similar phenomenon can be found in the "most popular" videos and photos on YouTube and Flickr, respectively. This voting principle becomes more literal on social news sites like Digg, reddit, and StumbleUpon, where users *vote up* stories they like and *bury* ones they don't. You could never keep up with every technology story submitted to Digg. But you could subscribe to and monitor the RSS feed of the most popular stories about Apple. We cover these services in more detail in Chapter 13.

Setting up an RSS reader and subscribing to various feeds gives you a firsthand look at how Web 2.0 technologies alter the way you consume content. Subscribing to blogs you're interested in and learning to aggregate online content is a useful first step in your social media immersion.

Entering the Blogosphere: The Basics of Launching a Corporate Blog

Companies often try out Web 2.0 and social media marketing by writing a blog or publishing a podcast or videocast. Corporate blogs can be the perfect introduction to the world of social media because they offer more control than any other social media tool. Think of a typical corporate blog as a literal soapbox on a street corner. Even though passers-by—your readers—can talk back, corporate bloggers have an elevated position from which to speak. Plus, bloggers can choose not to publish certain comments or can turn off comments altogether! They're in a position of power. The relationship of blogger to reader is more traditional, or top-down, and less democratic than in a number of more conversational and egalitarian online channels, like forums or social networks. Starting your own corporate blog also preps you for social media marketing activities to come. You develop the right mindset—hey, now you're a blogger—and you improve your organization's online credibility when it comes time to launch your first blogger outreach campaign.

You can find a bookshelf's worth of how-to guides and hundreds of websites discussing how to start a blog (check out "Recommended Reading" on page 263 for some of our favorites). Here, however, are some answers to questions that our clients always ask when starting a blog for their organization.

How Do You Start?

Start with an internal-facing blog on your company's intranet; this will permit only employees to read the blog. This approach ensures that:

- Neophyte bloggers can practice in a safe environment. They can come to grips with the time demands that their blog will require and make mistakes without any serious ramifications.

- The idea of outward-facing blogs can be gently introduced to the rest of the organization.

- Achieving companywide support for blogging when there's a positive example available is easier.

- The IT and web teams can become familiar with a blogging platform.

If you want to take baby steps, you can subsequently run a *private beta* of your outward-facing blog. Open it up to a small external audience. This external soft launch should be targeted to an informed and sympathetic audience. A password-protected partners portal or premium support zone on your website is a natural spot for this limited public trial.

Use this soft launch to solicit feedback (directly on the blog, through comments, ideally) and introduce the company's bloggers to a larger audience. Once you do this, however, the cat is out of the bag. You can ask your chosen readers to treat the blog like a closed beta program, but anything that's said could end up on other blogs or in the mainstream media.

Should You Build Your Own Blogging Software?

We're surprised how often this question is asked. Web designers and developers seem to adore the challenge of crafting a blog platform or content management system from scratch. We urge you to give this some serious thought first. A plethora of popular, cheap (or free), and reliable blogging platforms are available for every scenario. For instance, Blogger (*http://www.blogger.com/*) and WordPress.com (*http://www.wordpress.com/*) offer the platform, domain name, and hosting for free, but the URL will usually be a combination of their URL plus the name of your blog. WordPress.org (*http://www .wordpress.org/*—confusingly, different from WordPress.com) offers the platform for free but not the hosting and domain name. Similarly, MovableType (*http://www.movabletype.com/*) charges a license fee for the platform, depending on the usage scenario, but doesn't include the domain name and hosting. If you already use a content management system for your corporate website, like Drupal or Joomla, a blogging solution is probably already available as an add-on module.

Who Should Blog?

As a general rule, not the corporate communications people—that means you. Communications folks have typically been inculcated to be consistently "on message" and to speak in the safe, dry language of the press release. This approach is poison to a blog, which thrives on an authentic individual voice. Who writes the blog depends on why you're starting a blog: Establishing industry expertise? Providing technical tips and tricks? Polishing the company's image for recruiting?

We've found that the best corporate bloggers are:

- Informed about their area of expertise. They probably already participate in associations and online communities that relate to their profession.

- Passionate about their work.

- At least a little opinionated.

- Good written communicators.

- Well educated about the company's position in the marketplace.

- Already experienced personal bloggers.

Pick the staff members who can deliver on your goals. We've found that employees who advocate for the customer—product managers, technical support staff, technical writers, and so forth—often make great corporate bloggers.

Starting with a group blog, where at least three or four people contribute, is a good idea. This distributes the burden and ensures that the blog doesn't go dry because someone is away on vacation. Additionally, you'll likely find that one or two staffers discover a passion for blogging. They'll inevitably write most of the posts, respond to comments on the site, and so forth. For group blogs, highlighting the individual bloggers is important. Readers want to get to know the people behind the blog, and so each blog post should prominently feature the blogger's name and photo.

Why Should You Write a Blog?

First, consider why you're launching a corporate blog. These are some common objectives:

Foster customer relationships

Customers crave timely, candid dialogue with a company. They want greater access to and more information about your organization's activities. Blogs can increase customer goodwill toward your company. They're also an excellent place to educate customers informally about new concepts and industry trends.

Solicit user feedback

Here's an old Internet truism: If you don't give your customers a place to talk about your products and services, they'll find their own place. Wise companies enable public discourse with their customers, ensuring that they can "own" or oversee as much of the online conversation as possible.

Establish expertise

Blogs are an excellent means of promoting particular staff members as experts or pundits in a given industry sector or niche.

Research the market

Blogs provide an ideal venue to try out new ideas and pitch new features to your most passionate supporters (they're the likeliest blog readers). You'll get immediate, generally informed feedback—blogs can be a focus group without the room rental and doughnuts.

Provide technical support

Blogs can become another channel for your support staff to communicate with users.

Connect with journalists, analysts, and industry bloggers

Journalists and analysts were some of the earliest consumers of blogs and RSS. Additionally, many bloggers have become de facto journalists in their area of expertise.

Deploy damage control

For companies of all sizes, blogs make quick-and-dirty tools for damage control. This is partially due to their one-button publishing model, but also because of the transparency and authenticity blogs tend to foster.

Improve interdepartmental communication

When various teams are blogging for a company, you foster a natural exchange of information and a better awareness of other company projects.

Increase staff profile

Blogs can help the stars inside your company shine and make them feel recognized for their contributions.

Recruit new employees

A company's blogs should reflect its culture. Blogs written by passionate employees help possible new hires get an inside look at your organization.

What Should You Write About?

People often make a mistake when writing corporate blogs and website content: They write about their company from the perspective of the company. This trap is an easy one to fall into. Instead, corporate blogs should focus on clear communication and delivering value to the customer. Value doesn't only mean discounts and deals—it means content that's compelling, entertaining, and possibly helpful. Stonyfield Farms runs the Baby Babble blog. The company rarely discusses its products, but instead uses this blog to provide infant health information for readers. The blog doesn't directly sell dairy products, but it does establish Stonyfield Farms as an expert in the field and engender positive feelings in customers.

Popular topics include company news, product tips and tricks, your take on the industry and your competition, and what we call *corporate dark matter*. Dark matter is all the compelling stuff about your company that doesn't make it onto your website or into high-level marketing messages. Sales and tech support are good departments to mine for dark matter content, such as email messages explaining product features in plain English, or answers to commonly asked support questions.

Also, emulate others. Take your content and style cues from a blog or podcast you like.

How Often Should You Blog?

Ideally, three times a week. If you have a team of four bloggers, then each blogger can write three blog posts a month (though, as we mentioned, that will shift over time). Three blog posts a week makes the site feel healthfully alive without overwhelming readers. If you can't reliably blog at least once a week, you should reconsider whether a blog is the right fit for your organization.

How Will You Manage All the Feedback?

This question is the one we hear most frequently. We can assure you, as a new blogger, you won't be buried in comments and feedback. Consider this data point. General Motors' FastLane Blog (*http:// fastlane.gmblogs.com/*) has been around more than three years and was one of the early examples of corporate blogging done right. On the blog, senior GM executives offer opinions on corporate and industry news. For American car enthusiasts and industry workers, the blog is a compelling read. It's made even more compelling these days by the site's frank discussion of GM's bankruptcy filing. The site claims roughly 5000 daily visitors. Yet the average post on this well-promoted blog for a Fortune 500 brand receives about 15 to 20 comments per post.

The so-called 1 percent rule of the online community applies here. The 1 percent rule says that out of any 100 online users, only 1 person will create content; the rest will be *lurkers*, or site visitors who read without interacting. The relationship obviously varies from site to site, but our experience confirms that you'll be lucky to get 1 comment for every 100 visitors on a corporate blog. If you plan for this ratio, you'll be in good shape. And remember, when you launch a new blog, you always start with a readership of zero (or one, if you're counting your mom). Too many comments is a nice problem to have—and a rare one. Lots of comments means your readers are truly engaged with what you're writing.

Where Should the Blog Live?

Should your blog function as part of your corporate website, or should it live at its own domain name? Most of the time, hosting the blog as part of your main website is to your advantage. Companies just add an extra item—*Blog*, typically—to their main site navigation, and the blog's home page (with the most recent entries) becomes just another page on the website. What are the advantages of this approach? You can generate instant readership by encouraging site visitors to read and subscribe to the blog.

Blogs are an excellent tool for improving your site's search engine optimization (SEO). Search engines love blogs for their frequently updated content. Nearly every business owner we know, regardless of the size of the company, recognizes the importance of SEO to his company's website's success.

The blog helps to reinforce, in an informal way, your corporate messaging. Mountain Equipment Co-op is one of Canada's largest retailers of outdoor equipment, a cooperative, and a boisterous advocate of corporate social responsibility. The co-op runs an ethical sourcing blog at *http://blog.mec.ca/*, the goal of which is "to encourage an informed dialogue on what's happening in factories everywhere."

Why would you launch a blog at its own discrete domain? One reason is shelf life. Maybe you're running a short-term blog as part of a microsite for a marketing campaign. Credit union Vancity launched a community blog at the aspirational URL *http://www.ChangeEverything.ca/*. The credit union initially launched the site to reaffirm its brand as an organization that truly cares about community. The distance between this site and the corporate site meant that if Change Everything didn't catch on, or if things didn't go well, VanCity could quietly shut it down. Instead, the site was a success, so the company kept it running.

Another reason to run an offsite blog is if you want to provide some measure of independence from your corporate site. Back in 2005, when podcasts were big news, we launched *QA Podcast* for QA Labs, a software consultancy that specialized in quality assurance. The podcast featured short, informal conversations between an industry expert and senior staff from QA Labs. The discussions were technical and rarely mentioned the company itself. We intentionally kept the corporate messaging to a minimum—a brief "sponsored by QA Labs" message in the introduction and a small logo on the associated blog. In short, the podcast was a soft sell to establish the expertise of QA Labs staff. We hosted the site at *http://www.QAPodcast.com/*, reinforcing the podcast as a resource that gave back to the community.

A Few Blogging Don'ts

Hundreds of corporate blogs are launched every day. As such, we see lots of the same mistakes repeated time and again. In this section, we point out some practices to avoid.

Don't Fake It with a Character Blog

You don't have to watch a marathon of *Roxanne*, *Shrek*, and *Shakespeare in Love* to recognize that pretending to be someone you're not is folly. Similarly, you can kill a social media campaign by bungling a character blog. A character blog is written by a fictitious character—human, animal, or mascot. Character blogs sound like a fun, catchy campaign idea, but they are hard to get right. Some have hit home runs. For example, the Dwight Schrute character blog for NBC's *The Office* has had millions of views. But for every success, you can find plenty of fizzled attempts: the defunct Captain's Blog written by rum magnate Captain Morgan, McDonald's terrible Lincoln Fry blog, and the mundane Moosetopia blog from Moose Tracks ice cream.

Character blogs often fail because getting the right tone is difficult, they're rarely entertaining, and readers just don't seem to stick with them. Now, if Ronald McDonald divulged what his hamburgers and fries were really made of, that'd be some compelling reading. The final blow for character blogs is that they run contrary to what online communities are trying to achieve. Fictionalized blogs are not about real conversations or authenticity. We support marketing guru Steve Rubel's verdict that where marketing is concerned, "character blogs are a complete waste of time."[*]

---

[*] Steve Rubel, "Character Blogs are a Complete Waste of Time," Micro Persuasion, April 17, 2005, *http://www.micropersuasion.com/2005/04/character_blogs.html*.

Incidentally, the same advice goes for Facebook. Facebook administrators have consistently and aggressively deleted fictional or non-human profiles. The site has specific language about fake profiles in its terms of use.

Don't Give In to Flame Wars

If you're writing about controversial or contestable topics, expect disagreement from blog readers. When the ensuing debate is civil, it's terrific. You earn readers who are passionate enough to leave detailed comments challenging your views. Assuming they're not just troublemakers trying to ruffle your feathers, you should always—respectfully and professionally—engage with commenters.

That said, beware the *flame war* (we also like the term *nerd fight*). The Web's anonymity fosters a certain cocky confidence in online debates, and civil discussion can quickly devolve into name-calling. Getting caught up in the moment and saying something you'll later regret is easy. Here's our best piece of blogging advice when you're neck-deep in a heated online debate: Never blog or comment in anger. If you find you're getting upset, step away from the blog for a few hours, or even a day or two. The blog isn't going anywhere, and you'll get a fresh perspective after a little break from the flame war.

Don't Obsess over Perfection

The natural voice of the blog post is informal and conversational. Part of the appeal of reading a blog is watching the blogger work through an idea in a kind of real-time improvisation. Don't spend too much time trying to craft the perfect 500-word essay for the corporate blog. The blog isn't the same as the company's About Us page. It's messier and more unpredictable, and it has fewer content requirements. Don't be afraid to experiment a little and make a few mistakes along the way.

Prepping Your Website for Social Media Outreach

Getting social media ready isn't just about becoming familiar with the tools and technologies associated with social media, like RSS and blogs. You also have to prepare your website for the online marketing activities you're about to undertake. You're not ready to launch a campaign if your organization's website is wildly out of date, if it doesn't provide bloggers with the content they need in order to write about you, or if it's a classic *brochure website*—a static site that doesn't offer opportunities for two-way conversation. In this section, we'll discuss the bases you should cover to get your website social media ready.

As discussed at the beginning of this chapter, starting your own corporate blog is an ideal way to prepare your website for social media marketing activities. Running a blog is an education in social media. Plus, blogging opens up a channel for two-way conversation and shows other bloggers that you get this social media stuff. If blogging sounds like a too-scary first step, here's some good news: You don't have to blog to be current. You can make your website social media ready in other ways, without committing to the ongoing demand of writing blog posts.

Link Me Up

The ability to link from one website to another is fundamental to the Web. URLs are the road signs visitors use to find precisely the information they're looking for. If each page of your company's website doesn't have its own distinct URL, then you're working from a deficit. Unique page URLs make it easy for other sites—like the blogs you pitch—to reference and link to specific content on your website. For instance, if your website is entirely built in Macromedia Flash without unique URLs for each page, then online influencers probably can't point to your service description page or your slick new product demo. This problem sometimes occurs on fashion and art websites and sites with online catalogs. Although websites built with Flash often look great and can be fun to use, they don't always include unique URLs for each page. Flash can even negatively impact search engine optimization because search engines may have difficulty indexing pages created with multimedia tools. Don't get us wrong; some wonderful user interactions can happen when Flash and Ajax are used on a site. Just don't get carried away with slick design and user interactions unless you know they won't hamper your marketing activities.

A word of warning: Sometimes web designers have a tendency to put less emphasis on social media and search engine optimization than on building a site with a major wow factor. Don't get talked into slick animations and interactions if they make finding you and your products harder for customers.

The Social Media Resource Page

Another great place to start your social media facelift is your online media page or new media press page. Remember printed press kits? Those were heady days when journalists had the time and inclination to page through our carefully prepared and creatively designed company overviews and executive bios. Now you can resurrect some of that dusty corporate messaging and modernize it for your website's social media resource page. If you're already posting press releases and media coverage on your website, good for you. Still, you can do more. Some new developments in online press kits make it easier for journalists, bloggers, and other online influencers to share you with their audience.

Here are some guidelines for creating your new, social-media-friendly press kit—also called a *social media resource page*. Include these elements on your social media resource page, and content creators will have everything they need to cover your story.

Everything Old Is New Again

Conventional marketing tools shouldn't be completely eclipsed by shiny new social media toys. Traditional and new marketing tools can work together to make an even greater impact than when used separately. For example, the elevator pitch—a one-sentence overview of your product, service, or project—is still useful, so it should appear front and center on your social media press page. Remember, many bloggers, podcasters, and videocasters are hobbyists who don't have hours to spend researching and writing content. If they can excerpt your elevator pitch or link to a thorough description of your new baby buggy or barbeque without doing much legwork, they may be more inclined to cover your story. If you're concerned about staying on message in this crazy Web 2.0 world, the elevator pitch might be your only chance to get an approved corporate message out to the online world.

The elevator pitch isn't the only traditional marketing tool to include on your social media resource page. Add product brochures, corporate overviews, management bios, relevant company PowerPoint presentations, and any other content you'd include in a traditional media kit. Even links to technical documentation work here. All of these collateral pieces should exist on their own unique pages, which bloggers and journalists can access via a link from the social media resource page. These documents should also be available as downloadable PDFs that can be both viewed digitally and printed. Good web etiquette calls for indicating beside a link whether it's a PDF download. You should also include the file size if the downloads are more than 1MB.

Get a Multimedia Hook

If you've worked in media relations or on the newspaper side, you know that a good photo can make a story. A borderline story can end up on the front page if fantastic art is available to accompany it. The same thing can happen in the blogosphere. You don't need to spend lots of time and money on professional photography, but you should try to rustle up a few compelling visuals.

Whether you're selling a hardware security device or a new sports coupe, include a good selection of product photos on your media resource page. Make sure content creators can easily download or embed your photos in their posts. A mistake some companies make is to copyright their product shots, which makes reposting them legally difficult—or impossible—for bloggers. Most bloggers, podcasters, and online journalists are familiar with Creative Commons–licensed photos in Flickr. So we encourage you to upload photos to Flickr, assign them a Creative Commons license, and allow content creators to pull photographs from Flickr to use in their articles and blog posts. You can, of course, embed photos on your own social media resource page and link them back to Flickr.

What if your product isn't a "thing" that can be easily photographed? Depicting services, for instance, can be tricky. That's why so many websites are littered with corny stock photography of

What's the Deal with Creative Commons?

Creative Commons (CC) is a nonprofit organization "devoted to expanding the range of creative works available for others to legally build upon and share."* Creative Commons has released free licenses that range from traditional copyright, which restricts the use of copyrighted content entirely, to licenses that allow you to retain your copyright, but let others copy and distribute your work. You can choose to include restrictions, like not allowing others to use your work for commercial purposes or to make derivative works. Although Creative Commons licensing is often associated with photographs, the licenses can be applied to any content—text, software code, song lyrics, tunes, and so on.

On a personal note, when we upload our photographs to Flickr, we give them a Creative Commons license that allows others to use, modify, and share our photos as long as we are credited as the photographers. By licensing our vacation photos in this way, our personal snapshots have appeared as artwork in *Let's Gozo Magazine* (Malta), a Danish travel brochure, and a Czech business magazine.

* "Creative Commons," Wikipedia, *http://en.wikipedia.org/wiki/Creative_Commons/*.

attractive models shaking hands and giving each other the thumbs up. Instead, try posting relevant graphs or charts that support your marketing message. Or take photographs of your customers—yes, the real human beings that use your products and services. Not only do photos of real people confirm that you actually have customers, but also they adhere to the transparency and authenticity model we tout for online campaigns.

If your offering is virtual, like software, include screenshots that show your product in action. Product videos also work well. After all, according to YouTube's website, people watch "hundreds of millions of videos a day on YouTube." Before you hire a fancy production team, remember that the YouTube generation doesn't expect production-quality web video, so don't feel obliged to spend thousands of dollars to produce yours. Similarly, simple and affordable screencasts can be made in-house with software like Camtasia Studio or ScreenFlow.

RSS-Enable Your News

Journalists, online influencers, and your customers may want to have your corporate news delivered directly to their news readers via RSS. So make sure you've put your news feed, or feeds, front and center on your press page. You can even create a corporate news feed separate from your blog feed, which journalists monitoring your news often prefer. Your RSS subscribers make up the ultimate opt-in list. They've visited your website and purposefully subscribed to your corporate news feed. Any email marketer will tell you that kind of highly targeted audience is golden. Don't abuse your corporate news subscribers by distributing lame announcements like photos of your new office space. Save lightweight news for your blog.

Show You're in the Loop with a Blogroll

Bloggers commonly link to the websites they read on a regular basis or to blogs that complement the content on their own sites, podcasts, or videocasts. By adding a *blogroll*—a list of links to other relevant blogs—to the sidebar of your social media resource page, you demonstrate that you're active in the blogosphere. We often include the blogs of journalists and online influencers we'll be pitching on our clients' blogrolls.

Here's the logic behind that move. Almost all bloggers have an *ego feed*; they use tools like Google, Yahoo! Pipes, or Technorati to look for online mentions of their names and for websites that link to theirs. By adding their websites to your blogroll, you're on their radar even before you begin your outreach project. We'll talk more about how blogrolls can help your blogger outreach campaigns in Chapter 3.

Share the Wealth with a Linkroll

A *linkroll* is a list of bookmarked links accompanied by brief descriptions. Posting a linkroll on your resource page is akin to clipping articles from the newspaper and passing them out to your colleagues. You can create a linkroll with social bookmarking tools like Delicous. Simply bookmark relevant articles you find online using one of these tools, and then aggregate those bookmarks on your social media resource page. We explain more about social bookmarking in Chapter 13.

Building a good linkroll works best when product managers and developers get in on the action and bookmark relevant articles, photos, and video connected to your product, company, or industry. Why bother? First, referencing third-party mentions of your company on the Web affirms its legitimacy. If ReadWriteWeb covers your product, then TechCrunch might decide to write about it too. On a more altruistic note, social media is about being open and generous. If a visitor has come to your site to read about ergonomic chairs or herbal supplements, you offer them a richer, more rewarding experience by providing links to other useful resources—yes, even if they reference one of your competitors.

What Does It Look Like When It All Comes Together?

A social media resource page should be a one-stop shop for traditional press kit info, relevant links, and new media goodies, like RSS feeds and YouTube embeddable videos. Journalists, bloggers, podcasters, and video bloggers can then easily use your information in their stories. If content creators have good resource materials on hand, they may be more inclined to write about your product or organization. If you provide easy access to solid, well-written background materials, you also improve the odds of getting an accurate story.

The Social Media News Release

Even the humble press release has been influenced by Web 2.0 and social media. Enter the *social media news release.* A social media release complements a traditional news release with content new influencers want to see—RSS feeds, video, embeddable images—and tools that make your release easier to share on the Web. Here are some tips for creating an effective social media release:

Pack the headline full of good keywords. Your goal is to get online visibility, so keep search engine optimization in mind when you write your release headline. Choose keywords, not company acronyms or marketing buzzwords, that will help your release get maximum coverage on Google and Yahoo! News.

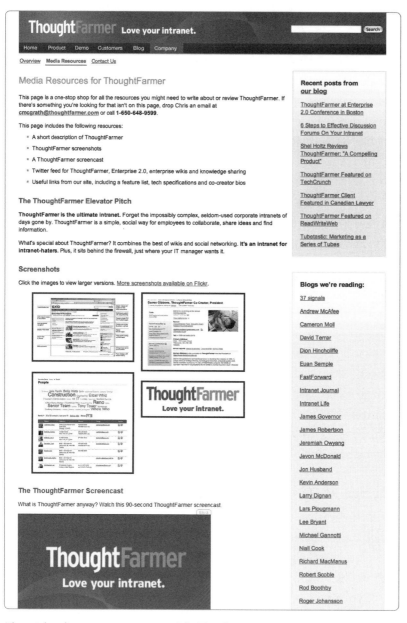

The social media resource page we created for ThoughtFarmer, an intranet provider

Make sharing your release online easy. You can do this by adding a bookmarking widget (shown in the following figure) that allows readers to save and share the link to your release within social networks.

Marketwire's own social media release, announcing its new Web 2.0 news release service

Embed video and images to further spread your release. By posting video and images on YouTube, Vimeo, and Flickr, people in those communities can stumble upon your content. Be sure to link these assets back to your release.

If creating a social media release on your own website feels technologically overwhelming, a variety of services are available that will do it for you. Most of the traditional wire services are getting in on the action and, for a hefty fee, will add all these bells and whistles to your release.

We're actually not huge fans of the prepackaged social media press release, however. We find that old-school marketers use it as a crutch; the social media press release enables them to feign genuine engagement while still hanging on to the rapidly aging traditional press release. The social media press release also feels like a desperate bid by wire services to remain relevant. In 2008, SHIFT Communications' Christopher Lynn created a handy snapshot of the

SMR Capabilities Across Major Wire Services

	marketwire	PR Newswire	BusinessWire	PRWeb
RSS Feed to Corp Newsroom	●		***	●
Comments	●			●
Comments with RSS/Email	●			
Trackbacks	●	●	●	●
Sharing	●	●	●	●
MP3/Podcast/Audio	ADD $	ADD $$$	ADD $$	●
Video	ADD $	ADD $$$	ADD $$	●
Video hosted on Major Sites	●	●	●	
Graphic	●	ADD $$$	ADD $$	●
Tags	●	●	●	●
Updated News Ticker	●		●	
Archive	●		●	●

***if BusinessWire maintains the online newsroom

SHIFT Communications' 2008 snapshot of wire service social media offerings

social media news release services offered by wire service vendors.[*] While the service offerings will change over time, this illustration offers a comprehensive cheat sheet of social media tools you can add to any news release.

The number of social media assets you can add to your website and news releases can seem overwhelming. But don't get discouraged by the task of incorporating social media into your traditional PR activities. Remember, the point of all this technology adoption is to make your job easier. By making your news easy to share and spread around the Web, you'll allow more people to see it. All these technologies work together to help you get the job done.

You've learned how to use RSS; you're ready to launch your own corporate blog; and your website is social media ready. Now you need to devise a campaign strategy that will get you in front of bloggers, online journalists, and other new influencers.

---

[*] "Untangling Claims About Wire Services & Social Media," PR Squared, February 11, 2008, *http://www.pr-squared.com/2008/02/prsquareds_social_media_tactic_6.html.*

3

FLAGGING A RIDE: FINDING THE RIGHT

BLOGGERS AND COMMUNITIES

You've given your site its new media makeover, you've reviewed the rules, and you've been getting to know your industry's online communities. Now is the time to find the right roads to travel and the right online influencers to meet along the way who will help you get the word out. In this chapter, you'll learn how to find popular bloggers and online communities in your industry and to discover which tools to use to build a prize blogger contact list.

Three Buckets of Blogs

Sometimes we think of the blogosphere as being divided into three different types of blogs. This kind of thought experiment may help you contextualize your social media research. The three kinds of blogs are:

Personal blogs   These are mostly diaries of one's life or a particular period or aspect of one's life (a blog about a mother's pregnancy or building a house). Reflecting the particular interests of the blogger, personal blogs may cover a range of topics. One of the world's most famous English-language personal blogs is Dooce, written by a stay-at-home mom in Salt Lake City.

Topical blogs   Usually more journalistic in nature, these blogs cover a particular topic (cars, pets, identity politics, and so forth). They are often, but not always, updated more frequently than personal blogs. Examples of this category of blog include The Amateur Gourmet, Autoblog, and The Unofficial Apple Blog.

Corporate blogs   These blogs are written by and officially associated with a company. They usually combine company and industry news. For instance, Google has many blogs for its various teams and projects.

Most of the time, you should start by looking for the topical blogs for a particular industry or geographical region. Why topical blogs? First, they're easy to find. If you run a ski lodge, you're looking for blogs about travel, outdoor equipment, and winter sports. Second, topical blogs are, by their nature, tightly focused. Every post on Ski-Blog.com is going to be about—you guessed it—skiing. Their readership is obviously interested in that topic and thus a desirable audience for your marketing message. Third, topical bloggers are generally more accustomed to being contacted by marketing folks. Finally, topical bloggers tend to have daily or weekly demands for content. They tend to write more often because they are, or aspire to become, probloggers. They may want or need relationships with companies and marketers to satisfy their constant content demands.

Arieanna Schweber is a professional blogger and entertainment editor at b5media where she writes for a variety of entertainment and celebrity blogs. Here, she gives us her take on the kind of content probloggers need for topical sites:

> Topical blogs demand a greater commitment from bloggers because they have set parameters. If you are going to cover a topic, you have to be an expert in something. That requires posting on all the relevant news in your niche, whether that be one post a day or ten posts a day. The task of a blog is to bring together a community with accurate and timely reporting on a topic infused with enough personality to set it apart from traditional media offerings.

If you can help a topical blogger fulfill this mandate, then that's a relationship you should try to foster.

We're not saying you should ignore personal blogs. They're especially good if you're trying to reach a particular region or demographic. They just require more research. You need to be as sure as possible that a given personal blogger or diarist will be interested in what you're offering. How do you determine that? Read, search their archive, and read some more. If you're promoting a Portland film festival, find some local bloggers who often write about movies. And if it's a gay film festival, you might want to steer clear of the neoconservative blogger. Don't make assumptions, mind you. Just draw informed, well-researched conclusions.

As for company blogs, we mostly avoid them. They often have small audiences and tend to write about themselves and their products. They're certainly not inclined to write about the competition.

Size Matters, and Yes, It Is a Popularity Contest

Back when you were penniless and backpacking around Europe, you consulted with your fellow hostellers about the best spot for cheap schnitzel and grappa. When sizing up bloggers, podcasters, and video bloggers, use the tools in this chapter to vet your targets. These tools will give you a green light or stop you in your tracks.

Finding the right blogs and online communities to contact with your story is the first hurdle to clear on your journey toward a successful campaign. Yes, size matters. You want to identify content creators who have the greatest readership and influence within your industry. A link from these bigwigs can send thousands of visitors to your site and also help to bolster your own search engine ranking. The challenge here is getting noticed by these sites. Grabbing the attention of a popular blog like CrunchGear or Gawker is analogous to being covered by the *New York Times*. So, although this chapter focuses primarily on finding the big guns, don't count out smaller blogs entirely, as you'll likely see some good success with them. A story from a minor site sometimes bubbles up through the blogosphere to über blogs and even infiltrates traditional media. In 2006, a New York concert raising funds for AIDS research was canceled when a handful of bloggers blogged in protest. Apparently, some of the artists participating in the concert were known for songs with violently anti-gay lyrics. In less than 48 hours, A-list blogs and the media had picked up the story and the event was canceled.

So, how do you find the sites that best fit your marketing mandate? We wish there were one easy answer. Sadly, no single tool reliably measures readership and audience. Instead, you'll need to combine tools and tactics to compare blogs and draw conclusions about which bloggers you'll want to contact.

Learn to Read the Road Signs

Here's a summary of tools and sites you can use to locate and compare blogs. You may not want to hear this, but all of the blog-finding tactics we discuss are imprecise. As we write this book, we have yet to see a comprehensive, reliable tool that can satisfy all your research and monitoring needs. Your best strategy is to apply as many different measures as possible and then add a big dose of intuition. The intuition part is crucial because, in the short term, someone can fool any of these tools. For this reason, we're extremely skeptical of vendors who claim to have a canonical system for categorizing and ranking websites. These tools might be useful, but you should never generate a list of blogs without visiting each and every one to verify its appropriateness. Would you pitch a magazine columnist if you'd never read her articles? Would you run a PR campaign without vetting the journalists from a purchased database? Probably not. Appraise bloggers in the same careful way.

Finding Blogs with Google

Believe it or not, Google is the most useful and reliable blog-finding tool around. Nobody does a better job of ranking websites in order of popularity and authority. Every Internet user grasps—consciously or otherwise—that the websites Google displays first in its search results are usually the most relevant. Those top links are the likeliest ones to answer your search query. In another sense, relevancy in Google means these links are the most popular, authoritative, or reliable links.

Of course, millions of people are busy trying to influence Google's rankings. An entire industry has been built around *search engine optimization* (*SEO*), a variety of strategies—some legitimate, some nefarious—aimed at bolstering a site's position in Google and other search engines. Why? Because higher rankings mean more authority and popularity, and those qualities translate to more visitors, which in turn translate to more revenue. Despite this, Google remains a remarkably effective tool for organizing the Web in a meaningful way.

So how can you use Google to find the blogs you'd like to contact? There's nothing magic about it—but you will have to do plenty of digging. Finding and comparing blogs is as simple as entering a search query like *<subject> blog* and paging through the results. Search for *knitting blog* and you'll find Yarn Harlot, Chic Knits, and the Knit Witch blog. To get an idea of how popular a site is, type this into Google:

```
link:http://www.yarnharlot.ca
```

The results will tell you how many other sites link to this blog. Simply put, the more links, the more popular the blog. At the time of this writing, Google shows 4550 sites linking to *http://www.yarnharlot.ca/*. Compare that with *http://chicknits.com/rambles/* and you get 837 incoming links. Now you know that Yarn Harlot is probably more popular, or authoritative, than the ChicKnits blog.

Typically, the sites listed on the first page of Google are more popular than the sites listed on the tenth page. Google's inherent ranking system is very helpful in narrowing down your search for popular topical blogs.

Google Blog Search is another free tool you can use to search for relevant topical blogs, but we haven't found it as useful as old-school Google Search. Google Blog Search doesn't rank search returns in the same way as Google Search; this tool is more focused on displaying recently updated blog posts than on displaying relevant posts. As such, it finds blog content that matches your search query but tends to return less relevant and popular results. For instance, if you search for *knitting* on Google Blog Search, you'll find that many of the results on the first page aren't sites specifically about knitting; they may simply mention knitting in passing. Spending some time with this tool to make sure you're not missing opportunities is worthwhile, but in our experience, you'll get the best results from Google Search.

Metrics: Making a List, Checking It Twice

When we're researching blogs and bloggers for clients, we usually build a spreadsheet that includes several metrics based on a variety of free tools. These metrics help us compare and filter blogs based on their popularity.

Blog Name	URL	Technorati Rank	Google PR	Alexa Ranking	Compete Visitors
TreeHugger	http://www.treehugger.com	16	8	4070	910289
Inhabitat	http://www.inhabitat.com	50	4	11231	299343
EcoGeek	http://www.ecogeek.org	3768	4	53690	67361
Lighter Footstep	http://www.lighterfootstep.com	27612	6	109128	13724
MetaEfficient	http://www.metaefficient.com	18552	4	88498	58618
The Ethicurean	http://www.ethicurean.com	16490	6	266905	17409

A spreadsheet we created to compare the popularity of similar blogs

A spreadsheet is a critical tool in the execution of your blogger outreach campaign. In addition to the rankings on various services, include as much information as you can about the blog in question. You can also use the spreadsheet to track your contacts and follow-ups with bloggers. A typical spreadsheet should include this information:

- Name of the blog

- Blogger's name, if available

- Blog URL
- Contact details (email address, contact page on site, and mailing address if you can find it)
- Topics the blog covers
- Regional range of the blog, if applicable
- Google PageRank
- Technorati Authority
- Alexa ranking
- Compete visitors
- Pitch policy describing how the blogger likes to be approached
- Notes

Although none of these ranking tools is foolproof on its own, their combined results give a more precise overall picture of how blogs compare in relation to one another.

NOTE   *More and more bloggers are including pitch policies on their site as a way to steer PR folks in the right direction.*

Google PageRank and Trends

Google offers two free metrics tools that can help you compare target sites: Google PageRank and Google Trends.

PageRank = Popularity

Google PageRank is a link analysis algorithm that assigns a numerical ranking to a web page. The higher the PageRank number, the more popular the site. The algorithm Google uses to generate PageRank is rather complex. Here's Google's explanation of how it works:

> PageRank reflects our view of the importance of web pages by considering more than 500 million variables and 2 billion terms. Pages that we believe are important pages receive a higher PageRank and are more likely to appear at the top of the search results.

PageRank also considers the importance of each page that casts a vote, as votes from some pages are considered to have greater value, thus giving the linked page greater value. We have always taken a pragmatic approach to help improve search quality and create useful products, and our technology uses the collective intelligence of the web to determine a page's importance.*

In a nutshell, the greater the number of incoming links a site has from important sites, the higher the page's PageRank is likely to be. The PageRank scale is like the Richter scale, meaning it's logarithmic, so a blog with a PageRank of 6 has 10 times the authority of one with 5. To give you some context on how difficult increasing your Google PageRank is, Facebook and the *New York Times* have a Google PageRank of 9. Any blog with a PageRank of 4 or higher is worth a second look.

You can check Google PageRank in two easy ways:

- Use any of a number of free web tools like PageRank Checker (*http://www.PRChecker.info/*). Click the **Check Page Rank** link and then type the web address of the site you want to check. Click **Submit**, and the PageRank result immediately appears.

- Integrate Google's PageRank checker into your browser using Google Toolbar (*http://toolbar.google.com/*).

When you're trying to get a picture of a blog's popularity, Google PageRank is one of the metrics that can give you a general idea of where a site sits in the blogosphere.

Compare Websites with Google Trends

Google Trends (*http://www.google.com/trends*) is a fast, easy, free way to compare the popularity of websites based on Google's own data. Enter two or more websites into the tool, and Google Trends generates a report displaying an estimate of how many visitors each site receives from the search engine. For this to work, you will need to choose **Websites**, not Searches, at the top of the page. If the site isn't particularly popular, there may not be enough data to render a

---

* Google Technology Overview, *http://www.google.com/corporate/tech.html*.

comparison, so this tool is most useful for comparing popular sites. Be warned that this report only shows traffic from Google searchers, as opposed to site visitors who come from other websites, RSS subscribers, and so forth, so you're only comparing a fraction of the sites' traffic. Still, we've found a strong correlation between the number of visitors to a site from Google and the total number of visitors to the site.

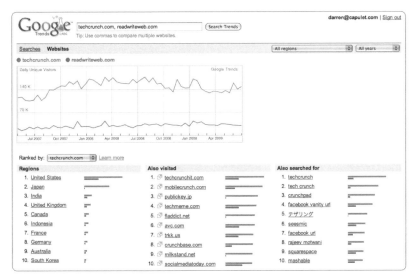

Google Trends compares visitor traffic to TechCrunch and ReadWriteWeb.

Technorati, BlogPulse, IceRocket . . . the List Goes On

Technorati (*http://technorati.com/*) is a search engine that focuses on blogs and other popular social media channels. Its slogan is "search the live web." As of late 2008, Technorati, considered one of the leading blog search engines, indexes more than 112.8 million blogs. Technorati can help you find topical blogs because it searches blog content for keywords and phrases, but we find it most useful for measuring the popularity of blogs we've already found using Google Search. Technorati is ideal for finding out who's saying what online about a specific topic. So, if you search for *Shania Twain* on Technorati, you won't be sent to her website, but you will get results from the latest buzz about albums, concerts, and gossip.

Technorati has a handy feature called Technorati Authority that helps marketing folks measure a blog's relevancy. If you enter a blog's URL into the search bar on the home page, Technorati will display the blog's *authority*, or the number of other blogs that linked to that site over the last six months. The higher the number, the more Technorati Authority the blog has. Technorati also displays a rank for each blog. This rank indicates where the site stands in the blogosphere.

Several Technorati competitors are out there: IceRocket, Google Blog Search, Nielsen BuzzMetrics, BlogPulse, and so forth. We encourage you to experiment with each service to see which you prefer, though Technorati continues to be our tool of choice. Compare the search results for your industry, and stick with the service that seems to generate the most useful and reliable results.

Alexa, Compete, and Quantcast

Alexa can be a rather confusing tool. What the heck is it, and is it actually useful? Alexa, owned by Amazon.com, provides information about the web traffic to other websites—not unlike Google PageRank. But it differs from Google PageRank in a fundamental way: Internet users choose whether or not to install the Alexa Toolbar in their browser. Alexa can only monitor the user behavior of those who have installed its Toolbar. Alexa then generates statistics about site visitors based on that data.

Alexa has a few problems. First, the Alexa sample group is often too small to be meaningful. As such, a small bump in visitors with the Alexa Toolbar installed in their browsers represents a huge change in the Alexa rating. Second, Alexa Toolbar installation appeals to a particular demographic of web users, which doesn't offer a true picture of web user behavior. On its website, Alexa describes its target demographic as "Web masters and computer professionals" and "professional males between 25 and 34 years old." That's a pretty specific profile. These shortcomings make Alexa a questionable measurement tool, which is why we don't put a lot of stock in Alexa rankings. We still sometimes include Alexa on our blogger contact spreadsheet—often, admittedly, at our client's request.

Compete is akin to Alexa as it offers competitive metrics based on consumer behavior data; like Alexa, the Compete Toolbar tracks and records the online behavior of more than two million users. Compete displays web analytics data from two or three competing websites in an easy-to-read graph, though Compete suffers from the same reliability issues as Alexa. Similarly, Quantcast is a rating service that estimates and reports on audience metrics, such as traffic and demographics, but this service is primarily designed for advertisers. These tools can still be useful if you measure their *relative* results rather than the hard numbers.

Count RSS Subscribers

For any kind of content creator, RSS subscribers are very precious audience members. They have, after all, opted in. They have voluntarily agreed to receive blog posts, podcasts, videos, and so forth regularly. For the average blogger, RSS subscribers comprise the core, most loyal part of his community. As such, checking the number of subscribers that a blog has is another means of evaluating its popularity.

Many bloggers use FeedBurner to measure the number of RSS subscribers they have. Think of FeedBurner as web analytics for RSS. It enables RSS publishers to track their subscribers' behavior—where they came from, what RSS reader or website they use, and so forth. FeedBurner also enables users to publish a little widget or *chicklet* that displays the number of subscribers to a particular blog. This is the simplest way to check the number of subscribers—look for a little blue or orange button that displays the number of readers.

The FeedBurner chicklet

You can also search a blog for the phrase *RSS subscribers* or ** subscribers* to see if the blog's author has volunteered this information. As with other statistics, some bloggers will choose not to disclose this information. You will find, however, that the more commercial blogs (which are therefore interested in advertising revenue) will want to pull back the curtain on their statistics.

Be a Bit Skeptical

For all of these services—from Google to Quantcast—remaining somewhat skeptical is important because the numbers are more relative than absolute. Search guru Vanessa Fox tells us what she thinks about these measurement tools and explains how they can still be useful, if not entirely reliable:

> All of the services are fairly notoriously unreliable. They all use different methods for gathering data that make them inaccurate by nature. Alexa, for instance, uses the Alexa Toolbar, which is skewed toward a certain user demographic. These tools are useful in a couple of ways, however: for trending over time and for comparisons. If you use one tool to gather data on these two things, then although the data will be unreliable, it should be equally unreliable over time or among sites, so the trending should be fairly accurate.

Don't Overlook Anecdotal Evidence

Anecdotal evidence can be exceedingly useful when growing your blogger contact list. The metrics tools mentioned previously go a long way toward helping you compare sites once they're already on your list, but these less empirical tactics can put some ideal targets on your radar.

Blogrolls: Who Is Your BFF?

Bloggers commonly link to other blogs they read on a regular basis or that complement the content on their own blog. They often offer this link-love in the form of a *blogroll*—a list of websites usually found in a sidebar on the blog. Once you find a few promising blogs via Google Search or other means, check out their blogrolls. Bloggers in a particular industry, location, or affinity group will often link to each other, so blogrolls

Blogroll

- + John Bollwitt
- 2Bit Studios (Mel)
- Adult ADD Strengths
- Amateur Geek
- Ariane
- Awake & Dreaming
- BC Brit
- Boris Mann
- Chillaxin
- Condo Hype
- Confessions of a Monkey
- Creampuff Revolution
- Dan Lilly
- Darren Barefoot
- David Drucker
- Dr Beth Snow

Think of a blogroll as a blogger's recommended reading list.

can provide a gold mine of sites to read and potentially add to your contact list.

Some signs indicate, however, that blogrolls are beginning to go out of style. Popular personal blogger Rebecca Bollwitt of Miss604.com had this to say when we spoke to her about disappearing blogrolls:

> Perhaps this is because blogrolls were social to begin with—a "blogs I like" or a "my friends" list. Now that we have so many other social networks where we can show off our friends, maybe people aren't finding blogrolls as useful. I discovered recently that deleting someone from your blogroll is like a big virtual slap in the face. So link lists are becoming more trouble than they're worth, even to clean them up or consolidate them.

If that's the case, we encourage you to mine blogrolls for the underlying relationships now before they disappear.

A Little Help from Your Friends

Get out of your chair, step away from the computer, and have some real-world conversations with your colleagues about what blogs they're reading. An informal, in-house survey won't give you comprehensive results, but chances are some of your colleagues know exactly which blogs and online communities are talking about your industry, your competitors, and maybe even your company. Consider keeping a shared, private in-house blogroll to encourage your colleagues to monitor the social space. You can do this easily. Post the blogroll on your intranet. If you don't have an intranet, create a private pagecast in Pageflakes (*http://www.pageflakes.com/*), which is simply a personal collection of web favorites, and share it with your colleagues. Or use FriendFeed (*http://www.friendfeed.com/*) to distribute an RSS feed or single view of links, photos, and video content that you think is relevant to your business. Alternately, you could maintain and share an OPML file, which is essentially a computer-readable list of RSS feeds. Storing the feeds in this format means that it's easy to import feeds into an RSS reader. Keeping all this information in one place will ensure you're not duplicating research or misplacing key content.

You could repeat this process at industry events. "What blogs are you reading?" is a goofy but effective icebreaker. Be sure to ask analysts and journalists as well. You should definitely include these sites on your list.

Trust Your Instincts

You're a marketer with good instincts. Don't forget to pay attention to more subjective indications of a blog's popularity:

How many comments does the average post receive?

Obviously this varies based on the blog's topic and writing style. A blog post about presidential candidates or the superiority of Windows over Mac is likely to garner a lot more attention than a description of last night's calamari. So take time to browse through the blog's recent archives to get a sense of the conversation over time. You can bet a blog that averages five comments per post has more readers than the one without comments.

How often does the blogger write blog posts?

If the blogger only posts twice a month, he probably—but not necessarily—has a smaller audience. The author and software developer Paul Graham posts essays periodically on his website. They're very popular, even though he doesn't write more than six or eight a year. The practical reason for considering posting frequency is that if the blogger is an infrequent poster, it will be more difficult to interest him in your story.

How long has the blogger been blogging?

Generally speaking, the older the blog, the more the readers it has. Exceptions to this rule exist, but other factors—lots of comments or incoming links, for example—will make new yet popular blogs obvious.

How much stuff—widgets, blogrolls, and so forth—is included in the blog's sidebars?

A blogger who's aware of and active in her community will tend to advertise affiliations and connections this way. More "stuff" suggests the blogger has a broader reach.

How many other services can you find the blogger on?

Does the blogger use FriendFeed, Twitter, Last.fm, or any of the other social media and Web 2.0 services? If the blogger is engaged on other services beyond his blog, the blog's network of readers is probably bigger too.

Have you seen the blog design before?

The popular blogging services—WordPress, Blogger, MovableType, and so forth—enable bloggers to change the look and feel of their site by installing a design template or *skin*. If you visit a lot of blogs, you'll begin to recognize the difference between off-the-shelf templates and custom designs. If a blogger has gone to the trouble of creating a unique design for her site, the blogger is more serious about blogging.

If you combine metrics tools with Google Search, Google Blog Search, anecdotal evidence from friends and colleagues, along with a healthy dose of good instinct and common sense, you'll be well on your way to pitching the right people, which is half the battle! On the flip side, if you opt for an easy way out—like purchasing a blogger contact list—we can assure you that you'll be disappointed with the returns. In here somewhere is almost certainly a life lesson about being rewarded for your hard work.

Now that you've got a list of promising contacts, you can create your pitch.

4

NETIQUETTE: MISS MANNERS FOR THE WEB

Welcome to the world of the new influencers. The reason the social web is sometimes called the "wild west" is that we're still working out the kinks of how best to communicate with one another online. The rules of conduct may not be set in stone, but the social web isn't a total free-for-all either. You should be aware of some key, often mystifying, communications protocols before striking up conversations with the locals. This chapter provides some lessons on how to communicate with *new influencers*—bloggers, YouTube stars, Facebook friend magnets, and Digg superstars. Think of this chapter as finishing school for Internet communication. If you understand the social innuendo, you've got a much better chance of breaking into the inner circle and getting mentioned or reviewed by powerful online influencers who can send thousands of visitors—and potential buyers—your way.

We will run through a variety of communications techniques here, but if you take one lesson from this chapter, take this: Listen first. Thankfully, nearly all new influencer communications occur in the Internet's public forum, so you can adopt an anthropological approach. By emulating the influencers' behavior and learning their dialect, you can be confident when you approach them. As Jane Goodall discovered, the best way to learn about a species is to live among them. So you're going to start being active online right now. Have your computer in front of you while you read this chapter, because we're going to put you to work.

Lesson #1: Listen First

The golden rule is "listen first." Start by finding some blogs and online communities that are discussing your product or organization. In Chapter 3, we lay out a strategy for searching out the relevant new influencers in your industry, but here are a few quick pointers so you can reconnoiter a few corners of the Web right away:

- Start with Google, of course. Unless you're IKEA or General Motors or in the entertainment industry, you probably won't find blogs dedicated specifically to your company or brand. Still, doing a complete search for *<your company> blog* can't hurt. You'll probably discover some blog posts that reference your company. Poke around the associated blogs, and see if they mention your organization on a regular basis. If they do, start reading them.

- Can't find any blogs exclusively dedicated to your company? No problem. Do you have larger competitors in your industry? Try searching for *<your competitor> blog*. Start reading the corporate blogs written by your competitors, as well as the third-party blogs that cover them.

- You can almost certainly find blogs covering your industry. Don't believe us? Pick the most unlikely industry and do a search for *<industry> blog*. Our favorite way to prove this is by doing a quick search for *funeral blog*. Try it—you'll find dozens. If your industry has newsletters, magazines, and conferences, at least a handful of bloggers are writing about it, too. Find a few, and start reading them today.

With just a few clicks, you've got a virtual stack of reading material that will help you get to know the new influencers in your industry, what they're talking about, which companies they're watching, and perhaps most importantly, what they're *not* writing about. If you do your homework and read these blogs weekly, you're laying the groundwork for good future encounters with these folks.

Lesson #2: Take Baby Steps

In Chapter 1 you learned about the Conversation Prism, which illustrates a variety of social media channels. Rules exist for communicating within the different channels. For this beginner lesson, let's look at Digg. Digg is the most popular social news site on the Web. Users submit their own news stories to the website, and others vote for or against the news stories (we explain Digg's full marketing potential in detail in Chapter 13). The best way to understand how folks communicate within Digg is to set up a user account. To begin, visit *http://www.digg.com/* and click the **Join Digg** link in the top navigation bar. Complete the registration process, and upload a photo to make your profile a little more personal.

Next, browse the site using the topics listed in the navigation bar. Digg uses somewhat peculiar categories for organizing its stories (for instance, Technology has Apple and Microsoft categories, but no Google). Each section displays items including news stories, videos, and images that have recently been voted up or *dugg* within that section. Likewise, the front page displays popular stories that have been dugg for the whole site. The stories that appear on Digg's home page can send hundreds of thousands of visitors to a website. On Digg, the community chooses which stories become popular and which stories get voted down, or *buried*.

Now's your chance to get your hands dirty. Drill down into a section that interests you, or use the **Search Digg** text box to locate stories. Given the demographics of the Digg community, you're going to find more stories about astronomy than ballet. Once you find appealing stories, click the link associated with each story summary to visit the story's originating website. If you like the story, return to Digg and click the **Digg It** button associated with the story. The number of diggs will increase by one (or more, if the story is rapidly receiving many votes from other users).

Congratulations! You've just participated in your first careful, discreet social media discourse. By voting up a story on Digg, you've become part of the community by saying which stories deserve to be promoted. The lesson here is to start small. If you haven't already been commenting on blog posts or participating on social news and bookmarking sites, begin conservatively in a social media channel like Digg. Participating on Digg is a safe way to look before you leap.

Tips for Choosing a Username

If you're shy about getting active online, then take baby steps. You can always register using an alias on Twitter, Digg, and MySpace while you check out the services. Remember, everything you do online is tied to your personal reputation, so choosing a username can be very important.

What if you want to get up to some hijinks on the Web—antics that your employer, customers, or online contacts might frown on? Don't worry, your social life doesn't have to come to an abrupt halt. Consider creating an alternative, anonymous persona that allows you to express yourself without causing repercussions for your professional life.

Alternately, building your personal brand online can be a powerful tool for making inroads with new influencers. If you're working hard to make valuable contributions on social networks, blogs, and Twitter, then don't hide behind a screen name. People like to know who's behind a profile and often engage more readily with "real" people than with handles. If you use your real name, you'll begin to enjoy the professional benefits of online exposure, including building stronger online relationships.

Before you choose a username, consider your goals. Are you trying to obscure your identity to keep your personal life separate from the professional sphere? Or are you trying to make a name for yourself in specific web communities so you have more influence with the right crowd?

Lesson #3: Make Friends

Making friends online can be a lot easier than making friends in the real world. That's one of the reasons social networking and online dating is so successful. Thankfully, online small talk is considerably less awkward than real-world cocktail chatter. You can extend your hand to online influencers by linking to their websites, subscribing to their blogs, adding them to your blogroll, following them on Twitter, or joining their Facebook groups. Before you start forging online relationships, you should familiarize yourself with these tools. Now is a good time to sign up for Twitter and Facebook accounts if you haven't already.

Bloggers, podcasters, and video creators notice these connections because they are constantly monitoring their growing audience. Think of these low-key, first moves as your calling card; they break the ice when contacting new influencers with your story. We've discovered that if the new influencers recognize you as a regular reader, a Facebook group member, an RSS subscriber, or a Twitter follower, they're more likely to give you the benefit of the doubt and hear what you have to say. A word of warning: Unless the person you're trying to befriend has hundreds and hundreds of Facebook friends—and is obviously not very discerning about who he friends—we suggest holding off on sending him a Facebook invitation. For most, a Facebook invitation is one step too far into the inner circle. Wait until you've had one or two email conversations before getting too friendly.

Lesson #4: Lay Your Cards on the Table

Pop quiz. What are the two critical tenets of new PR? If you said "authenticity and transparency," then kudos for paying attention and thoroughly reading Chapter 1. These tenets apply to all your interactions with social media creators. You've got to be completely up front about who you are, what company you're working for, and what your motivations and goals are. For starters, the message needs to come from you, not *info@yourcompany.com* or *news@yourcompany .net*. You're trying to forge a personal, lasting relationship with the person at the other end of your outbox. If you appear to be hiding anything (and that includes hiding behind a generic email address), your email will likely be filed among the Viagra and Rolex ads.

When we're contacting bloggers for the first time, our opening line is often something like this:

> Hi, My name is Darren Barefoot and I'm a blogger (*www*
> *.darrenbarefoot.com*) and a marketer (*www.capulet.com*). I'm
> working with ACME Blow-Up Toys (*www.acmeblowup.com*)
> to help them get the word out about their new line of . . .

Our goal is to divulge as much information as possible as quickly as possible. The URLs are key because links are the language and currency of the Web. Bloggers can immediately visit any of the sites we provide to confirm our identity. Links work like little tokens of trust—a personal detail disclosed that helps to strengthen a connection.

Clarity is key. If your goal is to get a blogger to review your product, simply ask him. Don't send him tickets to the opening night of your play as a gift. Explain that free tickets are available for reviewers. If he wants free tickets, his intention should be to review your play. Whether you send a blogger a laptop or a new brand of dishwashing detergent, be sure to request a review or he might misconstrue the gift as a bribe. Take your lead from Andrew Milligan of Sumo Lounge International. Milligan wasn't selling enough bean bag chairs to make a go of it. But when he began approaching bloggers and offering to send them bean bag chairs to review, his luck changed. Two years later, after more than 250 blogger reviews or web posts about his bean bag chairs, the company's annual profits have tripled. In Shelly Banjo's *Wall Street Journal* article "Ripple Effect: Blogs Help Businesses That Can't Afford a Lot of Marketing," Milligan says, "This approach saved my business. It took Sumo from nothing to a fairly large and profitable company."*

---

* Shelly Banjo, "Ripple Effect: Blogs Help Businesses That Can't Afford a Lot of Marketing," *Wall Street Journal*, May 2008, *http://www.wsjclassroomedition.com/cre/articles/08may_cs_entr_blogs.htm*.

Lesson #5: Bloggers Aren't Journalists

Traditional journalists and bloggers have some obvious similarities, but recognizing that they're not one and the same is important. Here are some key differences:

Bloggers' requirements for content are less rigid.

A reporter on the entertainment beat has specific weekly requirements for articles. In an average week, she might write one celebrity profile, two movie previews, and two movie reviews. Bloggers are free from such stringent requirements. A movie blogger might preview six movies one week and none the next. That said, almost all of the top-tier bloggers publish lots of new content all the time. Conveniently, this means they're constantly on the lookout for new material and aren't tied to the same lead times and deadlines as print journalists.

Bloggers' writing is usually informed by their opinion.

Bloggers don't have to write about anything they don't want to. Instead, they tend to write about things they respond to emotionally (whether with outrage or adoration). So bloggers will not want to transcribe your media release announcing a new corporate partnership—press releases are utterly devoid of feeling (and, of course, are boring, manufactured news).

Bloggers make connections.

If you can't include a hyperlink in your pitch, don't target bloggers. They'll look for something to link to, and if you don't provide a link, they might link to your competition—or an unflattering article about your organization.

Bloggers reject marketing language.

In our experience, journalists are accustomed to the corporate hackery of the modern media release with its superlatives and glowing prose. Journalists typically receive dozens of corporate entreaties a day and are proficient at cutting through the noise and PR flacks to get to a story's source. They recognize biased marketing messages as a necessary evil.

Bloggers aren't as hardened to spin, but they aren't fooled either. In fact, bloggers can be publicly critical of your marketing process. We sometimes see naive marketers mercilessly mocked by bloggers because they've made unfounded or exaggerated claims in a press release. Journalists won't often ridicule you; bloggers aren't always so kind.

Will bloggers respect embargoes?

That is, if you ask them not to publish your news before a certain day and time, will they hold off? Probably, but aside from a few *probloggers* (those who blog as a day job), they may not know what an embargo is. Still, if your entire marketing campaign revolves around radio silence until a particular time on a particular day, select the influencers you pitch with extra care.

In practice, this rule is slightly tricky because sometimes you'll benefit from treating bloggers exactly like the mainstream media. For instance, you wouldn't pay a journalist to review your product, so in almost every case you shouldn't pay a blogger either. And just as you wouldn't dream of telling a journalist how to write her story, you also should not attempt to write a blogger's review for him. As a general rule, approach bloggers with the same professionalism as you would a journalist.

Lesson #6: Your Reputation Precedes You

A marketer's profile is a lot more public and personal than it used to be. Although some influencer communication happens via email, online communication tends to spill over into public spaces—like blog comments, Facebook profiles, and YouTube video responses. Your name is associated with every message and comment. The sun has set on the age of the "unnamed company representative." If you're just getting started in social media marketing, this lesson is important to learn immediately—before your online reputation gets sullied by impetuous blog comments, indignant posts, or too much information about your personal life.

The Internet never forgets, and that can be a problem. If you don't believe us, visit *http://www.archive.org/*. Internet Archive is an organization dedicated to, among other things, archiving the entire

Internet. And if that's not enough, Google can store old copies of websites for months or years. As the Web ages, definitively removing content—whether a social networking profile, a blog comment, or a video—is only going to get harder. Additionally, the Internet doesn't discern between personal and professional content, so your public persona online is your professional persona. They are inseparable. Of course, not all is doom and gloom, drunken spring break photos on MySpace, and unearthed sex videos; all the good works you do show up online too. If you're a member of your local town council, teach community salsa dancing lessons, comment astutely in forums and on blog posts, join affinity groups for good causes, or blog on a topic you're passionate about, that all bolsters your online reputation. When you work on the Web, remember that taking care of your digital reputation is good for your business and for your career.

Science-fiction novelist and world-famous blogger Cory Doctorow devised a name for this kind of digital credibility: *whuffie*. In his book *Down and Out in the Magic Kingdom*, whuffie is a reputation-based currency accessible to everyone. When characters meet for the first time, they instantly check each other's whuffie to gauge each other's reputation. We're not quite at that stage yet—where are those brain implants? But any sophisticated web user can, in a couple of minutes, paint a remarkably complete portrait of any other regular web user.

Lesson #7: Don't Be a Social Media Spammer

> I don't know the first thing about [*this company*]. But then this morning they spammed me. Any email that lands in my inbox that's written in marketing-ese and I don't know who sent it, that's spam.
>
> —Tim Bray, software developer, entrepreneur, and blogger

Spammer is pretty much the worst aspersion you can cast on a web denizen. In the online world, being called a spammer is like being called creepy, desperate, and corrupt all at once. Marketers rightfully worry about demonstrating spammy behavior and often ask us how to avoid looking like a shady online citizen. If you practice what we preach elsewhere in this book, you should be okay. For the sake of completeness, however, this behavior is the kind that will brand your forehead with a big red *S*:

- You send generic emails to bloggers and podcasters with salutations like "Dear Webmaster."

- You contact bloggers with grand promises of link exchanges. Bloggers value links, but offers of link exchanges have all the appeal and personality of pyramid schemes.

- You post promotions for your own Facebook group (or worse, your product) on the walls of other Facebook profiles, pages, and groups.

- You haphazardly respond to blog posts, podcasts, and videos that discuss your competitors and leave promotional messages about your services.

- You don't consider the topics a social media creator covers, and as a result, you pitch a chick lit novel to the guy with a hockey blog.

- You send press releases out to large lists you bought or culled from the Web without obtaining the recipients' permission.

- You sneakily insert links to your products and services into Wikipedia.

- You offer to covertly buy editorial coverage on a blog. On that note, you should be skeptical of anyone who accepts payment to promote your organization without first publicly disclosing that payment or sponsorship.

- You forget to listen first.

Lesson #8: Don't Fib

With all our talk of honesty, authenticity, and trust, this point should be obvious. But surprisingly, companies still try to deceive, misdirect, and spin conversations on the Web. Don't lie, because you'll get caught. And when you get caught, your online reputation will take a beating.

In addition to all the ways marketers usually lie, two related, insidious strategies seem increasingly prevalent in the social media sphere: astroturfing and sockpuppeting. The former refers to a PR strategy where a campaign tries to appear spontaneous and grassroots but is actually orchestrated by an organization. *Astroturf* is a metaphor for fake grassroots support. *Sockpuppeting* is the creation of fake web profiles for the express purpose of promoting or advocating for a particular company or organization.

Exposed examples of astroturfing are legion. In 2006, science journalist Antonio Regalado exposed a YouTube video critical of Al Gore as being produced by DCI Group, a public relations firm with ExxonMobil and General Motors on its client list. DCI Group claimed the video had been spontaneously created by an amateur filmmaker in California. What made Regalado suspicious? DCI Group was running advertisements on Google results pages shown to web users searching for *Al Gore*. Do a search for *DCI Group* on Yahoo! or Google. Consider how many of the top 30 results are unflattering accounts of this incident or otherwise critical of the company. That's the cost of astroturfing.

The simplest form of sockpuppeting in the blogosphere is also the most common. Company representatives leave fake comments using dummy user profiles in response to blog posts that are critical of their organization. Some pretend to be customers who are over the moon about the company's fantastic product; others ruthlessly bash their competitors. Many marketers aren't savvy enough to know that when bloggers look up their IP addresses, the sockpuppets' identities can become very clear. The *IP* in *IP address* stands for *Internet protocol*. They're numerical addresses that identify computers that are connected to the Internet. IP addresses can sometimes be used to determine, in general terms, the geographical location or Internet service provider associated with web activity such as posting a comment to a blog. In 2007, the CEO of Whole Foods, John Mackey, wrote anonymous online attacks of a smaller competitor, Wild Oats, in Yahoo! financial forums. He seemed to be trying to devalue Wild Oats' stock before Whole Foods offered to buy the company. In the end, Mackey was outed by the Federal Trade Commission when it investigated the acquisition. The sockpuppet debacle publicly embarrassed Whole Foods and Mackey and must have cost the company a fortune in legal fees.

Who Are These New Influencers, Anyway?

So who are these new media masters you want to communicate with, and why should you be so concerned about getting on their good side? Simply put, they're going to help you sell your products and services. They've got the power to send hundreds, even thousands, of potential customers to your website. That improves your chances of making sales. Plus, each link from a powerful new influencer is recognized by Google as a thumbs up for your website. Google rewards you by moving you up the search rankings, resulting in more visibility in search engines.

So how do these new influencers feel about marketers pitching them stories, products, and services? Margaret Mason, Muhammad Saleem, and Marshall Kirkpatrick let us in on what works and what totally turns them off.

Margaret Mason, Shopping Diva at Mighty Goods

Mighty Goods (*http://www.mightygoods.com/*) is a popular shopping and design blog that has been listed as one of *Time*'s Top 50 Cool Sites and has been selected best shopping website by both *BusinessWeek* and *Forbes*. Mighty Goods posts new content five days a week, so the site is always on the lookout for new products to feature. Margaret Mason is the brains behind Mighty Goods.

Q: How do you decide whether or not to cover a product on your blog?

A: If you send me something that I otherwise would have listed, I'll list it. If somebody sends me a big basket of body and bath products, and it's good, I almost always list it, especially if it's beautifully designed. I feel like I can say, "They sent this to me and it's something I would've bought myself, so I thought my readers would like it."

Q: Most of the time, do marketers get it right or wrong?

A: Mighty Goods has been running for three or four years. In that time, I've received only two things that I would not have bought with my own money. And I get several items a day in the mail. Anybody who has ever looked at my site understands what aesthetic appeals to me.

Q: What are you trying to accomplish with Mighty Goods?

A: The reason I started my style section was to give back to the community. There's a woman who makes these little bags in Japan who has, like, 10 visitors a day. I linked to her website, and she sold out of all of her stuff. She sent me an email saying "Awesome!"

Muhammad Saleem on Getting Dugg

Muhammad Saleem is a Digg superstar. We can give you a very good reason for enticing Saleem—and other top diggers—to vote up your posts. If Saleem diggs your article, you've got a much, much better chance of getting on the Digg front page. That's because Saleem's network is watching which stories he's digging and, in many cases, will follow his lead. We asked Saleem how he feels about marketers sending him stories and what criteria he applies to voting up content on Digg.

Q: How often do you get contacted by marketers who ask you to digg their stories?

A: I get asked to submit or vote on stories fairly often. However, I don't know how many of them are marketers and how many are just content producers and publishers just trying to get a little exposure.

Q: Do you ever digg on a marketer's request?

A: I don't care if a person asking me is a marketer or someone else; I usually submit or vote as long as the content is good.

Q: What criteria do you use to decide whether or not a story is digg-worthy?

A: The criteria is simple:
    Will the story be of interest to the general Digg community? Do I like the content? In most cases, I'll act if I think the community will appreciate it.

Q: What kinds of things would you say gets the Digg community the most excited?

A: The community's preferences are always changing. It used to be very technology-centric but has been leaning more and more toward world news (politics, business, etc.) and offbeat entertainment items.

Q: What's so great about Digg? Why do you dedicate time and effort to it?

A: There are several reasons I spend time on Digg. First, it's because of the platform. However flawed it may be, it's pushing boundaries and creating standards for how content is created and consumed online. Second, because by participating over the years I have built a fairly close group of friends. Finally, because it's just fun and allows you to keep up with trends in the social space.

For Marshall Kirkpatrick, It's Just the Facts, Ma'am

Marshall Kirkpatrick is the Vice President of Content Development at ReadWriteWeb, a blog that covers technology news, reviews, and analysis. ReadWriteWeb's got more than 275,000 RSS and email subscribers and is ranked by the blog search engine Technorati as one of the world's top 100 blogs. If you work in technology, getting covered by ReadWriteWeb should be at the top of your wish list. Though we've personally had good success with gimmicky, creative blogger outreach tactics, Kirkpatrick is a journalist at heart. He wants the facts. Here are his top tips on how to get your story on ReadWriteWeb:

Q: How many pitches do you receive each day?

A: I'm going to guess 40 or 50.

Q: Is getting pitched a drag or do you just see it as part of your job?

A: Bad pitches are a drag; good pitches are fabulous. Trying to figure out which is which quickly so I can move on to scanning RSS feeds is one of the most important parts of my job.

Q: What's the most original marketing pitch you've received? What about it made you want to write about the company?

A: Originality in a pitch is of very little consequence. The best pitch I've heard this year was when Eric Marcoullier from Gnip called me up while I was at the grocery store and he said, "This probably isn't very sexy, but I'm building a social media ping server that does data protocol transformation, including offering XMPP feeds from any participating source whether they publish in XMPP or not." I said to him, "Don't you dare forget to call me again two days before this launches; that sounds like the most awesome thing I've heard about in a long time." Just tell me in one or two sentences about what the technology does. I get excited about cool things for a living so don't try to trick me into getting excited about something unexciting, I won't appreciate it. Just tell me what it does, and if I like it, then help me get more information about it.

Q: If you could offer one piece of advice to marketers pitching news sites like ReadWriteWeb, what would it be?

A: Give me your client's RSS feed, make sure it's got interesting technology news in it from time to time, and put your phone number and IM in your email signature.

Q: If you could give marketing folks one tip about how *not* to pitch you, what would it be?

A: Don't refuse to tell me what the news is unless I talk to a CEO first.

Etiquette Cheat Sheet

Be respectful. Be honest. Don't lie. Send good content. This advice seems like common sense (or even common courtesy!), but we've seen so many examples of duplicitous marketing on the Web that we feel we have to say it again. One of the oldest and most reliable pieces of advice for online conduct is this: Treat the people you're talking to as though they're in the room with you. At a cocktail party, you probably wouldn't wield a megaphone to broadcast your commercial message, constantly interrupt conversations with a product plug, or tell stories that simply aren't true. And surely you've watched enough sitcoms or read enough Shakespeare to recognize how foolhardy it is to pretend to be someone you're not. Be authentic, and you (probably) can't go wrong.

We encourage you to dive into these new landscapes and meet the locals. Whether that's signing up for a StumbleUpon account, posting your first photos to Flickr, or launching an internal blog on your corporate intranet, participation is key to comprehension. Plus, becoming involved in these communities is essential to establishing your online credibility and that of your organization. We can't learn about new cultures or how to speak their language if we don't leave our living rooms, and that's the first step in engaging with the world of social media. So get off of your virtual couch and explore the social web.

5

STICK OUT YOUR THUMB:
DEVISING YOUR PITCH

A successful social media relations campaign needs a good story. If reality TV has taught us anything, it's that any story worth telling needs good characters and a compelling plot, and it should be at least a little entertaining. Think of your pitch as a narrative, your executives as characters, and the person you're pitching as the skeptical audience who needs to be won over. Then spin a good yarn.

So, what makes a good pitch?

The pitch is compelling and relevant.

"You should write about our new product" definitely won't cut it. Think critically, and focus on a specific feature that will capture the recipient's attention. Ideally, that feature should be unique. Few bloggers will care if the new car you're selling gets a couple more miles to the gallon than your competitor's. But they might be intrigued if it comes with a polka dot paint scheme. Keep your story relevant by contacting bloggers and online communities that are already interested in your topic.

The pitch is timely.

A new product offers some mystique and can improve your chances of being noticed.

The product is still a secret.

Just like journalists, bloggers care about exclusivity. The rivalry between top gadget blogs Gizmodo and Engadget is legendary, as each blog tries to scoop the other with coverage of the latest technology news. Because that kind of competition is common on the Web, consider offering an exclusive to the most popular and relevant blogger on your list.

The pitch is personal.

Bloggers don't want to be blasted with press releases or mass pitches. Address a blogger by his first name. Introduce yourself right at the start. Show bloggers you're familiar with their work by referring to a relevant post on their site.

The pitch is short and sweet.

Time is precious, so don't waste words on pleasantries and small talk. Cut to the chase.

The pitch is comprehensive.

This point might seem to contradict our tip about short and sweet, but ensure that the new influencer you contact has all the information he needs to write a story. If you don't want to include all the details in your initial message, you can always provide links to web resources.

The pitch is conversational.

Social media is much more informal than traditional business communications. So sound like a real person, not a marketing team run by committee. Heather Armstrong, author of Dooce, one of the world's most popular mommy blogs, offers this advice: "I'm looking for the personal email. Not the pitchy email, just 'Hey, what's up, I was thinking that you might be interested in this because of this or that post that I read on your website.'"

The pitch leads with a link.

Include a link in the first paragraph of your pitch. Anyone you contact online should be able to click through quickly to your organization or product announcement. Leading with a link shows you can speak the blogger's language. Don't start pitching until you have something to link to.

The pitch includes an incentive.

This can be tricky, as you don't want to offer to buy a mention. An effective incentive is a limited free offer, such as a software license that expires in a week or after so many uses. Never, ever send cash or expensive gifts. In our experience, inviting bloggers to review a product works really well. MOO, a printing company based in London, England, turned a giveaway into a successful marketing campaign that boosted prominence and sales in the company's first year. One way MOO differentiated itself in a busy, competitive sector was by integrating with social media services like Flickr, Facebook, and Vox. If you already have images hosted on one of these services, MOO makes it extremely easy to have them printed as postcards, greeting cards, and in many other formats.

When MOO launched in September 2006, Flickr was one of the few services with which it integrated. Wanting to make a splash and recognizing the power of free stuff, MOO gave away 10,000 packs of 10 mini business cards to Flickr users. Targeting Pro (that is, paying) users was a wise move. If users are willing and able to pay for photo hosting and sharing, they will be more likely to pay to have their photos printed.

MOO Vice President of Sales and Marketing Lisa Rodwell describes the power of this strategy:

> By giving early adopters free MOO cards, they were quick to become advocates for what MOO is all about. They took photos of their MOOs; they shared them in groups, in their blogs and in real life. The freebies injected MOO into many conversations that lead to more sales.[*]

MOO didn't buy any advertising or apply traditional marketing tactics in its first year of operation. The company achieved early success by partnering with Flickr and motivating users to talk about MOO by offering a giveaway for review.

The pitch offers access to executives.

As we've mentioned already, bloggers, podcasters, and video bloggers like to be afforded the same benefits as journalists. Reward them with access to the CEO or product manager. Extend social media creators the same privileges you offer journalists. Invite them to media events, give them products to review, and make top company staff available for interviews. This benefit costs your organization precious little in terms of time and resources, and it demonstrates your respect for online opinion.

Drums or Smoke Signals: Which Channel to Choose?

As more social media tools emerge and become commonplace, pitching becomes more complex. Do you stick with email, try to get new influencers' attention on Facebook, or start tweeting your pitches?

Most of the time, you can contact social media creators using email. Email is, after all, still the lingua franca of the Web. Email enables you to satisfy the criteria we just described for creating a good pitch. Nine out of ten bloggers and podcasters either publish an email address somewhere on their site or provide a contact form for you to fill out and submit. If given a choice, we almost always use the contact form. The form is probably more resistant to spam filters and most likely prefilters the email message for the blogger—the

---

[*] Author interview, November 18, 2007.

subject line indicates the message is from her site. In the next section, we provide an example of an effective email pitch.

We discourage you from contacting influencers through other online messaging channels unless they explicitly request it. If you contact bloggers via Google Chat or another instant messenger tool, be respectful of their time. Don't demand their instant, complete attention. Don't ping them on Skype or AIM or send them a message via the email services in Flickr or Facebook unless you know they're cool with that. With the exception of Twitter, we've found these alternative routes to be less successful than traditional email pitches.

The microblogging platform Twitter became very popular in the second half of 2008, especially among technology enthusiasts. Twitter is part instant messaging client, part social bookmarking application, and part real-time status update. For a detailed discussion of Twitter, see Chapter 12. Like many emerging social media channels, Twitter is becoming another vehicle for pitching new influencers. More and more newspapers, like the *New York Times,* the *Star Tribune*, and even your local paper, are on Twitter, tweeting about stories they're covering and interesting tidbits in the news. Likewise, new influencers use Twitter to promote their blog posts and muse on the day's happenings—so nothing is stopping you from responding with relevant story pitches. Just be brief and on topic. From Mashable.com, here are some examples of Twitter in action for PR folks:

> Rafe Needleman (@rafe) of CNET tweeted that he would be attending the Web 2.0 Expo in NYC and that he'd be interested in meeting startups. Sachin Agarwal (@sachinag) of Dawdle.com (@dawdledotcom) was listening and approached Needleman based on that tweet. Agarwal got a one hour sit down, and Needleman wrote a great overview of his business.

> Marketing rep Ashley Skiles (@ashleyskiles) has been following a medical reporter at the Atlanta Business Chronicle for one of her clients, Susan G. Komen for the Cure, a fund dedicated to fighting breast cancer. One night the reporter tweeted there was a run on milkshakes at Chick-fil-a, a popular restaurant chain in the southern U.S. Next morning, Ashley ran to Chick-fil-a, picked up a milkshake for

the reporter and left it at his office along with a press release from her client. She didn't get any press (until now), but she did get the attention of the journalist.*

Given Twitter's 140-character restriction on messages, you have precious little space to compose the perfect pitch. That's one Lilliputian elevator ride. So, for example, if you wanted to pitch a technology journalist about the iPhone, you might compose your message like this:

```
@reporter Apple's iPhone just might revolutionize the world of
mobile devices. Plus, it looks awesome.
```

This short, direct pitch makes the context of the message clear to the recipient, which is probably why pitching via Twitter is gaining in popularity with new influencers who are already bombarded with email pitches.

What about calling social media creators to deliver your pitch? Ninety percent of the time, the answer is no. Exceptions to this rule exist, but only if you meet all of these conditions:

- You already have an established relationship with the social media creator.

- The creator has given you permission to call (if she publishes a phone number on her website or profile page, that qualifies).

- You've got timely or exclusive information that the blogger will appreciate. Timeliness is tricky to judge, but try to be honest and objective. Your company comes out of stealth mode and launches a public beta program? That's newsworthy. You sign up a new partner in your reseller program? Not so much.

Don't write pitches in the comments area of a blog post, podcast listing, or video. Like socks with sandals, this is just plain tacky. The comments section exists for discussing the relevant post, not for you to sell your products and services. Marketers sometimes resort to pitching in comment forms when a blogger doesn't provide a publicly

* David Spark, "Sixteen Great Twitter Moments," Mashable.com, October 31, 2008, *http://www .mashable.com/2008/10/31/great-twitter-moments/*.

available email address or other means of contact. That's known as the cold shoulder—an explicit sign the blogger doesn't want to be approached. Scratch that blogger's name from your little black book (though keep reading the blog if he is influential), and move on.

Pitch Tactics We've Tried

At Capulet, we work with new media folks all the time. We run online contests and handle blogger relations; we've even ghost-written a Facebook profile for, ahem, a dog.

In this section, we're opening our trunk of tricks to show you what's worked for us. We hope some of these examples will inspire you to be creative with your own social media relations campaigns. These pitches range from traditional emails to less conventional, attention-getting tactics. These examples also show that social media outreach can be pretty fun.

An "Illuminating" Email Pitch

Here's a standard email pitch that gets the point across with little fanfare, but was effective with the audience of travel bloggers we were pitching:

> I'm Julie Szabo, a marketer (*www.capulet.com*) and blogger (*www.bootandblade.com*), and I'm helping out the folks at Litebook.com.
>
> In the spring, you had a couple of posts about jet lag and British Airways' nifty body clock calculator. A more robust version of the hack-your-body-clock approach to beating jet lag is using full-spectrum LEDs.
>
> Litebook is a portable "light box" that uses bright white LEDs of a wavelength identical to sunlight. Use the Litebook at the appropriate time, and it'll reduce the nasty effects of jet lag. There's also a jet lag calculator on Litebook's site that enables users to figure out when they should use the device, and when they should avoid light to overcome jet lag as quickly as possible.
>
> Would you like to give the Litebook a test drive the next time you're changing time zones?

Some links:

Litebook and jet lag: *http://www.litebook.com/light-therapy/jet-lag.asp*

Media resources like products shots and the like: *http://www.litebook.com/support/bloggerresources.asp*

If you have any questions or want to try it out, let me know.

Cheers. Julie

Other Ways to Woo

Email pitches are our stock and trade, but we've also had success being more creative. Why go to so much trouble? Because everyone is really busy. Sometimes you need to be creative, even elaborate, to get an influencer's attention. And when you work hard to craft an original approach, people tend to respond to it. Think handmade versus Hallmark. Plus, investing effort demonstrates respect for your audience. The subtext says, "We value your attention, so we went to a lot of trouble to earn some of it." On a personal note, being creative is also a lot more fun—and one of the reasons we prefer social media relations to traditional PR.

Video Killed the Email Star

In 2007, we manufactured some playful videos to promote Elastic Path, an e-commerce platform vendor. Instead of going with the conventional email pitch, we created a series of informal, personalized video pitches for a group of prominent bloggers. Each video was less than two minutes long and featured Darren sitting on our back patio in Malta and talking to the camera, YouTube style. We intercut a few scenes from the Elastic Path videos, uploaded them to a video sharing site, and passed the link (and not much else) on to the bloggers.

As with so many aspects of the Web, the idea matters as much as its execution. Our backyard videos weren't particularly slick or sophisticated, but they were personal and engaging. The campaign was very successful—nearly 80 percent of the popular bloggers we contacted wrote about Elastic Path's videos. A few talked more about

Darren sends personalized video clips from Malta.

our personal, face-to-face pitch strategy than the videos themselves. Obviously, we don't want to star in our clients' projects, but this technique exemplifies how authentic, creative communication can be effective.

The video pitch worked so well that we continue to use it in new campaigns. In a campaign we ran for a client in the competitive intelligence space, we sent bloggers a URL to a personalized YouTube video starring the talking head of "Agent Headsov." She tells each blogger that he or she has been selected to be a secret agent to fulfill a special mission—to examine our client's software and report back on his or her blog. Again, the personalized videos caught some of our new influencers' attention. Who doesn't dream of being 007, even just for one fun blog post? The personalized visual approach has proven an effective way to get in the door.

Bam! Kapow! Here's My Pitch!

A printer manufacturer hired us to get the word out to Canadian bloggers about its new line of color laser printers. Seeking a pitch style that coincided with the offer of test-driving a new printer, we created a personalized, one-page comic strip for each blogger. Obviously no direct correlation existed between the printer and the comic strip, but we built on the tangential sense of the latter being something

Darren pitches a printer review to a couple of bloggers in comic form.

that was usually printed. As you'll see, a campaign becomes more effective not only when it's personalized, but also when reviewers can literally see themselves in the message.

Using Flickr photos of ourselves and the bloggers and easy-to-use comic building software, we created 20 comics to send to our target bloggers. The dialogue in each comic referred to past interactions and the topics the bloggers often wrote about. In this example, Darren contacts a husband-and-wife blogger team who share his love of ice hockey.

As an introductory contact, this strategy may be risky (and slightly creepy), but we already had a relationship with most of these bloggers. Because we'd pitched these folks before, the bloggers received the pitch as we intended—as an inventive and whimsical greeting card. And it worked. Of the 20 bloggers we contacted in this campaign, 17 of them agreed to try the printers and write reviews.

Alternate Reality Marketing

ThoughtFarmer is a technology startup that makes intranet software that includes wikis, blogs, and other social networking tools. It's like a business-oriented Facebook on your corporate intranet.

ThoughtFarmer asked us to help increase its visibility online by securing reviews and write-ups from some top technology bloggers. IT department heads figured prominently among their potential customers. Our market research (and our intuition) indicated that these IT professionals kept a close eye on technology blogs and social news sites like Digg or that venerable geek community, Slashdot. We then developed an unorthodox campaign predicated on three assumptions:

What do we care about most? Ourselves. Marketing works best when we can see ourselves in the context of the campaign.

Find what's funny. Campaigns that entertain, amuse, and inspire curiosity are most effective.

Marketing messages work best when the message bears similarity to the topic. The best way to advertise a skywriting company is in big smoke letters.

Working with ThoughtFarmer, we invented a fake company called Tubetastic Inc. and a fake corporate intranet for the company at *http://www.wemaketubes.com/* (now defunct). Savvy readers will recognize this as a nod to US Senator Ted Stevens' infamous metaphor for the Internet. Stevens described the Internet as "a series of tubes" and was mercilessly mocked for it by web citizens. Tubetastic's slogan was, "We make tubes. A whole series of them."

For each of the 50 influencers we planned to pitch—bloggers, analysts, and journalists—we created a fake employee profile. Each profile included a photo of the person, recent items from the Tubetastic blog, and a fictitious employee interview. We left one question unanswered in the hopes that some of the bloggers might log on to the intranet and answer the final interview question themselves.

The Tubetastic intranet also featured some amusing news stories on its home page ("Tubetastic Opens New Office in Chile, Operations Team Nonplussed") and an org chart showing all of the influencers. Many of the bloggers would recognize the other names on the list. We were extra cheeky and assigned the lowest-level jobs—mascot, janitor, and so forth—to the most popular bloggers.

A fake employee profile for ThoughtFarmer's social media marketing campaign

Having created the fake intranet, we then sent each blogger a package via old-fashioned snail mail. Because online communications channels have become overwhelmed, a snail mail package stands out. Plus, when you create and customize something for a recipient, you demonstrate how much you value his attention.

We sent each blogger these items:

- A new employee welcome letter, with prominently featured login details for the Tubetastic intranet

- An employee badge with the blogger's name, fictitious job title, and photo

- The org chart with the blogger's name circled

The campaign was complicated and risky, but the strategy worked. ThoughtFarmer was reviewed and referenced by many of the bloggers we contacted, including two of the top five technology blogs. ThoughtFarmer's website traffic tripled, and the company has enjoyed increased attention from the technology blogosphere ever since.

The Tubetastic campaign worked because it amused, engaged, and enticed the new influencers. When they visited our fake intranet, they saw themselves and their peers instantly. More important, as soon as they logged in to WeMakeTubes.com, they were using ThoughtFarmer's product. When you promote a product using the product itself, you are already halfway to a sale (or in this case, an online review), which is why free giveaways have always worked.

NOTE   *This campaign bears a superficial resemblance to the more complex world of alternate reality games or ARGs. These games are often used for viral marketing strategies and increasingly include social media aspects. For more information, we recommend reading the work of Jane McGonigal, game designer and ARG guru. You can find her blog and research writing at* http://www.AvantGame.com/.

Other Blogger Outreach Campaigns We Like

Here are a few more blogger outreach case studies that offer examples of effective techniques:

Blogging from the press box
  In the face of declining mainstream media attention and attendance, the NHL's Washington Capitals undertook an aggressive blogger relations strategy. They invited several Capitals bloggers and podcasters to watch and report on games from the press box and gave them full access to players—previously the exclusive domain of sports reporters.

Digital press junket to the future
  Syfy, the cable channel previously known as The Sci-Fi Channel, flew 25 bloggers and podcasters to Vancouver for a weeklong media junket. They enjoyed set tours, meet-and-greets, and interview opportunities for five locally shot shows, including the geek favorite *Battlestar Galactica*. The project generated massive online coverage including set tour reports, cast interviews, and hundreds of photos posted on Flickr.

NOTE   *Here's one way SyFy could have improved the digital press tour: The channel should have created a microsite that aggregated all of the bloggers' content from the junket—photos, audio, video, and blog posts—in one place. That way, one blogger's readers could easily access the material created by the other attendees.*

Comic shop mashup

Hijinx Comics is a pretty ordinary brick-and-mortar comic-book shop in San Jose, California. In order to build visibility and incoming traffic online, the shop created a Google Maps mashup entitled *The Ultimate Comic Shop Map*. A *mashup* is a web application that combines data and functionality from multiple sources into a single view. The Hijinx map shows you the locations of comic shops in almost every state in the country. It gave Hijinx a story to talk to bloggers about and something unusual and engaging for them to link to. Internet marketing professionals sometimes refer to this tactic as creating *link bait*, but that term is unnecessarily pejorative. The reality is simple: If people like something, they'll link to it.

Coaster community outreach

SeaWorld San Antonio had a problem. The new roller coaster, Journey to Atlantis, was opening a month early, and the traditional marketing efforts weren't ready. SeaWorld turned to online marketing in the meantime by contacting 12 websites for roller coaster enthusiasts, inviting any local Texans to try out the ride, and offering plenty of custom video clips and photographs to those from out of state. Basically, SeaWorld targeted the early adopters—those who would be most excited by the prospect of a new ride. Of course, those are the same people who are likeliest to evangelize about their experience to others.

In an interview about the project, Kami Watson Huyse, the PR consultant who assisted SeaWorld San Antonio with its social media outreach for the launch, talked about how SeaWorld measured success:

> We measured everything. We measured how many times these things were downloaded. We measured how many comments we had. We measured how many

people came to the site. We measured all the analytics. Now, those are just outputs. What really matters is: Did they come to the park? Did they ride the ride? And did they enjoy the ride? Those are the questions we asked here in the park.

During the launch period for Journey to Atlantis, SeaWorld surveyed visitors when they exited the park. For the first time in the park's history, they cited the Internet as the number one source of information about the new ride, evidence that they successfully connected with a new audience thanks to online outreach.

It's Not Always About the Pitch: Finding Other Creative Ways to Get Noticed

Social media relations doesn't have to revolve entirely around the pitch. If you want to build an audience or increase the number of visitors to your site, be creative with your online marketing tactics.

DeSmogBlog is an advocacy website and blog dedicated to "clearing the PR pollution that clouds the science of climate change." We've worked with DeSmogBlog on a variety of social media relations initiatives. Many of these campaigns don't center around a pitch. For example, the "Greenest Photo Ever Contest" encouraged visitors to submit photos to DeSmogBlog's contest for a chance to win a new digital camera. Readers could then vote for their favorite photos.

Here's why this campaign worked:

The contest was hosted on Flickr. Engaging an established community brought some Flickr *alpha users* (folks who use Flickr every day, participate in groups, and comment on others' photos) over to DeSmogBlog to check out the contest.

Many Flickr users are also bloggers. To encourage their friends, families, and readers to vote for their photos, the users blogged about the contest and linked to DeSmogBlog in the process.

Engaging your community generates goodwill. In this case, we invited readers to showcase their photography and potentially win a prize. Your contest might ask users to come up with a name for your new product or participate in a survey.

The lighthearted Stars and Stinkers Flash game is another traffic-generating tactic for DeSmogBlog. The premise is simple: Players rate celebrities based on their environmental friendliness. Complete with bells, fart sounds, and banjo music, the game has brought a bunch of new visitors to the site. We also let bloggers embed the game on their own sites like a YouTube video, and we released the source code so designers can build their own climate change mashups. More than 15,000 people have played the game.

These are examples of campaigns that did not revolve around a story pitch but still helped meet a crucial objective—bringing new visitors to a site from outside the site's core readership.

Stars and Stinkers worked as a traffic generator for DeSmogBlog.

What Not to Do

By now, you've got some good ideas about how to contact bloggers. Now, here's an example of what not to do. This pitch came in to Darren's personal website, *http://www.darrenbarefoot.com/*. We've excerpted parts of the email and made it anonymous so we don't embarrass the poor sender.

> My name is Regina Phalange and I'm a writer and marketer.
>
> I'm hoping to build a blog club that can review indie films, fashion events, and culture unique to the Canadian experience. This database of select blog writers will become a mini media distribution platform as it grows.
>
> And so I ask you to join my club and perhaps post a blog on (*name of an independent Canadian flick, plus URL*).
>
> WHY? The club is supported by 3rd party links from other marketers on discussion posts and in niche content forums . . . the more you participate the more your blog will be linked.

Seems okay, but then she offers text about the film to be inserted verbatim into Darren's blog. If bloggers wanted prewritten text, they'd all be posting press releases. You wouldn't tell a journalist exactly what to write, so don't pull that on a blogger either.

Then she promises to improve Darren's Google PageRank. The pitch was starting to sound like an SEO racket or a marketing scam. With a bit of prying, the sender disclosed that she worked for the film distributor and was trying to build online buzz for the film.

In truth, the idea of a blogger club wasn't a bad one, but not being truthful in the pitch cooked her Canadian goose. Avoid this disaster by following these rules:

- Remember what mom said about lying: You'll always get found out. Disclose who you're working for and what your goals are. Trying to dupe new media folks isn't kosher. Lying shows you're not interested in building relationships. Similarly, don't approach bloggers and podcasters as an individual if you're running a business. If you do, you're misrepresenting yourself and your company.

- Don't "require" someone to blog about your product.

- Don't make it appear that you're trying to help the blogger you're pitching when you're really helping yourself. Such a claim is disrespectful and disingenuous.

- Do your research. Too often marketers blindly send out pitches to bloggers who may have only written a single random blog post about their industry or market. One post among hundreds or thousands doesn't demonstrate interest in a topic.

Don't Bribe the Border Guard

Bloggers are akin to journalists, not advertisers. You wouldn't give a reporter money to review your product, so don't make that same embarrassing mistake with a blogger. Offering money is a tempting, quick-fix approach, but few legitimate, well-connected social media creators will accept under-the-table compensation. Many will be offended if you approach them this way, and you may suffer some very public criticism. The same goes for other social media services. Don't try to buy off top Digg, StumbleUpon, or Twitter users. PR on the Web is all about relationships. And relationships built on mutual respect and trust are stronger and more reliable than those built on the promise of a quick buck.

This is a hard-and-fast rule, right? Okay, just to complicate matters, we know of a few situations where it may be okay to pay for reviews.

These services connect vendors who want their products reviewed with bloggers:

- ReviewMe (*http://www.reviewme.com/*)

- PayPerPost (*http://www.payperpost.com/*)

Vendors can choose the blogs they want their products reviewed on, and these sites facilitate the paid review. Before you sign up for this service, be aware that these sites don't promise good reviews, just reviews. Reviewers are instructed to tell their readers that they're being paid for the review and to honestly assess products and services. So if you sign up, be ready for the good, the bad, and the scathing.

Sponsored conversations (a term coined by Forrester) are a variation on ReviewMe and PayPerPost. In this case, a company compensates a blogger in return for write-ups. This only works if bloggers disclose the relationship and if they review your product without bias.* So, go ahead and give a blogger a new laptop, a car, or a year's supply of laundry detergent, as long as everyone knows about it and the blogger is free to can your product if it doesn't measure up.

Rules for Following Up

You send off a targeted, creative personal pitch. You wait and wait and don't hear back. Are they just not that into you? Don't worry, this result is pretty common. In fact, we generally consider a response rate greater than 30 percent to be a success. What should you do if you get radio silence?

If you haven't heard anything after a week or two, follow up with a brief, friendly email. Please don't ask the blogger why he hasn't covered your story yet. If he publishes contact details for alternative channels, consider following up by instant messenger or with a microblogging platform like Twitter. Sometimes these mediums can be less clogged than bloggers' email inboxes.

One or two follow-ups is generally enough. If the folks you contact haven't responded after the initial pitch and two follow-ups, then let it go. Remember, unlike the mainstream media, new media folks probably aren't used to constant hassling by marketers, which means they'll take to it even less kindly.

Just as in PR, the pitch is your best instrument for getting bloggers' attention and starting to build relationships with them. The less formal communications customs in the blogosphere make it easier to be creative, even fun, with your pitches. In our experience, a unique pitch idea can go a long way toward getting noticed. But new influencers aren't tricked by style over substance. Sending a tailored message to the right blogger is the most effective pitch, which is why you'll be glad you worked so hard to research and vet the bloggers on your list.

---

* In 2009, the Federal Trade Commission provided clarification of the FTC Act and its oversight of online reviews. They stated bloggers and advertisers who do not disclose "material connections" in testimonials and advertisements can be fined or held liable. In other words, disclosing payments and freebies is very important, to the tune of several thousand dollars in fines.

6

So you've identified 50 of the most influential, eligible bloggers in your industry, you've devised a creative pitch, and you've contacted them all via their preferred channel. Now you can sit back and relax because your job is done, right? No way! You still have to execute another key component of your campaign: measuring success.

What Does Success Look Like?

Here's the superb thing about measuring online PR campaigns: numbers. The numbers are one reason we prefer web marketing and social media relations to offline marketing and PR. Doing the latter, we'd wonder about the exact value of an advertising campaign or mention on the evening news. Did editorial coverage result in actual revenue or just brand awareness? Metrics on the Web aren't completely infallible, but we find more precision online. In this section, we discuss some common measurements for social media marketing.

Many marketers are familiar with the notion of the *marketing dashboard*: watching the status of ongoing marketing activities, including spending and sales, to measure the return on marketing investment. Social media expert and former Forrester analyst Jeremiah Owyang uses the metaphor of a modern car's GPS to explain how social media monitoring and measurement differs from the traditional marketing dashboard: "The dashboard in a car measures key health metrics but the most important screen is the GPS (global positioning system). It tells me where I'm headed, where I am, and how to get there."* The hard numbers from online metrics tell you which roads to take—they are the ultimate marketing map.

To build your own online marketing map, you must first determine your goals. Forrester analysts have invented an excellent approach for developing social media objectives called POST:† people, objectives, strategy, technology. POST encourages marketers to get to know their customers and to set concrete goals up front. First, figure out who your customers are. Where do they spend their time online, and how do they like to interact when they're there? How can you engage with them in a positive, meaningful way? Second, specify your ideal campaign outcome. Do you want a two-way relationship with your customers and potential customers? Do you want to reach a new audience? Do you want people to start talking about your product? In the strategy component that follows,

---

* Jeremiah Owyang, "Social Media Measurement: Dashboards vs GPS," October 16, 2008, *http://www.web-strategist.com/blog/2008/10/16/social-media-measurement-dashboards-vs-gps/*.

† Charlene Li and Josh Bernoff, *Groundswell*, Cambridge, Mass.: Harvard Business Press (2008).

create a plan for what you will do if customers embrace online initiatives. How will you keep them engaged? What will you do to strengthen those relationships? Answer these questions before you start blogging, tweeting, or posting on Facebook. The results you want should drive your critical technology decisions. If you choose to become active in a social network where your customers don't hang out, you won't be successful. If you want to build buzz, then a blogger outreach campaign is probably a better choice than starting a corporate blog. By taking all these factors into account and then measuring results against concrete objectives, you'll know whether you're on the right track.

Image courtesy of Forrester Research, Inc.

Forrester's four-step approach to developing a social media strategy

So, once you've determined your objectives, what should you measure? Here are eight possibilities, starting with the most common. In all cases, we encourage you to be as specific as possible. For instance, instead of simply gathering more incoming links, identify the kinds of sites you want to link to yours.

Visitors

Everyone wants more visitors to their website, but not all visitors are equal. Obviously you want visitors who are likely to be interested in your site's content and offerings. As marketing guru Seth Godin says, your website should turn a stranger into a friend and a friend into a customer. You measure visitors with analytics programs like Google Analytics or Webtrends. Setting up analytics only takes a few minutes and provides accurate, real-time data about the number of people visiting your site, what links they're clicking, and whether or not they're buying anything while on your site. Reviewing your web analytics is like looking over a visitor's shoulder. You can find plenty of books on web analytics and online metrics, and we've included a couple of them in "Recommended Reading" on page 263 if you want to explore web analytics more deeply.

Incoming links

As we've said before, links are the currency of the Web and are essential to generating online buzz. For sophisticated web users, incoming links indicate your authority and expertise. As we discussed in Chapter 1, you can track incoming links to your site by typing `link:http://www.yoursite.com` into a Google search. Google will return a list of the web pages linked to your site. Remember, you can exclude internal pages from your website that link back to your homepage by adding `-site:http://www.yoursite.com` to your search.

Social network activity

How many friends does your Facebook group have? How many followers does your Twitter feed have? When you add an event to Upcoming.org, do people join? When measuring success here—and on other social media channels—whether you've got 40, 400, or 4000 followers doesn't really matter. While the goal is to increase the number of followers, blog mentions, incoming links, and so on, don't forget to evaluate the quality of that conversation over time, as well.

Conversations and contributions

These might be comments on your blog, Facebook page, YouTube video, or Flickr photos. Alternately, you might measure how often your customers add to or modify your public wiki or Wikipedia entry. When others engage with you via social media channels, you're reaching your target audience online and interacting in meaningful ways.

References in the blogosphere

How often do other blogs mention your organization? Are you generating buzz? The City of Calgary developed a process for tracking the blogosphere. Paul Newmarch, an integrated marketing strategist for the city, shared its approach to new media with us. He says his team delivers a social media issues report each week that examines how a particular topic is being covered in social media and compares that to mainstream media coverage. "We often find that the opinions expressed in social media don't match the tone of the coverage we receive in traditional media," Newmarch says. If clearing snow off the roads is a major issue in the blogosphere, the city addresses that issue online, both on its website and by contributing to existing discussions on blogs.

The City of Calgary monitors more than 200 blogs a day and uses BackType and daily Google and Technorati alerts to keep on top of online mentions. But the number of incoming links isn't its holy grail. "The city tries to go beyond actual clicks and numbers to examine the quality of the conversation, not simply the volume of conversation," says Newmarch. But that doesn't mean measurement isn't critical. Before rolling out a social media campaign, the city clearly defines measurable goals, like raising awareness or stimulating conversation about an issue, such as water conservation. For the City of Calgary, influencing public opinion is a more meaningful metric than visitor stats.

Views on social media sites

How many times has your video been played on YouTube? How many people have downloaded your latest podcast? Many sites allow the audience to rate your content as a way to express whether or not they find it useful and enjoyable. Are you getting the thumbs up on Digg? If the results and reviews are favorable, you've probably got the right idea.

RSS subscribers

These folks are extremely valuable. Like newsletter subscribers, you have permission to contact them regularly, which means they're interested in what you're doing or selling. Their actions should influence your site content and design; they are your online focus group. FeedBurner, owned by Google, is the de facto free tool for tracking RSS subscribers and their behavior. FeedBurner tells you how many subscribers you have, where they're coming from, and what they like best. *Burning* your RSS feed, or creating a feed that others can subscribe to, is free and easy:

1. Register for a FeedBurner account at *http://www.feedburner.com/*.

2. Follow the instructions to enter your blog or RSS feed address into the text box.

3. Click the button to activate your feed.

Your RSS feed has now been burned, and you can track subscriber numbers and activities on your site.

Social bookmarking

How often do your customers add links about your organization to services like Digg, Delicious, and StumbleUpon? In other words, do others find your content compelling enough to share with friends or bookmark for future reference?

Be sure to measure several indicators of success. Just as a GPS gives you step-by-step driving instructions, use a combination of data points to generate a map of where your marketing campaign needs to go next. For instance, you may double the number of visitors to your site, but see only a tiny increase in RSS subscribers. Perhaps you're able to lure new visitors to your site, but once they get there, they're disappointed with what they see. We recently posted a fun and provocative post to one of our clients' blogs that resulted in a major traffic increase—80,000 visitors in just one month read that post. The trouble was, hardly any of those visitors were actually interested in our client's service—they just read the post and then left. Seeing the traffic spike was fun, but ultimately, the blog post didn't attract the right kind of audience. So despite the impressive number of visitors, the tactic wasn't very successful. By measuring the results of *all* your social media tactics, you'll see which ones provide the most value. One dugg article might generate more results than time-consuming blogger outreach. If you know which tactics bring you closest to your specified marketing goal, you'll know where to spend your precious marketing dollars and time.

Be Realistic. Be Humble.

Companies new to social media often have misconceptions about what's achievable. They tend to believe that if they upload a video on YouTube, that video will automatically get a million views. That's simply not the case. As more and more content goes online, earning audience attention gets harder. For this reason, testing your strategies before committing to target numbers and setting goals is a good idea. Companies often immediately expect thousands of visitors a day, when a much more realistic starting point is a couple hundred. And of those visitors, only a subsection will be the ideal target audience. Still, a couple hundred visitors to your website each day is a good start, so don't get discouraged early on.

Tricks of the Trade: Tools for Measuring Success

A variety of free tools—thanks, in part, to Google—are available for monitoring mentions of you and your company online. This section offers an overview of these tools.

Web Analytics: Your Foreign Language Phrase Book

Web analytics is the primary tool you'll use to track your campaign's success. These statistics provide real insight into your website. No matter which tool you choose—we're fans of Google Analytics—you need to learn to interpret all its data and delve into all its features. Web analytics don't just tell you how many visitors come to your site each day; these numbers provide enlightening data about what visitors do once they're on your site. Where do they go? What do they like? How easily can they accomplish what you want them to?

Are the right people coming to your site? How long are they staying? This treasure trove of information will help you shape online marketing efforts, web content, and even web design and development.

Google Alerts: An Oldie but a Goodie

Google Alerts is a free, ubiquitous tool you're likely already familiar with. It provides surprisingly accurate, almost real-time web monitoring for keywords and phrases. Google Alerts is getting increasingly faster at serving up results daily, weekly, and as they happen. These alerts are delivered to your email inbox and cover news from mainstream online media, blogs, videos, and other websites.

Web Monitoring 2.0

A fail-safe way to monitor blog mentions is to return to your blogger contact list and subscribe to their RSS feeds. Not sure how to subscribe to an RSS feed or how to read feeds? Go back and review "RSS 101" on page 22, sign up for or download a free RSS reader—like Bloglines or Google Reader—and start reading. But don't stop there. You also need to monitor the entire blogosphere for keywords that apply to your company, your products, and your industry. If you don't know what's going on in the wider world, you'll miss out on both company mentions and potential social media marketing opportunities. Fortunately, this kind of monitoring will catch references from your target group of influencers. If you read carefully, you'll probably spot blog posts that result from your pitch. Of course, we're not all good about keeping up with our reading. We've all had weeks where, on Friday, we open our RSS reader and discover the count of unread items has reached 873.

Happily, shortcuts are available, and you'll need to take them. These tools help you track the social media sphere. Not only will they detect posts you should respond to, but they'll also find new blogs and online communities to subscribe to and possibly pitch. A caveat: This section of the book is subject to rapid change. New social media channels emerge constantly, and new ways to monitor them soon follow.

The following table introduces tools and URLs for monitoring the most popular social media channels. To begin, identify keywords that pertain to your company, competitors, and industry. If you're already running an online contextual advertising campaign using a service such as Google AdWords, use keywords from those campaigns to monitor blogs, too.

Social Media Channel	Search Tools	Notes
Blogs	http://blogsearch.google.com/ http://technorati.com/ http://www.bloglines.com/ advsearch/ http://socialmention.com/	These tools allow you to search for specific content in blogs.
Photos	http://www.flickr.com/search/ http://photobucket.com/ http://www.socialmention.com/	These tools help you find photos tagged with your keywords.
Video	http://www.youtube.com/ http://video.google.com/ http://www.metacafe.com/ http://www.blinkx.com/ http://www.socialmention.com/	These tools allow you to find videos tagged with your keywords.
Podcasts	iTunes Podcast Directory	The iTunes directory and Google will help you find podcasts, though no reliable tool for searching within podcasts exists yet.
Events	http://www.facebook.com/ events.php http://upcoming.yahoo.com/ http://www.socialmention.com/	You need to log into your Facebook account to search for events inside Facebook.
Discussion forums	http://www.boardtracker.com/	There are millions of old-school message boards and discussion forums on the Web. No tool can search all of them, but we've found that BoardTracker.com offers the best returns.
Twitter	http://search.twitter.com/ http://www.socialmention.com/	You can also use the *track* command in Twitter. See the Twitter help documentation for more information on using commands.

Social Media Channel	Search Tools	Notes
FriendFeed	*http://friendfeed.com/search*	You can use the parameter **who:everyone** to search all of FriendFeed, or replace **everyone** with a particular username to search just one feed. Because FriendFeed is mostly an aggregator of content from other RSS feeds, you're liable to replicate results from other tools.
Social networks	*http://search.myspace.com/* *http://www.facebook.com/s.php/*	You can search these networks from nearly any page on the site, using the text box in the upper right corner. These pages in particular enable you to search for and add friends on these social networks.
Wikis	*http://www.google.com/*	Assuming the wikis are public, Google is your best bet. You can always use the parameter **site:http://www.sitetosearch.com** to narrow a Google search to a specific site.

SpyFu, SEODigger, and Google AdWords Keyword Tool are other tools that can help you identify relevant keywords.

Here are some tips for monitoring the Web with these tools:

- Search for names of senior executives and company spokespersons.

- Consider common misspellings of the search terms you're monitoring. Some tools will include misspellings in search results, whereas others won't.

- Search for specific product or service categories. Use terms that are as narrow as possible, or else you'll be bombarded with too many results. A search for *flooring*, for example, would be unmanageable. On the other hand, a search for *reclaimed hardwood flooring USA* might reap rewards. Similarly, a brand manager at Nike should include the product family or model she is keeping an eye on in addition to the term *Nike*, to avoid drowning in results. A more specific search also helps you avoid *spam blogs*—websites where spammers list thousands of terms to try to lure you to their site.

- Where applicable, search for incoming links to your organization's web properties. You can do this via Google, as mentioned on page 102. You can, of course, also mine data from analytics programs. Google Analytics, for example, provides a list of traffic sources, showing which websites your visitors are coming from.

- Current web technology doesn't enable you to search video or audio content yet. For now, you must rely on the *metadata*—title, description, tags, and so forth—that's associated with video and audio clips.

Does all this sound like too much work? Take heart—you don't need to be a senior executive to get this done. You can even share these tasks among departments. For instance, a marketing assistant or business analyst can set up and monitor the Web for company, competitor, and industry mentions. As long as the person has an understanding of the company's business and goals and a grasp of the competitive landscape, he can do the job.

On the development side, technical support engineers or technical writers are often a good choice for responding to web mentions. They're good communicators, tend to have a broad awareness of the company's products, and can even reply to basic support-related posts. Of course, before anyone responds to web mentions, decide how you want your organization to engage online and what topics you should avoid to stay out of trouble. Many companies write blogging and commenting guidelines to keep everyone on the same page. We discuss this more in "Talking Back: How to Respond to Posts" on page 111 and in Chapter 8.

The One-Stop Web Monitoring Shop

As of mid-2008, we've been relying on a kind of hack called the Social Media Firehose for our social media monitoring. Social Media Firehose is a Yahoo! Pipes project by Kingsley Joseph.[*] Yahoo! Pipes (*http://pipes.yahoo.com/*) enables nonprogrammers (like us) to remix,

---

[*] Social Media Firehose, *http://tinyurl.com/firehose/*.

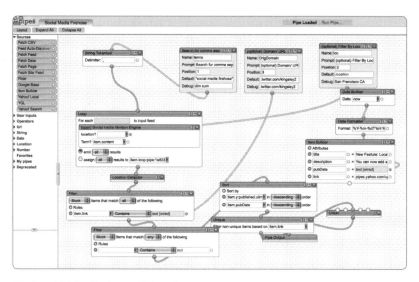

The Social Media Firehose on Yahoo! Pipes

filter, merge, and otherwise play with RSS feeds. You can share anything you create with Yahoo! Pipes, so others can use or even build upon your newly created project.

Kingsley's Social Media Firehose project provides a constantly updated RSS feed that displays references to your brand in almost all of the popular social media channels: blogs, Flickr, YouTube, Twitter, and so forth (Facebook is the most obvious exception). To get started, sign up for a Yahoo! account (if you don't have one already) and construct a Pipe for your company or product. Assembling a Pipe isn't entirely intuitive, so we suggest watching the introduction video before you begin. The advantage to this aggregated approach is obvious—you get all your brand-related news in one place, instead of having it trickle in from a dozen different feeds.

In many cases, more than one person in your organization will want to monitor mentions. You can do this easily. First, you can create a group login for your Social Media Firehose, which works well if you're monitoring across departments. You can give those who understand social media and RSS feeds monitoring access to the account. However, if you're concerned that an engineer or an intern will start mucking around with Pipes, you can also keep everyone in the loop but far away from your monitoring setup.

Bookmark all client web mentions using an online bookmarking tool like Delicious. By tagging web mentions with a keyword, such as *acmeblowupQ309*, clients can go directly to Delicious for an up-to-date view of web mentions, along with direct links to those mentions. You can make this bookmarked information public or password protected.

If this process sounds like something built from LEGO pieces and duct tape, that's because it is. If you've got marketing dollars to burn, you can purchase one-stop monitoring solutions such as Radian6 and Techrigy. Both let you search for keywords and phrases and produce a dashboard of data, including recent online mentions and origination categories for data (Flickr, blogs, Twitter, and so on). Currently, Techrigy offers a free account that includes searches for a few phrases or keywords, and you can upgrade to a more robust professional account. Paid solutions are a good fit for big brands that need to measure intensive social media activity, where their products and services are mentioned hundreds or thousands of times a day. For small- to medium-sized businesses and organizations, though, we haven't found these enterprise-class tools to be enough of an improvement over the free alternatives to make them worth the cost.

Talking Back: How to Respond to Posts

If everything goes according to plan, the blogosphere will be buzzing about your campaign. The bloggers you pitched will post about you and your product and others will tweet in response. Because this is the social web, responding to the chatter is important—you're building relationships, after all. You've immersed yourself in the blogosphere and have a good grasp of the language and etiquette, so you're ready to respond to posts. Here's how:

Be gracious. When you earn a mention, don't be shy. Leave a comment thanking the blogger for noticing and noting your pitch. A short "thanks for the mention" will do. Or, if the content isn't accurate, you can cordially clarify the information along with a thank you.

Get the right person in your company to respond. In most cases, marketing folks are the worst commenters and bloggers.

We're trained in the art of spin, and breaking old habits is hard. The blogosphere values authenticity, so matching the right blog post with the right person inside the company is wise. Say you find a blog post written by a software professional criticizing a particular product feature. Ideally, a product manager or senior developer should respond. Before you let a colleague loose to comment, however, review etiquette guidelines and company privacy policies. You may even ask them to read Chapter 4 of this book.

Always identify yourself. Don't pretend you're a happy customer who just loves the feature getting panned online. Check out some unfortunate anecdotes about astroturfing and sock-puppeting in Chapter 4.

Exercise good manners. Your reply should be professional, friendly, and courteous, just as with any staff-customer interaction.

Treat the person as if she is standing in front of you. Apply all those customer-service skills you learned while folding sweaters at the Gap. Acknowledge any problem, explain the rationale behind whatever led to the issue, and, if possible, offer to resolve the unhappy person's concern.

Consider an example from Todd Sieling; he was the product manager at the social bookmarking website Ma.gnolia.[*] Here's how he responded to a huffy comment to an otherwise flattering blog post.

> Hi all, I'm the product manager for Ma.gnolia, and appreciate the conversation you have going here. I wanted to respond to a couple of comments specifically.

He then goes on to address a few points and questions raised by readers and offers a way to contact him personally at the end of his post. Here's why we think Todd's response is first rate:

- He's the right guy to write this post. As a product manager, he's got insider info on new features and release schedules. He's also well aware of what he can and can't share with the public.

---

[*] Due to a trademark dispute, Ma.gnolia is now known simply as Gnolia.

- He introduces himself right away and thanks contributors for checking out Ma.gnolia.

- He focuses on a specific topic and explains what Ma.gnolia is doing to address the issue in future releases.

- He writes (and sounds) like a real human being, not a marketing hack spinning a rosy response.

Here's Todd's advice on responding to posts:

> Where the conversation is happening is where you have to be. Because you're a guest on someone else's blog or forum, you need to be up front about who you are and be a voice that people can trust by responding to their points and not trying to "work your message" into things. Any expectation of controlling the conversation has to be abandoned, as someone else owns and manages the channel you're using when you get into blog and forum conversations. Being genuine about problems and solutions, without being a doormat to abuse, is the best way to be relevant and earn the respect of readers.

One of the joys of social media marketing is that you get the opportunity to engage in real and effective conversations with new influencers and their readers. If they don't "get" your product, explain it to them; if they don't like your product, let them know what you'll be doing differently in the future; if they love it, thank them for their exuberant support. Go ahead and rub shoulders with these web denizens; this is how you'll become part of the gang.

If You Don't Measure, You Can't Manage

As marketers, you've been told time and again that if you don't measure campaign success, you won't achieve your goals. After all, if you don't know what works, how can you possibly know what avenues to pursue? Sure, run your online campaign for a little while without many expectations in order to obtain a starting point for tracking performance. But once those initial numbers become clear, you need to devise your desired outcome.

Remember, some of the success factors to measure in your online campaigns are:

- Number of visitors

- Number of incoming links

- Number of mentions on social networking sites

- Number of RSS subscribers

- Social networking activity

- References in the blogosphere

We know numbers can be unforgiving, but if you don't track performance, then investing resources, finances, and creativity into social media marketing initiatives simply doesn't make sense. You'll also find, joy of joys, that more of the marketing budget will come your way for online campaigns if you can prove with hard numbers that social media is improving visitor counts or online presence.

7

IS SOCIAL MEDIA MARKETING

RISKY BUSINESS?

When we talk with new clients about social media marketing, they almost always ask this question: What are the risks? For many, starting a company blog can feel riskier than shelling out tens of thousands of dollars on advertising campaigns. But when you consider measurability alone, online marketing gives you considerably more empirical data than any billboard ad. Still, we fully understand and appreciate that venturing into the unknown can be scary. You don't need to be nervous about blogging or participating in online communities, but you do need to know the common pitfalls of social media marketing and how to avoid them. In this chapter, we'll cover 10 common risks that go hand in hand with launching and running a social media marketing campaign.

Risk #1: Your Campaign Doesn't Get off the Ground

You put energy and money into launching your social media relations campaign. You read this book; you create a Facebook group for your company; you compile a list of bloggers; and you create a resource web page with videos, photos, and plenty of compelling links. You even develop some creative programs you're sure will make waves online. In short, you undergo a complete social media makeover.

Then you start contacting bloggers. You submit your gadget story to Slashdot, your tech story to TechCrunch, your eco-friendly story to TreeHugger. You wait for responses and posts to appear. You wait a little longer. You follow up with the bloggers. You wait. Nothing happens. Your social media campaign isn't getting off the ground.

Don't panic, and don't be disappointed. If you've run a traditional media relations campaign, you know that not every press release gets traction. Neither will every online outreach activity. The good news is that you can choose from a menu of tactics for promoting your campaign online. Unlike media relations, where your success rests in the hands of a few journalists, you have a variety of ways to resuscitate your online campaign.

Start by reexamining your strategy and considering a campaign using a different channel from the Conversation Prism. Try them all and see what sticks. If you've already pitched your A-list bloggers, move to your B and C lists. News bubbles up from all kinds of sources on the Web, not just Digg and reddit. If bloggers aren't responding, take a different approach. Try running an online or real-world event and promoting it on Upcoming.org. Record viral videos for the YouTube community, or launch your own podcast. You might find that you have more success promoting a video or podcast to online influencers because you're giving them something unique to talk about, which can help build more buzz.

Secrets to Building Long-Term Relationships

Like working with conventional media, social media relations is primarily about building relationships. Just as you build affinity with journalists by devoutly reading their work, you get to know bloggers and social media moguls by reading and commenting on their blogs, photos, and Twitter streams. All this "getting to know you" stuff takes time. The good news is that if you do your homework and understand the kinds of stories your target bloggers cover, you'll send them relevant information that captures their attention.

Similarly, putting up a Facebook profile doesn't mean the rest of the world—and potential customers—will immediately begin friending you. You must first post valuable information and then seek out interested parties to invite into the conversation. This all takes time. As with any relationship, patience is key. If the big blog hits don't come in right away, don't lose heart. Keep building those relationships and prove that you're a reliable source of valuable information.

Relationships are a two-way street. Even if your outreach to bloggers, podcasters, and video bloggers is authentic, informative, and thoughtful (and you abide by all of the rules), your contacts may develop relationship fatigue. They may grow bored if all they ever hear from you is news about your company and products.

Carnival Cruise Lines began using Twitter (*http://twitter.com/ CarnivalCruise/*) to notify customers about special deals, facility upgrades, new routes, and so forth. Using Twitter to get the word out was a great idea, but the company received some criticism for navel gazing. Over the last year, Carnival Cruise Lines has begun to tweet two-way conversations. The company sends direct messages to followers planning holidays via Twitter and communicates with customers to find out how their vacations went. It also recommends travel blogs and highlights cruise-related articles in travel magazines. The company occasionally offers value outside of what's happening at Carnival Cruise Lines, and that improves content quality.

To build a stable, long-term relationship, you need to stay interesting. Provide online influencers, Twitter followers, Facebook friends, and RSS subscribers with valuable industry news that maps to their interests and has little to do with your corporate communications plan. Pass along analyst reports, surveys, and trend stories. If you use Twitter, tweet a link to today's most compelling industry article. Make yourself a valuable resource beyond your pitch, and social media creators will read your emails and answer your phone calls.

You're Just an Average Joe

Your campaign may have stalled because you don't have a good enough story. Most companies and products are unremarkable, even boring. Don't feel bad; we can't all be Apple. You'll just need to be more creative about running campaigns and attracting the attention of your online community. One misconception is that "anything goes on the Internet," but that's simply not true. If your story isn't compelling enough to send to a journalist, don't send it to a blogger. If your product or service is blasé and you can't change it, find a creative way to tell your story. Happily, the Web gives you an opportunity to push boundaries with creative marketing campaigns. If you're looking for inspiration, read "Alternate Reality Marketing" on page 88 for an example of a creative online campaign that paid off despite a rather run-of-the-mill product.

Risk #2: Blogger Backlash

If you're a marketer to the core, then your heart skips a beat when Google Alert notifies you of an online mention. (You're not monitoring your company online with Google Alerts, Technorati, SocialMention.com, or a Twitter search? Stop. Do not pass go. Return to Chapter 6.)

First, you'll want to know who mentioned you. Is the news good? Does the blogger like you? Is he influential? Unfortunately, not every day is a great day, and inevitably, heartbreaking results will appear in your inbox.

We had our first bitter taste of blogger backlash in the early days of blogger relations. We were working with a company about to launch a publishing tool for marketing and PR professionals. We'd been successfully pitching the story to journalists, but we also wanted to get the attention of bloggers writing about blog marketing. They seemed the perfect fit for our pitch, so we searched for bloggers posting about new media marketing and sent out pitches—just as we'd done with journalists.

We didn't, however, take time to get to know the bloggers we were contacting. We picked bloggers within a targeted category, but we didn't read their blogs thoroughly or religiously enough to get to know their likes and dislikes. If we had, we would never have contacted a particular blogger with a real loathing for PR folks like us. Our email to this blogger backfired with an acidic post about stupid PR people not getting the blogosphere. We got clobbered, right down to criticism of the press release's "dumbass" headline.

We'd assumed professional bloggers would behave like journalists—if a reporter doesn't like your pitch or isn't interested in your story, she simply and mercifully ignores you. But unlike journalists, bloggers don't have any editorial checks and balances, so they can—and just might—say anything. Now, we don't think bloggers should have to abide by any particular editorial standards on their personal websites, but at the time, we were quite shocked. The blogger not only mentioned our company by name in the post, but she was influential enough that her negative post showed up on the first page of Google results for *Capulet Communications* for several months. Burying her post took time and some hard work. We don't

---

What Was Old Is New Again

More journalists are becoming bloggers and vice versa, so the line between journalism and new media is beginning to blur. In the fall of 2007, Chris Anderson, editor of *Wired* magazine, posted a bitter rant about PR people randomly spamming him with irrelevant, untargeted media releases. He went so far as to publish the email addresses of 329 people who flooded his inbox with releases in just one month.[*] Other bloggers followed suit. Gina Trapani, editor of the popular website Lifehacker.com, also published a list of PR professionals she blocked.[†] Read Mr. Anderson's blog post to find out which outreach tactics infuriate editors and bloggers.

[*] Chris Anderson, The Long Tail (October 29, 2007), *http://www.longtail.com/the_long_tail/2007/10/sorry-pr-people.html*.

[†] "PR Companies Who Spam Bloggers," prspammerswiki, *http://prspammers.pbwiki.com/FrontPage*.

---

want to scare you with our unhappy incident, but as you launch your social media marketing campaign, remember two things about the Internet. First, plenty of people online will respond negatively to any form of outreach. Do your research and leave them off your list. Second, the Internet never forgets.

Risk #3: The Crowd Talks Back

PR professionals are accustomed to crafting and honing their corporate messages carefully. They are like overprotective parents who won't give their toddler enough space to find out just how resilient he really is. This kind of obsessively controlled marketing compels PR professionals to stick with traditionally safe activities that offer full control over how their company's message is broadcast. Trade shows are a perfect example of "command and control" marketing. You design the booth, print the brochures, brief the staff, and choose the perfect swag. But how effective are trade shows? How many genuine leads drop their business cards into your fishbowl? Or are random attendees exchanging their cards for branded bags of almonds just to avoid the vending machine?

In social media marketing, you don't get complete control over the message; you give some of it to your customers and critics. Why on earth would you do this? Because, by inviting the crowd in, you get real, measurable feedback, maybe for the first time. You may even discover that the message you've been forcing on customers doesn't work; it may not resonate with the people you're trying so hard to impress.

Flickr's wild success as the Web's largest online photo sharing site is an example of what can happen when the crowd talks back. Flickr was the brainchild of Ludicorp, a software company that began developing a video game called *Game Neverending* in 2002. This web-based massively multiplayer online role-playing game (MMORPG) was a predecessor to *Second Life* in that it was more of a social space where people could interact and play than a traditional video game with specific objectives. While developing *Game Neverending*, Ludicorp built a side product that took advantage of software they'd already created. That product was Flickr. When Ludicorp first launched Flickr, it had a stripped-down *Game Neverending*–like interface with photo sharing instead of game object sharing. Flickr immediately captured and overshadowed interest in *Game Neverending*, which was shelved in 2004.

The first incarnation of Flickr was a chat environment with photo sharing. People could meet, talk about photos, and make updates to their photographs that friends could see in real time. The Flickr team then listened to what users said on the forums and learned that although lots of people signed up, few of those sign-ups turned into active users. As soon as Flickr introduced more traditional features, like unique URLs for each photo and asynchronous photo viewing (that is, being able to view friends' photos whether or not they are logged on), users stuck around. Ludicorp decided where to go next by listening to what users were saying. Flickr has since become a massively multiplayer online photo sharing world. Just how big? If you printed every photo hosted on Flickr as a snapshot and laid them side by side, they would encircle the earth eight times. When you invite customers into the fold, you've got a chance to improve your relationship with them. In Flickr's case, the company took user feedback and altered its development direction.

Here's another example. Unless you're new to the Web, you've probably heard of superblogger Robert Scoble. His rise to fame began at Microsoft in 2003 when he started blogging within the company. Scoble pitched the occasional Microsoft product, but he was staggeringly frank and critical of the Microsoft Corporation itself. He pulled back the curtain on the world's biggest corporate giant, which made Microsoft seem a little less wicked. By allowing Scoble to depict the company as imperfect and fallible, Microsoft was able to shift public opinion in its favor—something its marketers had been trying to do for years without much success.

Risk #4: You Get Rejected

A bad product review in an industry journal is tough. Usually, though, after a month or two, the hardcopy magazine article disappears and you can (sort of) pretend it never happened. Unfortunately, if an online influencer reviews your product poorly, or a customer rants online about a bad experience with your company, those posts don't go away. Thanks to Google's caching system and the Internet

Archive, which takes and stores snapshots of the Web at various points in time, the Internet remembers everything forever. The benefits you reap when online feedback is positive—lasting online praise, increased community interest, and good buzz—can backfire when the news is negative.

On the bright side, social media is based on two-way relationships. Remember the many-to-many model we discussed in Chapter 1? You can respond to a poor review or negative post and begin meaningful discourse with the reviewer and your community. Undeserved criticism is often called out by happy customers who feel you've been judged unfairly. This happens all the time on RateMyProfessors.com, a website that enables students to grade their university and college professors. When a professor gets an unfair review, satisfied students often post stories about their positive experiences in the classroom.

So what happens if an online influencer pans your product? Share your point of view. Silence says you're not monitoring the Web closely enough to know what's going on, and more importantly, that you don't care enough to do a Google search on your company name. It also says you're not part of the community and that you're not willing to engage in the online conversation. Comment astutely on negative posts, discuss improvements, or defend your product. You don't have to accept a bad review as the last word; you can participate in the ongoing conversation.

Risk #5: Your Initiative Dies on the Vine

Many company blogs, Facebook groups, and Twitter accounts launch with a bang and then fade away, with more time passing between updates. You spend less time commenting on others' blogs, and you ignore profiles on social networks. The success of a social media marketing campaign rests on your company's genuine interest in engaging its audience and becoming an active member of an online community. You can sleepwalk through the steps and follow all the rules, but if you don't connect with colleagues and customers, your campaign will die.

Stay engaged by clearly demonstrating to your boss, your colleagues, and your team why social media matters. Use examples

Where's Your Tribe?

The easiest way to kill a social media marketing campaign is to shout out to the wrong crowd with the wrong medium. Communities exist around almost every topic, and choosing the right audience for your message is key.

- If you're marketing to 30-somethings, you'll find them on Facebook or LinkedIn, not MySpace.

- If you're selling a line of bejeweled bodices, submit to Stylehive, not Digg.

- If you're promoting a new author, distribute a short reading as a podcast, not a video. No one wants to sit in front of YouTube for 20 minutes watching someone read. But your audience may want to listen while on their morning walk or doing the dishes.

from this book to illustrate how a good social media marketing campaign can build buzz for a product. Don't leave out the stories about what can happen when you ignore what's going on online. A common complaint from the marketers we work with is that they're too swamped with offline marketing activities to keep social media marketing initiatives afloat. Giving your team enough time and the right tools to monitor the Web, comment on blog posts, and so forth is critical. You may want to cut back on less effective offline marketing activities or get more help to make sure social media marketing tasks get completed. Another good way to stay committed to your online community is to find people inside your organization who are already active online. The barrier to entry is lower for those who have their own blogs and already know their way around social news sites and Facebook.

Social media marketing campaigns lose their gusto for many reasons. Maybe your organization makes personnel changes or introduces new projects, or maybe you simply give up too soon. Your task is to build a culture of engagement inside your company and inside your marketing department. We think you'll be surprised by how effective your marketing strategies and activities become when you start to consider what your community really wants.

Risk #6: Ignoring Other Marketing Channels

Blogs and social media are ideal for initiating direct, informal, engaged conversations with your customers. But they're not a panacea. They're an additional communications channel and shouldn't replace e-newsletters, static web pages, or other collateral materials and marketing programs. Plenty of potential customers aren't looking for you online.

By counting on social media alone to connect with your community, you alienate potential customers trying to find you in other ways—at trade shows, in industry journals, at events, and by real-world word of mouth. The online audience is definitely growing. A Miniwatts Marketing Group study based on information from the US Census Bureau and Nielsen/NetRatings found that by December 2007, 71 percent of people in North America regularly used the Internet. That statistic is compelling, but many potential customers still find online reviews and third-party web commentary dubious. They want to see how a product is reviewed in *InfoWorld*, *Pets Today*, or *Cigar Aficionado* before buying. They want the official word, and for many, that word doesn't come from the Internet—not yet anyway.

In 2004, Dove launched the worldwide Campaign for Real Beauty. Primarily a billboard, magazine, and television ad campaign, the advertisements pictured normal women of all body types, hair and skin colors, and cultures. The idea was to celebrate the natural physical variation in women's bodies and to inspire women to be comfortable in their own skin. One billboard in the series asked viewers to phone 1-888-342-DOVE to vote on whether a woman on the billboard was "fat" or "fab." The results were posted in real time on the board.

The campaign moved from billboards and magazines onto the Internet where Dove set up the Girls Only Interactive Self Esteem Zone and created a series of successful Internet-based short films promoting self-esteem. The Dove campaign is a good example of offline marketing initiating and integrating successfully with online attention. You too can integrate the Web into offline campaigns by including a "find us on Facebook" tag in your print ad or by posting additional or follow-up content on your website.

Risk #7: Too Much Success, Too Soon

Too much success? Sounds crazy, we know. But not being prepared for an online home run can be a disaster. The Twitter fail whale is an example of what can happen when you experience overnight success. When Twitter crashes and the site goes down, a whimsical image of small birds trying to hold up a whale appears as an error message. The term *fail whale* has become synonymous with frustrating user experiences—not quite the brand reputation you're after. The fail whale has inspired poetry, T-shirts, tattoos, songs, and even short YouTube films. While Twitter can be forgiven for not anticipating such a massive, immediate uptake, you must do everything you can to avoid your own fail whale.

In the spring of 2008, the Irish start-up Dial2Do.com created a nifty application called TwitterFone. After completing a quick sign-up process, you can call a local phone number and speak your tweet to TwitterFone, and it will transcribe and update your Twitter stream. For those who want to stay active on Twitter but aren't always online or don't have time to log in to the Internet just to update their stream, this idea is great. On launch day, TwitterFone was covered on TechCrunch, the biggest tech news site on the Web. Within 24 hours, TwitterFone had more than 10,000 new sign-ups.

The infamous Twitter fail whale

Luckily, TwitterFone was ready. If you're not prepared for that kind of response, you can miss your big chance. First, your site might crash. This consequence is sometimes called the *Digg effect* or *Slashdotting*. It happens when a popular website links to a smaller site and causes the small site to slow down or crash because the servers can't handle the extra traffic. Liaise with your IT department to make sure your servers are ready for an onslaught.

A successful online campaign calls for considerable community outreach from you and your company. You'll need adequate resources for monitoring mentions and responding to blog posts and comments. Within 24 hours, there were 148 comments on the TechCrunch article about TwitterFone, 148 blog mentions, and 1,690 Google mentions. You must participate in these conversations right away. Make sure you've got access to resources so you can make this happen.

When the Web gives you the nod, make sure your product is ready for review. In TwitterFone's case, the company only had three customer problems in the first 24 hours. Plus, when online influencers tried out the service, it worked like a charm. If you're selling a real-world product, make sure you've got a plan in place to deal with unexpected orders and have enough demo products available to send to reviewers. Keep the momentum going!

The week after a successful social media campaign can be a letdown. When your web traffic goes through the roof, you can't help but hope to maintain those numbers. But this effect is called a *traffic spike* for a reason. Though the attention will have a long-term positive effect on your web traffic, the numbers will inevitably soften. Don't be disappointed. Use your newfound popularity and new relationships with online influencers as a springboard for your next campaign.

Risk #8: Not Being Proactive

Just like in the real world, the 21st-century Web is littered with stories of companies that responded too slowly to crises. "Getting out in front of a story" is good PR practice that applies online as well.

Corporate blogs and podcasts are a great way to address such situations rapidly. They tend to foster informal and frank conversations, and they're easy to post to and update. Plus, the advantages of the underlying publishing and syndication technology means your message reaches your stakeholders—customers, industry journalists, and so forth—rapidly.

Here's a great example of being proactive from a Canadian company. Hand Maiden Fine Yarn is a wool wholesaler with a strong and loyal following in the large online knitting community. A quick web search of the name produces glowing praise for its yarn. However, Hand Maiden Fine Yarn is also a recognized vendor of yarn that contains seaweed. In November 2007, news broke in the *New York Times* that yoga-wear giant lululemon had made unsubstantiated claims about the therapeutic benefits of its seaweed-infused clothes.[*]

lululemon was pilloried in the mainstream media and across the blogosphere, and the company's stock faltered. The proprietors of Hand Maiden Fine Yarn became concerned that, just as the online and mainstream media had turned on lululemon, the media might also slam its seaweed product.

Instead of battening down the hatches and hoping to avoid a PR storm, Hand Maiden Fine Yarn promptly posted to its blog with an honest, forthright discussion of the issue. Here's an excerpt:

> I think that it's interesting that with an increasing interest in "alternative fibres," there seems to be backlash against them. Bamboo? Cultivated soy? Organic Wool? Even the carbon emissions let off by sheep have been touted as problematic. Sustainability is complex, but at Hand Maiden and Fleece Artist we're doing our best to make good choices and communicate to our customers honestly.
>
> Our seacell fibres are great to work with, feel good to wear, and have been certified by the European Union as a reduced-impact fibre. The health claims are currently unresolved. Whatever the conclusion, we feel good about the product, largely due to the great response we've gotten from our customers.

The result? No backlash, online or off, and the response from Hand Maiden's community has only been supportive. The lesson here is that responding to stories before they happen can save you

---

[*] Louise Story, "'Seaweed' Clothing Has None, Tests Show," *New York Times*, November 14, 2007, http://www.nytimes.com/2007/11/14/business/14seaweed.html.

from a crisis. We'll be covering online crisis management in more detail in the next chapter.

Risk #9: You Will Be Measured

Measurement is one of the biggest problem areas in marketing today. Print advertising is a perfect example. You carefully design an ad, painstakingly massage the copy, and systematically choose the insertion rate and placement. But in most cases, marketers don't design systems to measure offline advertising success effectively, such as setting up campaign-specific landing pages. So they don't know how many people responded to their print advertisements. Why do marketers continue to depend on activities that are so hard to measure? We think it's because fuzzy results are safe results. And if you're hiding from the hard numbers, then social media marketing will make you sweat.

New clients always want to know how we measure success. Our primary deliverables are more site visitors and more incoming links. With trackable links, source-specific landing pages, and tracking codes, it becomes very clear whether or not we've reached our goals and delivered on our promise. These hard numbers are conveniently and intelligibly displayed in web analytics programs, such as Google Analytics, so the client doesn't have to guess about an online campaign's success or failure. If hard numbers and direct questions make you nervous, you'll need to toughen up before your social media marketing campaign gets underway.

Risk #10: Someone Gets Cold Feet

You've devised a masterful social media marketing campaign. You've done your research, and you've got your resources in place. Maybe you've already started pitching online influencers.

And then somebody gets cold feet.

Maybe it's a business partner or senior management or a client that starts to question your tactics. Whomever it is, they've got serious concerns and the power to stop your campaign. To most people social media marketing feels a bit like navigating the surface of the moon: The terrain is foreign and scary.

We used to do traditional media relations, and clients often got nervous in that arena, as well. The reasons tend to be the same: They lack confidence in their product; the results are unpredictable; they want to tweak the messaging endlessly; and so forth. Building relationships and landing a product review on a popular blog, only to have your boss pull a runaway bride at the last minute, is extremely frustrating.

To avoid this phenomenon and the arguments that may ensue, you need to prepare your superiors and colleagues. Introduce them to the concepts of social media marketing and how these principles differ from other promotional channels. Show them online prominent mentions of your competitors. Get them to read the first three or four chapters of this book. If we've done our job correctly, they'll learn why online marketing is important and how social media outreach works.

Proceed with Caution, Not Cowardice

Don't let this chapter scare you away from social media marketing. Yes, risks exist. But if you do your homework, follow the basic rules, and get some help navigating the social media waters, you'll see that it provides an effective, measurable, and extensible platform for marketing campaigns. The real risk is pretending that the social media revolution isn't happening. That only puts you further behind your competitors and impedes your relationship with existing and new customers.

8

DAMAGE CONTROL IN THE DIGITAL AGE

When you start thinking about taking marketing risks, do you automatically dwell on the worst-case scenario? I know, I know, you can't help it. Thinking the worst comes part and parcel with your marketer's mind. And that's not a bad thing. Every marketer should have a crisis plan in place just in case all hell breaks loose. In this chapter, we'll discuss the role social media can play in a crisis. We'll also introduce strategies to help ensure your social media marketing tactics don't cause catastrophes.

A Crisis Management Primer

Crisis management comes into play whenever something goes wrong. Sometimes the calamity is real, like mad cow disease in the United Kingdom in 2001 or the madman who poisoned bottles of Tylenol in Chicago in the early 1980s, causing several deaths. Other times the crisis is less cataclysmic, like when the media inadvertently jumbles their facts or a vice president misspeaks. Whether the news is dire or just misinterpreted, your objective in a crisis is to get your message out loud and clear to a wide audience of customers and stakeholders as fast as you can.

Dr. Vincent Covello is a renowned crisis management master. He's the founder and director of the Center for Risk Communication and has authored and edited over 25 books and more than 75 published articles on risk assessment, management, and communication. He's identified seven pillars of crisis management—also called *risk communication*—to follow when things go sideways.

Involve the public as a legitimate partner. The public is your family. They're the ones who buy your stuff. They're loyal. They're your tribe. They recommend you to their friends and rate your books, holiday resorts, or kitchen appliances on forums and consumer websites. Think of the public as stakeholders in your business and you'll be inclined to give them the respect they deserve.

Plan and evaluate your efforts. In Chapter 6, we discussed the importance of measuring the success of your marketing activities. If you don't know what works, you can't evaluate your actions and manage outcomes. Ditto for crisis management efforts.

Listen to the public's concerns. If you're willing to listen, your customers will tell you exactly what information you need to release to the public to quell their concerns and squash a crisis.

Be honest, frank, and open. Enough said.

Coordinate and collaborate with other credible sources.
Whether the *LA Times* or the Huffington Post, getting your
message broadcast via trustworthy media sources will help you
set the record straight. Before contacting the media, however,
consider which sources your audience considers trustworthy.
What's the blog of record for your industry?

Meet the needs of the media. This pillar is so easy to get right,
but we get it wrong so much of the time. Flip back to Chapter
2 for a quick review of the information that should be on your
website, ready and waiting for mainstream media and new
influencers to use in their stories.

Speak clearly and with compassion. Translation: Make sure
your spokespeople receive some media training, please.

Can Social Media Make Your Crisis Worse?

The answer to this question depends on who you ask. Social media
naysayers will insist that using social media puts you in harm's way.
After all, you can find plenty of examples of social media marketing tactics going off the rails. Plus, the Web can hasten and fuel a
crisis by spreading it faster and wider than any regional newspaper
or radio program can. Here's the kicker: Even if you choose not to
get your hands dirty writing a blog, using social networking sites,
or building relationships with new influencers, the Web will still
impact your crisis.

The Internet Insta-Crisis

News travels fast, especially bad news and especially online. That
means when you're managing a crisis, you've got less time to react
than ever before. Today, with so many communications tools like
email, YouTube, and social news sites—where a misstep can attract
thousands of eyeballs in minutes—the chance that a gaffe will go viral
and amass a huge audience is greater than ever. A notorious example
of this is the story of Comcast's sleeping technician. In June 2006,
Comcast customer Brian Finkelstein uploaded a video of a Comcast

technician who'd fallen asleep in Finkelstein's home while on hold for his own company's tech support.* Finkelstein edited the video to include the pop song "I Need Some Sleep," and added slides in Comcast's signature font that read, "Thanks Comcast for two broken routers, four-hour appointment blocks, weeklong Internet outages." The embarrassing video has since been taken down, but the *New York Times* reported that half a million people viewed the video in the first week alone![†] And that's not the worst of it. The story will never really die because it's become part of Comcast's Wikipedia entry and shows up in tens of thousands of search results on Google.

The Predictable Pile-On

As well as hastening the blow, the Web amplifies a crisis because everyone seems to like getting in on the action. Here's an oldie but goodie. Kryptonite Locks sells bicycle locks. In 2004, a blogger published a step-by-step explanation of how to pick a Kryptonite U-lock with a Bic pen in 30 seconds or less. The juicy story was too good for the wildly popular Engadget blog to pass on, so they posted it, too.[‡] Unfortunately, Kryptonite was slow to react; days went by before the company made a public statement. The silence gave the blogosphere plenty of time to make Kryptonite a laughing stock. By the time of Kryptonite's response, the *New York Times* had printed the story, and hundreds of print and online publications had picked it up as well. Kryptonite Locks was forced to launch an extensive lock exchange program that the company predicted would cost them about 10 million dollars.[§] In Kryptonite's defense, these were the Neolithic days of online crisis management. Kryptonite spokesperson Donna Tocci thought putting a complete plan in place

---

* Sabena Suri, "Sleepy Comcast Technician Gets Filmed, Then Fired," CNET News, June 26, 2006, *http://news.cnet.com/8301-10784_3-6088136-7.html.*

† Randall Stross, "AOL Said, 'If You Leave Me I'll Do Something Crazy,'" *New York Times*, July 2, 2006, *http://www.nytimes.com/2006/07/02/business/yourmoney/02digi.html.*

‡ Phillip Torrone, "U-Lock Hacked by a Bic Pen," Engadget, September 14, 2004, *http://www.engadget .com/2004/09/14/kryptonite-evolution-2000-u-lock-hacked-by-a-bic-pen.*

§ David Kirkpatrick, "Why There's No Escaping the Blog," *Fortune*, January 10, 2005, *http://money .cnn.com/magazines/fortune/fortune_archive/2005/01/10/8230982/index.htm.*

before making a statement would be best,[*] which may have worked with traditional media. But in today's landscape, Kryptonite waited too long to get involved, and so the blogosphere took control of the story.

Blog swarms can be intense. Bloggers tend to magnify each other's energy (positive or negative), comment on each other's posts, and stir up a lot of attention along the way. Although the foofaraw often stays contained on the Web, the Kryptonite anecdote demonstrates that a story that begins as a whisper in the blogosphere can be picked up and amplified in the mainstream media as various newsmakers try to get in on the action.

The Internet Never Forgets, Remember?

In Chapter 4, we talked about the longevity of online records and the notion that the Internet never forgets. The Web is practically an archive of all notable mainstream media news since the mid-1990s. So if you can't make a crisis disappear—like the story of Comcast's sleeping technician—then what's the point? Instead of burying bad news, measuring crisis management success is becoming more about how well you manage damage control, because a record of that will be kept, too. If you're savvy, disciplined, and follow Dr. Covello's good advice, then the agility with which you manage a crisis will stand as a testament to you and your company. Alternately, if you make lazy choices and ignore what's happening on the Web, you risk being a case study in how *not* to manage a crisis in the next edition of this book.

We've demonstrated some of the ways the Web can exacerbate and amplify bad news. That's why we believe you've got to add social media to your crisis management toolkit—social media is an ideal instrument for today's fast-paced, Internet-driven world. The examples show that even when you're not actively participating in the social web, a negative story can emerge online, which is why understanding how social media works is critical for dealing with a crisis on the Web.

---

[*] Dave Taylor, "Debunking the Myth of Kryptonite Locks and the Blogosphere," The Business Blog at Intuitive.com, December 13, 2005, *http://www.intuitive.com/blog/debunking_the_myth_of_kryptonite_locks_and_the_blogosphere.html*.

Do You Really Have a Crisis on Your Hands?

Before we delve deep into crisis management dos and don'ts, it's worthwhile to ask what really constitutes a crisis. Is a bad online review a tragedy, or just a bump in the road? Overreacting to negative online feedback can create unnecessary confrontation and isn't always worth the effort, especially when a polite comment will go a long way toward calming the waters. Here are some rules for deciding whether or not you've really got a crisis on your hands.

Spotting your online adversaries is the first step in identifying a genuine crisis. We put antagonists into four categories: trolls, misinformed bloggers, unhappy customers, and scrutinizers. Being bashed by a troll is irritating, but not a crisis. The Web is laden with trolls. You can identify trolls by their aggressive, sometimes disrespectful posts. Trolls often delight in putting others down and occasionally belabor an argument just for the fun of it. Trolls tend to hide behind the anonymity of the Web and are often not taken seriously by other readers. The best way to deal with trolls leaving nasty comments on your blog is to ignore them. If they continue to harass you in a rude, disrespectful way, give them a public warning—the old three strikes and you're out rule applies here. The next step is to delete their comments and banish them from your blog. After all, your blog is your sandbox.

Next up is the misinformed blogger. These folks have made informational errors or inaccurate assumptions about products and services on their blog. You can fix factual errors by emailing misinformed bloggers privately or by making a correction in the post's comment thread. In most cases, bloggers don't mind being corrected; they want to offer their readers accurate information. The key here is to thank them for their initial interest and to point out the error politely.

What's worse than an unhappy customer? An unhappy customer with a blog. You've heard the adage that a happy customer tells two friends, but an unhappy customer tells ten. Ditto on the Web, only they tell more people. When a dissatisfied customer uses her blog or an online community to rant about your organization, you've got to engage. TripAdvisor is a website that ranks and reviews hotels and other travel services based on user feedback. These user reviews can be a headache for hotels that don't measure up to guests' expectations. The Golden Apple Boutique Hotel in Moscow received its first TripAdvisor review in 2005. The review wasn't flattering. From 2005 to 2007, the reviews were decidedly mixed. Then, in 2007, something interesting happened. The general manager began responding to reviews using the TripAdvisor management response function, which allows hoteliers to comment on a review publicly. Here's an example of a Golden Apple response:

> Dear guest! I appreciate that you took the time to post a comment here on your experience with us, guest feedback is a great help to improve the quality of our product! Just to let you and everyone know—a lot has changed since then: we significantly reviewed our pricing policies to reflect growing demand for better rate/quality ratio, we invested a lot in product quality improvement and introduced quality control procedures, we have also made lots of minor improvements to make our guests' experiences unique and truly memorable. And . . . We have finally been awarded [the] official 5 Star Deluxe rating! All these great achievements would be impossible without help and comments of our valued guests. Many thanks to everyone and welcome back soon![*]

About the same time the general manager began responding to criticism, the reviews improved. In fact, the Golden Apple Boutique Hotel did not receive one negative review in 2008. Positive changes implemented at the hotel obviously impacted reviews, but improving customer relations on TripAdvisor demonstrated that the Golden Apple cares about its guests' experiences and is ready to act. Compare the Golden Apple's response with this one:

> What a coincidence that the above was posted at the same time as the previous opinion. The reference to Travel Lodge again says it all really—an inability to comprehend fine food and service because the contributors are used to Travel Lodge and chips with everything. What a shame they were unable to enjoy this magical place.[†]

[*] Hotelier Review on TripAdvisor, July 2, 2007, *http://www.tripadvisor.com/ShowUserReviews-g298484-d530249-r7832859-Golden_Apple_Boutique_Hotel-Moscow_Central_Russia.html*.

[†] Hotelier Review on TripAdvisor, August 7, 2008, *http://www.tripadvisor.com/ShowUserReviews-g488311-d269262-r16058909-Saint_Martin_s_on_the_Isle_Hotel-St_Martin_s_Isles_of_Scilly_England.html*.

Yikes. That snide reply from the general manager at Saint Martin's on the Isle doesn't make me want to be a guest there. Here's a tip. Treat unhappy customers on the Web the same way you would if they walked up to your customer service desk with a complaint. Surely Saint Martin's on the Isle's general manager wouldn't say this to a customer's face! Polite interactions almost always neutralize a confrontation, online or off.

The last adversary is the scrutinizer. Scrutinizers are investigators. They're happy to point out thoughtless errors, even innocent mistakes. But they're not trolls. They have legitimate questions about products and services, personnel, and marketing processes. We believe they deserve an answer—or at least a thoughtful reply. At the end of 2007, Mark Zuckerberg, the creator of Facebook, responded to widespread criticism about an ill-conceived advertising program called Beacon with this apology: "We simply did a bad job with this release, and I apologize for it. While I am disappointed with our mistakes, we appreciate all the feedback we have received from our users. I'd like to discuss what we have learned and how we have improved Beacon."[*] Apologies are tough on the ego, but they demonstrate integrity. Remaining annoyed at Zuckerberg after this earnest apology would be hard.

If an apology isn't appropriate, then promise to investigate further or at least correct factual errors. Once you've responded, bring the conversation back to your site by publishing your point of view on your own blog, as Zuckerberg did. You may find that some of your true fans will come to your rescue, telling their own stories about good experiences they've had with your brand.

The lesson is this: Before you execute a multistep crisis management plan, take a moment to evaluate the gravity of the situation. If you're up against a single bad review or a couple of irate customers, do your best to address any problem in a polite, public way and then move on. Remember, monitoring the blogosphere and Twitter can tip you off to customer and blogger unrest, giving you a chance to

---

[*] Mark Zuckerberg, "Thoughts on Beacon," *The Facebook Blog*, December 5, 2007, *http://blog.facebook. com/blog.php?post=7584397130.*

solve the problem before it becomes a full-blown crisis. When a bad story goes viral, however, and attracts heaps of negative attention, be ready to get serious.

What Is Social Media's Role in Crisis Communications?

Marketers recognize the value of crisis management, but in today's interconnected world where bad news can spread so far in just a few hours, a responsive crisis management strategy is crucial. Here's where social media can help.

Bad news traveling at Mach speed on the Web can initiate a crisis. But the Web also allows you to respond quickly. No more necessary delays while press releases are drafted or press conferences organized. Follow Dr. Covello's rules to develop your content and then choose from a variety of channels to circulate your response to stakeholders immediately: post to your blog, message your Facebook group, send an email announcement to your newsletter subscribers, or tweet a link to your blog post from Twitter. Never before has telling your side of the story been so easy. By publishing your who, what, when, where, why, and how before the media does, you stay ahead of the news cycle and squash rumors that spread when the press and public try to fill in the blanks on their own.

Dr. Covello says, "Be honest, frank, and open." We feel the press release just isn't up to this task. A press release is the definition of corporate and the antithesis of authentic. We've written hundreds of press releases. While the information has always been honest and accurate, traditional releases lack heart and sincerity. In the first chapter of this book, we identified transparency, information sharing, and accountability as tenets of new media, and these attributes make social media a fruitful platform for damage control. The personal nature of a blog—even a corporate blog—trumps the stiff, corporate character of a press release. Not only does a blog satisfy the requirement for more genuine communication, but having open or moderated comments demonstrates that you want to hear the public's concerns.

In a crisis, social media can dramatically improve your response time, which can help you to get out in front of a negative news story.

Plus, social media gives you a direct line to your customers that you can use to communicate sincerely in a way that filtering your story through the mainstream media doesn't allow.

Rules for Making Social Media Work for You in a Crisis

How can you put social media to work for you in a crisis? We've devised six easy rules to follow to keep the Web on your side during a crisis.

Rule #1: Don't Hide

There are plenty of times on your social media travels when the best course of action is to blend in, not cause a scene, and keep your head down. But a crisis isn't one of those times. In April 2008, American Airlines was pummeled in the news when the airline had to cancel nearly 3000 flights because the Federal Aviation Administration deemed the company's planes unairworthy. American Airlines and its PR agency, Weber Shandwick, put a crisis-communications plan into action to deal with the cancellation debacle. They issued press releases, made sure front-line employees knew how to manage the onslaught of perturbed customers, and set their media relations program to full tilt. They also dabbled in online tools to get their message out, sending emails to frequent flyers with updates about the groundings (albeit signed by the EVP of Marketing, not the CEO), monitoring customer feedback on blogs, and even posting a video on YouTube of a press conference with the airline's CEO. In social media terms, the company actually did a few things right. But although it took a reasonably proactive approach in the mainstream media, American Airlines stayed quiet in the blogosphere. Here, from an interview in *Advertising Age* magazine, was American Airlines' strategy for not engaging in the online conversation, according to Mike Flanagan, senior vice president at Weber Shandwick:

> Mr. Flanagan said the airline's strategy included some new plays, including monitoring blogs, as soon as the crisis started. "That was an important part of our strategy," he said. "And we felt, in general, that the information was generally correct and balanced enough to where we didn't have

to get involved in the conversation. Some of the remarks were tough to take and on some blogs people were actually defending us.[*]

If a goal of crisis communications is to broadcast your personal message to the public, then leaving it up to the blogosphere to defend your business is very risky indeed. We would have counseled American Airlines to respond to both positive and negative online mentions (see Chapter 4 for more discussion on the right way to engage with new influencers). Why keep all the juicy updates for elite frequent flyers and the media?

American Airlines and Weber Shandwick did not alter their web strategy when the next crisis hit, just one month later. American Airlines was the initial US airline to start charging travelers $15 for the first checked bag—a wildly unpopular policy that caused even more PR headaches for the airline. Again, from *Advertising Age* magazine:

> Mr. Flanagan, who felt media coverage of the announcement and on some blogs was very fair, said American injected itself into conversations online only when inaccuracies were being reported. He said American hopes to have its own corporate blog operational within the next two quarters.[†]

Unfortunately, that corporate blog didn't work out. The American Airlines blog actually launched during the April 2008 cancellation crisis. The blog launched quietly—almost secretly—a month before Mr. Flanagan's *Advertising Age* interview, where he said he hoped an American Airlines corporate blog was in the plans. It launched on the Blogger platform and wasn't integrated with the rest of the American Airlines website, apparently because the carrier hadn't figured out how the blog would fit into its broader communications and marketing plan.[‡] In a baffling move, the blog, called AAConversation, was pulled after just a few posts. Web rumors claim the blog didn't

---

[*] Michael Bush, "'Tailspin' Gets a New Meaning," *Advertising Age*, April 14, 2008.

[†] Michael Bush, "American Takes Flak over Bag Fee—Despite PR Strategy," *Advertising Age*, May 26, 2008.

[‡] Suzanne Marta, "It's Official: American Has a Blog," Airline Biz Blog, April 14, 2008, *http:// aviationblog.dallasnews.com/archives/2008/04/its-official-american-has-a-bl.html.*

have senior management's support. So many examples of successful corporate blogs—Ford, Microsoft, and Southwest Airlines—are available that we're puzzled as to why American Airlines didn't follow in those companies' footsteps and use a blog to communicate more effectively with its customers during these two PR fiascos.

Rule #2: Use Your Blog as a Crisis Management Tool

The channels in the Conversation Prism (see page 13) provide a plethora of ways to combat errors and set the story straight when the media gets its facts wrong or the public makes inaccurate assumptions. We believe the most powerful channel for crisis communications is your corporate blog. If you have a blog, then you've got a soapbox and a megaphone. You can use your blog to react to the way the mainstream media covers your story. You can add forgotten details or draw attention to quotes taken out of context. If you've been writing a transparent and authentic blog all along, then your audience will be inclined to trust you now—when you need their support most.

If you don't have a blog, then you might consider starting one as a damage control tactic. But beware: Companies that have started blogging in the middle of a PR disaster have been criticized for launching a blog as part of the crisis spin. Even more important to consider is that when you launch a blog, you've got no audience, which means only a handful of people are likely to read your blog if you launch during a crisis. Building an audience takes effort and time, so starting from zero during a crisis can be unproductive.

Rule #3: Monitor the Web Closely

In Chapter 6, we presented some tools for monitoring online mentions and hopefully convinced you of the importance of tracking your brand on the Web. McNeil Consumer Healthcare (owned by Johnson & Johnson) learned this lesson in November 2008 when a mob of angry mommy bloggers went berserk over an ad created for the Motrin brand of pain medication. In an effort to get new moms to use Motrin, McNeil Consumer Healthcare ran an online and print ad that inadvertently offended moms. Miffed moms complained that the ad implied that mothers who carry their children in baby slings are wearing their babies as fashion accessories. The ad ran under the radar for weeks before drawing the attention and wrath of some influential bloggers. Interestingly, for the first time, the groundswell of outrage spread on Twitter, not just on blogs.

Timing was a big problem in this mess. All hell broke loose on Friday night, after marketing departments had gone home for the weekend. Oh, what a Monday was in store for them! On the Web, 48 hours is an eternity, and by Sunday night, news of the Motrin ad was everywhere, along with plenty of speculation about whether Motrin would respond, apologize, or even set up a crisis blog. So much damage was done in just two days that not only did Motrin take down the video and pull the print ad, but also the company begged forgiveness from the army of mommy bloggers calling for its head. On Monday, the Motrin home page displayed this apology from McNeil Consumer Healthcare vice president of marketing, Kathy Widmer:

> With regard to the recent Motrin advertisement, we have heard you. On behalf of McNeil Consumer Healthcare and all of us who work on the Motrin brand, please accept our sincere apology. . . . We are in the process of removing this ad from all media. It will, unfortunately, take a bit of time to remove it from our magazine advertising, as it is on newsstands and in distribution.[*]

This incident is a perfect illustration of how quickly news can spread and amplify online, even over a weekend. That's why you need to keep your ear close to the ground. If you don't know what's happening to your brand online, then you can't respond. And if you don't respond quickly, your story can gain a lot of momentum by Monday morning. The Motrin case does have a silver lining. Once the apology was issued, it spread through the blogosphere almost as quickly as the initial uproar and was pretty successful in quelling the mob. Here's a bonus tip: The apology would have spread even more rapidly if the company had issued it on the Motrin website as text rather than as a graphic. Rendering the apology as a graphic

---

[*] Jeremiah Owyang, "Motrin apology," Flickr, November 17, 2008, *http://www.flickr.com/photos/ jeremiah_owyang/3038360197/*.

made quoting it more difficult for bloggers and online media. In order to excerpt the apology and post it on their blogs, they needed to first transcribe it as text.

Rule #4: Clean Up Your Mess with the Right Channels

In the summer of 2008, a video showed up on the Internet of a (now former) Burger King employee taking a bath in the kitchen sink of an Ohio Burger King restaurant. In just a few days, the video gathered steam on YouTube and Break.com, and then appeared on MSNBC.com, CNN.com, FOXNews.com, and the Drudge Report. Burger King did what most companies would have done—it put a traditional damage control plan into play and launched a media relations campaign with the following statement:

> Burger King Corp. was just notified of this incident and is cooperating fully with the health department. We have sanitized the sink and have disposed of all other kitchen tools and utensils that were used during the incident. We have also taken appropriate corrective action on the employees that were involved in the video. Additionally, the remaining staff at this restaurant is being retrained in health and sanitation procedures. [*]

Mainstream media has the power to distribute Burger King's response far and wide, but we wonder if the company reached the right audience with this statement. Here's the thing—the Burger King video was an Internet meme, not a news story. The video was one of those amusing bits of miscellany you send to a friend to watch on his lunch break. Most likely the people who read Burger King's response in the newspaper or heard about it on the evening news never even saw the video and so weren't the target audience for Burger King's public relations efforts.

What would have worked better? Burger King might have tried fighting fire with fire by releasing its own video response on YouTube. For example, a response video showing the franchise owner walking us through the process of sanitizing the sink in question would have

---

[*] "Burger King Workers Fired Over Video of Teen Bathing in Sink," FOXNews.com, August 13, 2008, *http://www.foxnews.com/story/0,2933,402264,00.html.*

been well received. The video channel certainly worked for JetBlue Airlines when, during a particularly unlucky week, 1100 passengers were stranded at various airports. During the grounding, customers began uploading their own complaint videos to YouTube. JetBlue's founder, David Neeleman, responded by posting an apology on YouTube, which quickly became one of the top 10 most viewed videos that week. His apology received more than 85,000 views in 48 hours. By responding in kind, Burger King could have used the same video channels the infamous bather used to get attention in the first place. Of course, no corporate response video will ever rack up as many views as the original misdemeanor. But sending out a message via the right communications channel can go a long way toward making sure your target audience gets the message.

Rule #5: Consider "Search" in Your Crisis Strategy

In April 2007, Jen Bradburn, an author on Google's Consumer Packaged Goods (CPG) blog, offered some thoughtful search advice to consider during a crisis. We're expanding on her post "Product Recalls: Informing and Educating at a Crucial Time." Google's data confirms that breaking news fuels searches: "Concerned consumers are in record numbers using search engines to find recall information."[*] In other words, a peanut butter *E. coli* scare or a laptop battery spontaneously bursting into flames catapults news stories about brands in crisis—like Peter Pan or Dell—to the top search results. Here's the problem: How well you manage the crisis on your blog, whether you comment astutely on other blogs or actively engage with the online media, has little bearing on where your official crisis response shows up in search engines. If the *Guardian* writes an article about your product recall, that story is likely to turn up ahead of your press release in search results.

This is where ads on search results pages come in. You can use ads on search results pages, like Google AdWords or Yahoo! Sponsored Search, to make sure your official crisis response shows up in search

---

[*] Jen Bradburn, "Product Recalls: Informing and Educating at a Crucial Time," Google CPG Blog, April 12, 2007, *http://google-cpg.blogspot.com/2007/04/product-recalls-informing-and.html*.

engine results. You can't control search results, but you can still push your message by buying ads on search terms that are finding news stories related to your crisis. You can do this by:

- Purchasing ads on keywords related to your crisis. For example, Dell might have bought content-targeted ads on *laptop fire*.

- Ensuring your official response gets viewed by redirecting existing ads to a special landing page, a crisis FAQ, or your social media resource page.

- Running ads on crisis-related search terms even after the crisis is over. Though clear skies may be ahead, you should always have an accessible official response available for people searching for information about the incident.

Although you can do little to influence the outcomes of web searches like those for *pet food poisoning* or *mad cow disease*, you can try to funnel searchers to your website and your official crisis statement by running ads on the same crisis-related search terms that bring up bad news stories about your brand.

Rule #6: Outfit Your Website for a Crisis

In a crisis, you want to get your message out as quickly and as widely as possible. Your website is the natural place to do this, so make sure your response to customers and stakeholders is available and easy to access. In Chapter 2, we outlined the basics of a social media resource page. If you've already got that page up and running, then here are a few items you should add during a crisis:

Post your crisis response

Like the Motrin apology that replaced the doomed video ad, make your response ubiquitous. Give it real estate on your home page and place it front and center on your media resource page. If you want to be quoted verbatim, make sure your statement is made available as text on your site, not as a graphic. Text is easy for the media and online influencers to cut and paste onto their own websites.

Make prewritten scripts and FAQs available

People coming to your website during a crisis want information. Is their flight canceled? Has their dishwasher been recalled? How do they get their refund? Many of these questions have simple answers that can be written up as a FAQ and posted on your site. During a crisis, many marketers get bogged down with PR concerns—what is the media saying, how does it look, how has the brand been impacted? Instead, try to keep your customers at the center of the story. What do they need from you to get through the crisis and still feel good, even great, about being loyal to your organization?

Identify members of your crisis management team

Unless you want to spend oodles of time redirecting calls and queries through to your crisis management spokespeople, clearly indicate on your media resource page exactly who is available for comment.

Use social media tools already at your fingertips

Why not get your message out to the masses with the social media tools you're already using in your marketing efforts? Make a press conference video, upload it to your YouTube channel, and post it on your resource page. This option is a good one if you think stakeholders are more likely to watch a one-minute video than scroll through a lengthy page of text. If you already have a Facebook group, post your message there. Or, if your customers need to know about the crisis right away for health or safety reasons, send them a message via Facebook or Twitter.

Integrating social media into your crisis communications plan can help minimize the negative impact of a bad news story on the Web. Social media makes responding rapidly in a crisis and delivering your message to key stakeholders via numerous, direct channels easier than ever before. Unfortunately, if you haven't done the work to foster online relationships with customers and the media via a corporate blog, Twitter, or Facebook, then these tools become less effective in a crisis—at the time you may need them the most.

Making the effort to build a close and direct relationship with your supporters in good times can pay off when the tables turn.

Social Media Pitfalls and How to Avoid Them

We've talked a lot about how social media can work for you in a crisis. Mistakes, however, do occur. In the remainder of this chapter, we'll discuss common mistakes organizations make when they start using social media in marketing. By avoiding these blunders, you can be optimistic that your social media tactics won't inadvertently instigate a crisis of their own.

Get Yourself a Lightweight Blogging Policy

Social media pundits have mixed feelings about corporate blogging policies. Most consider them a wise step in educating employees about what topics can and can't be broached on a company blog. Organizations are naturally and rightly concerned about losing competitive advantage or exposure to legal action if an employee leaks a trade secret or defames a competitor on the corporate blog. On the other hand, a significant part of blogging's appeal is the blogger's unedited, passionate voice. This voice is, of course, what sets blogging apart from the corporate-speak on websites and press releases. Some blog pundits worry that a restrictive policy will discourage employees from writing on a corporate blog and will dilute the blog's personalizing effect.

For many years, Microsoft's unofficial blogging policy was simply "Don't be stupid." This was surprisingly effective, as thousands of Microsoft's employee bloggers have remained largely free of the controversies that have plagued some other tech companies. If a company has well-informed employees who understand a company's strategies and goals, then they'll know what they can and cannot say, whether on their blog or at the local café. Ensuring that staff is on the same page regarding project plans and strategic initiatives will go a long way toward diminishing risk. That said, a succinct policy helps blogging employees feel comfortable about their public writing. A policy also formalizes a code of ethics for your blog and puts some parameters around the project, which may help get the buy-in from your boss that you need to launch a company blog.

What Does a Blogging Policy Look Like?

Charlene Li was a vice president and principal analyst at Forrester when corporate blogging went mainstream. She is also the co-author of the *Groundswell* book and blog, both great social media strategy resources. Li was an early proponent of corporate blogging policies and developed this practical sample policy for the Forrester best practice report, "Blogging: Bubble or Big Deal? When and How Businesses Should Use Blogs."[*] Here's what she recommends:

- State clearly that the views expressed in the blog are yours alone and do not necessarily represent the views of your employer.

- Respect the company's confidentiality and proprietary information.

- Ask your manager if you have any questions about what is appropriate to include.

- Be respectful to the company, employees, customers, partners, and competitors.

- Understand when the company asks that topics not be discussed for confidentiality or legal compliance issues.

- Ensure that your blogging activity does not interfere with your work commitments.

We applaud Li's code of conduct for corporate bloggers. In particular, we like its clarity and brevity. As Li demonstrates, a blogging policy doesn't have to be a multipage document devised by senior management and delivered in a full-day seminar. Here are excerpts from two more policies that we encourage you to review and consider as you create your own blogging guidelines.

Sun Microsystems' Guidelines on Public Discourse: Advice on Where to Draw the Line

Common sense at work here; it's perfectly OK to talk about your work and have a dialog with the community, but it's not OK to publish the recipe for one of our secret sauces.

---

[*] Charlene Li, "Blogging: Bubble or Big Deal? When and How Businesses Should Use Blogs," *Groundswell*, Forrester, *http://www.forrester.com/Research/Document/Excerpt/0,7211,35000,00.html.*

Content requiring a non-disclosure agreement or considered Sun Proprietary should NOT be published on Sun's community site—even in spaces set up to restrict access to Sun employees only. If the judgment call is tough, on secrets or other issues discussed here, it's never a bad idea to get management or Sun legal help before you publish.[*]

Terms and Conditions for Blogging at Harvard Law School: Keeping Things Legal

You may not use the Harvard name to endorse or promote any product, opinion, cause or political candidate. Representation of your personal opinions as institutionally endorsed by Harvard University or any of its Schools or organizations is strictly prohibited.

As a general matter, you may post content freely to your blog and to those of others, so long as the content is not illegal, obscene, defamatory, threatening, infringing of intellectual property rights, invasive of privacy or otherwise injurious or objectionable.[†]

Another resource for blogging best practices is the Blog Council, a group of the world's largest brands that use social media, including Coca-Cola, Dell, General Motors, Nokia, State Farm, and Wal-Mart. They work together to develop guidelines around identity disclosure, outreach, and legal and policy issues. If you wonder how the senior executives in charge of social media at some of the biggest companies manage their corporate blogs and mitigate risk, read the "Disclosure Best Practices Toolkit," available on the Blog Council website at *http://blogcouncil.org/disclosure/*.

As you can see from these examples, designing a blogging policy doesn't have to be a time-consuming, monumental activity. The benefit of putting a policy in place is twofold: Not only will your guidelines ensure that all your bloggers know the rules, but also the act of writing the policy is a productive way to decide what your blog content should be, who should write it, and what tone, style, and character it should have. Writing a blogging policy is a solid first step toward running a productive and trusted corporate blog.

---

[*] "Sun Guidelines on Public Discourse," Sun Microsystems, *http://www.sun.com/communities/guidelines.jsp*.

[†] "Terms of Use," Weblogs at Harvard Law School, *http://blogs.law.harvard.edu/terms-of-use/*.

The Blogger's Code of Ethics

As a companion piece to her sample blogging policy, Li developed a sample blogger code of ethics that has been well received by most new influencers and would put any blogger, especially a corporate blogger, in very good stead. The folks at the popular GM FastLane blog liked it so much they adopted parts of it and adapted them for *http://www.gmblogs.com/*.

I will tell the truth.

I will write deliberately and with accuracy.

I will acknowledge and correct mistakes promptly.

I will preserve the original post, using notations to show where I have made changes so as to maintain the integrity of my publishing.

I will never delete a post.

I will not delete comments unless they are spam or off-topic.

I will reply to emails and comments when appropriate and do so promptly.

I will strive for high quality with every post—including basic spellchecking.

I will stay on topic.

I will disagree with other opinions respectfully.

I will link to online references and original source materials directly.

I will disclose conflicts of interest.

I will keep private issues and topics private, since discussing private issues would jeopardize my personal and work relationships.

Test-Run Your Campaign

Few social media marketing tactics are tried and tested because the arena is too new. A social media campaign is not like a direct mail campaign where you send out 100,000 flyers and expect an industry standard 2.15 percent return rate.[*] If you're not sure whether your campaign idea is a home run or a megaflop, test it first with a small group of new influencers—yes, an old-fashioned focus group! By

---

[*] "DMA Releases 5th Annual 'Response Rate Trends Report,'" Direct Marketing Association, October 13, 2007, *http://www.the-dma.org/cgi/disppressrelease?article=1008*.

now, you are building relationships with some of the online movers and shakers in your industry, so share your campaign idea with them and ask for honest feedback. Surely, if Motrin had tested its video ad with a group of mommy bloggers, it would have avoided the hassle and embarrassment of its ad disaster.

Own Your Social Media Campaign Assets

Discovering that a random enthusiast has created a Facebook group or MySpace page for your company, owns the *.ca* or *.uk* domain for your business name, or has set up a Flickr group or YouTube channel on your behalf is alarming. Just as you should register a variety of alternative domain names for your organization (for example, *acmelocks.us*, *acmelockssuck.com*, and so forth), secure your preferred accounts, pages, and communities on established and emerging social media channels. Even if you don't plan to use Twitter, YouTube, or Facebook today, reserving space in your organization's name is wise, so you have a degree of control over what the geeks call *the namespace*.

Brad J. Ward was the Electronic Communication Coordinator in the Office of Admission at Butler University in Indianapolis, Indiana. He also blogs about higher education recruitment at *http://SquaredPeg .com/*. With the help of some of his readers, Ward discovered that a company that publishes college review guides had, on the sly, created over 250 "Class of 2013" groups for various American universities, including Butler, on Facebook. The company's intent was unclear, but we have no doubt that if students joined these groups, they'd become a valuable asset to the group owner. Ward estimates that 250 well-populated Facebook groups might represent access to over 500,000 freshman college students. "That's huge," Ward says. "Sitting back for 8–10 months, even a few years, maybe friending everyone and posing as an incoming student. Think of the data collection. The opportunities down the road to push affiliate links. The opportunity to appear to be an 'Admin' of Your School Class of 2013. The chance to message alumni down the road. The list of possibilities goes on and on and on."[*]

---

[*] Brad J. Ward, "There's Something Going Down on Facebook. Pay Attention," SquaredPeg, December 18, 2008, *http://squaredpeg.com/index.php/2008/12/18/facebook-pay-attention*.

A core lesson of social media is that organizations must surrender control. You can't register every variation of your brand on every service. You should, however, create profiles and accounts so you've got a preferred or official name on these services and own as many of these assets as you can. Although you can't control the online conversation, you can contribute to and possibly shape it, especially during a crisis when owning and broadcasting your message is critical.

The Web's ability to amplify and spread bad news might make you nervous about using social media for marketing. Don't shy away. Instead, use social media during a crisis to broadcast your message to a wider audience faster than traditional media can. By incorporating social media into your crisis communications plan, you gain more agility and control over information bound for customers, stakeholders, supporters, and adversaries. Remember, never before has telling your side of the story been so easy.

To make sure your social media marketing activities don't cause a catastrophe, develop a simple but clear corporate blogging policy. Test-drive campaign ideas with new influencers when you have the chance, and take the time to register your brand on every social media service before a fan or foe does it for you.

9

DOES MYSPACE STILL MATTER?

Yes, MySpace still matters. MySpace is the still-growing social media monolith that catapulted social networking into the mainstream, and it's still relevant. Get your head around this number: MySpace has about 125 million users worldwide. Despite being surpassed by Facebook's meteoric rise in 2008, MySpace is America's second-favorite social networking site. As the Facebook uptake continues to soar, MySpace's relevancy will flag. But given the sheer number of Americans with MySpace accounts who visit the site on a regular basis, MySpace still matters—especially for marketers.

MySpace 101

If you're in an age bracket that missed the peak of MySpace mania in 2006, then you'll need to learn some basics. Let's set the scene. The year was 2002. Friendster launched and jumpstarted the social networking phenomenon. Other sites existed before Friendster— Tribe.com and Xanga, for instance—but Friendster popularized many of the features of today's social networking sites: a combination of user profiles, open comments, and a publicly viewable list of *friends*. Friendster was originally designed as a dating site, but members began using its social networking features in other ways: They instant-messaged and tracked down old friends with the Add Friend feature and sent messages to people they knew. Because of the dating component, many users were in their 20s and 30s. Today, Friendster is still an active and significant site, mostly in Asia. In 2009, the site reported having more than 85 million members.[*]

One year after Friendster launched, MySpace hit the Web. Its approach replicated many of Friendster's features—profiles, open comments, a friend list, and so on. Just one year after MySpace appeared, Facebook arrived on the scene. Unlike Facebook, which was initially a closed system for students at Ivy League universities, and Friendster, whose profiles were limited to individuals, MySpace achieved mass-market success almost immediately by gearing itself toward independent bands and their fans—a kind of "three chords and the truth" version of Friendster. The idea was that musicians, both those looking for their big break and those who were already household names, could use the site to share free music and videos with fans. Creating a website that displayed and played music and videos was, in 2003, still a challenging and expensive chore. MySpace provided musicians with a place to promote their music, list concert dates, and communicate with fans. And it worked. British pop bombshell Lily Allen got her first big break on MySpace. In 2005, MySpace launched its own record label, MySpace Records, to

---

[*] The Friendster Blog, *http://blog.friendster.com/about/*.

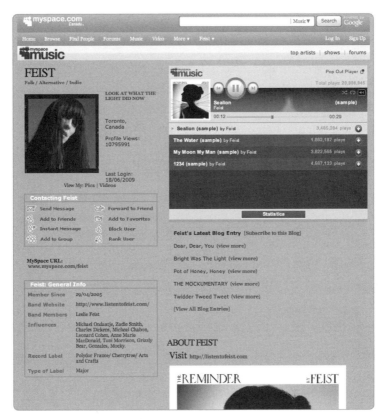

A typical MySpace music profile: Feist

promote new music from MySpace musicians. Dave Itzkoff, a writer for *New York* magazine and *Wired*, observed in his June 2006 piece in *Playboy*, "A MySpace Odyssey," that MySpace's music section was heavily weighted in favor of record labels, not up-and-coming musicians. Still, the focus on music—a topic that binds youth all over the world—was inspired.

MySpace quickly spun out to the mainstream. Just like the website says: You can do almost anything on MySpace. MySpace is free to join, and everyone is invited. The spirit of the site—the idea that everyone's welcome—is what makes it so appealing, especially to teens. Here's why we think MySpace has succeeded:

- Creating a profile page on MySpace is free. No credit card is required. Teens around the world don't need to consult their parents before creating MySpace pages. Plus, people from all economic backgrounds can join, helping to create a more diverse community.

- The MySpace embedded music player has been pivotal in making MySpace a favorite for bands and music lovers alike. Being able to stream music in a browser for free gave people a new, effortless way to share and listen to music online.

- The minimum age requirement is 14. Although the debate is ongoing about whether young teens are at risk by participating on social networking sites, inviting teenagers to participate on MySpace increased its cool factor and helped to spread the word.

- Mass adoption—MySpace began offering translated versions of the site in 2006. MySpace is currently available in 25 different countries and 15 different languages.

- Though most profiles are eyesores, the MySpace platform is well designed to create a complete, virtual social life. Every feature and design element makes hanging out with friends online easy—from the instant messaging feature to the Add Friend button—social interaction on the site is intuitive.

MySpace attracted major media attention when News Corporation purchased it in July 2005 for $580 million. News Corporation's acquisition put MySpace on the map and pointed to social networks as the next big Internet trend and an untapped source of ad revenue.

Demographics: Who Goes There?

The MySpace demographic skews young—younger than Facebook, anyway. But MySpace isn't all teens and tweens or geeks in their basements. danah boyd is a social network researcher at Microsoft who has done extensive research into how youth ages 14 to 24 use social technologies as part of everyday life. In 2007, she published a study showing that gender seems to influence participation on social networking sites.[*] Younger boys are slightly more likely to

---

[*] danah boyd, "The Significance of Social Software," *BlogTalks Reloaded: Social Software Research & Cases,* Thomas N. Burg and Jan Schmidt, eds. (Norderstedt, 2007), pp. 15–30.

participate than younger girls (46 percent versus 44 percent), but older girls are more likely to participate than older boys (70 percent versus 57 percent).[*] In June 2008, online reputation company Rapleaf released a gender and age study about social network users. Like boyd's, Rapleaf's research reveals that women considerably outnumber men on social networks. For every 100 males on MySpace, you'll find 175 females.[†]

How Does MySpace Work?

Like other social networking sites, MySpace revolves around the *personal profile*, a home page that presents the user's data. boyd makes an astute observation about the setup and design of these user profiles:

> Because the popularized style of these sites emerged out of dating services, the profile often contains material typical of those sites: demographic details (age, sex, location, etc.), tastes (interests, favorite bands, etc.), a photograph, and an open-ended description of who the person would like to meet.[‡]

But MySpace isn't just a billboard of personal details. It's a collection of friends. It makes a statement about the kinds of photos, music, and videos that you like. It's a way to meet people you would never meet in the real world. Most important, it's a fun way to spend your free time.

MySpace differs from other social networking sites in a significant way. Participants can design the look of their own profile pages. boyd claims in her report that this feature was a happy accident. On most social networking sites, users create their profiles by filling out forms that are designed to control the content's layout. But

---

[*] danah boyd, "Why Youth (Heart) Social Network Sites: The Role of Networked Publics in Teenage Social Life," *MacArthur Foundation Series on Digital Learning—Youth, Identity, and Digital Media Volume*, David Buckingham, ed. (Cambridge, MA: MIT Press, 2007), p. 3.

[†] Richard MacManus, "OpenSocial and Facebook Stats from Rapleaf," ReadWriteWeb, November 12, 2007, *http://www.readwriteweb.com/archives/opensocial_and_facebook_statistics.php*.

[‡] danah boyd, "Why Youth (Heart) Social Network Sites," *MacArthur Foundation Series on Digital Learning—Youth, Identity, and Digital Media Volume*, David Buckingham, ed. (Cambridge, MA: MIT Press, 2007), p. 6.

boyd says MySpace accidentally left open a technological loophole.*
MySpace's forms accept HTML and CSS code, which means users
can modify the look and feel of their pages. "By copying and past-
ing code from other websites, teens change their backgrounds, add
video and images, change the color of their text, and otherwise turn
their profiles into an explosion of animated chaos that resembles a
stereotypical teenager's bedroom," says boyd. Why is this so appealing?

At the time MySpace launched, if you wanted to create a personalized website with a unique design, the options were limited.
You could join LiveJournal, an online diary site that let users choose
from a variety of design templates for their pages. Or you could
select and buy a domain name, arrange for hosting services, and
learn enough HTML to cobble together your own site. However,
your site would live in a silo where no one else was likely to find
you or communicate with you directly. MySpace offered the best of
both worlds—a prepopulated social group, plus a way to customize
your own site to make a personal statement.

Once you set up a MySpace profile, you can do lots of things
to stay busy and engaged on the site. You can listen to music from
your favorite bands, send instant messages to your online friends,
play video games, blog, find friends from your past, redesign your
page, add videos and photos to your profile, post bulletins about
what you're doing, update your activity status, keep an eye on what
your friends are up to, run a poll, join MySpace groups and forums,
comment on your friends' posts, and more.

From Social Platform to Social Phenomenon

Despite its success, the MySpace platform isn't perfect. The general
design is, well, kind of ugly. Because you can personalize your profile, many users have difficulty implementing the layout and end
up with a hodge-podge profile design. Another unhappy reality
is that MySpace has been used on occasion by sexual predators to
meet young people online, which has caused the company trouble
in the press for years. More recently, MySpace was criticized when

---

* danah boyd, "Why Youth (Heart) Social Network Sites: The Role of Networked Publics in Teenage
Social Life," *MacArthur Foundation Series on Digital Learning–Youth, Identity, and Digital Media
Volume*, ed. David Buckingham (Cambridge, MA: MIT Press, 2007), p. 119.

it threw its doors open to advertisers and member profiles began to get bombarded with ads. Plus, many users are disenchanted with the increasing number of companies using MySpace to flog their wares.

So why is MySpace so successful? How did a web platform that leaves all its content and activity in the hands of its users become such a hit? *Wired* magazine contributing editor Spencer Reiss said of MySpace: "[It] is the biggest mall, nightclub and 7-Eleven parking lot ever created and the most disruptive force to hit pop culture since MTV."* And he's right. For teens, having a MySpace page is like being at the big weekend party. For adults, having a MySpace page says you still fit in with the cool kids. Maybe. MySpace succeeds because it's a genuine slice of humanity.

Marketing with MySpace

What does this all add up to for marketers? MySpace reports about 125 million users. Even if that figure is an overstatement, the number of users is huge, and MySpace is a powerful community. And for marketers, it's big money. Though social media marketing is relatively new, forward-thinking companies have been marketing their businesses online for years. Even in its early days, MySpace provided fertile ground for testing online marketing tactics.

One of the most compelling aspects of MySpace for marketers is the ability to find your perfect target demographic. MySpace users willingly give up huge amounts of personal data in their profiles—age, gender, education, even their zip codes. So, if you're looking for women ages 22 to 25 in Belmont, Washington, to join a focus group or to test-drive a Mini Cooper, MySpace can help you find them. All you need are good search criteria and some time.

In many marketers' minds, MySpace is synonymous with *viral marketing*. The right marketing message can spread through MySpace like a bad cold. The process is simple. MySpace marketers create a message that appeals to MySpace stars. These folks pass along the marketing message to hundreds of their friends, who then broadcast the message to their friends and so on. Although finding a marketing message that will stick with the MySpace community is tricky,

---

* Spencer Reiss, "His Space," *Wired*, July 2006, *http://www.wired.com/wired/archive/14.07/murdoch.html.*

marketers are charmed by the notion that their campaign will grow exponentially with just the push of a button. At the end of this chapter we offer up some marketing tips that will help you reach MySpace users without turning them off.

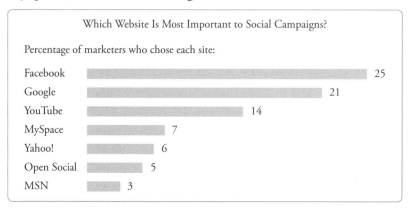

In a 2008 report published in the New York Times, Jupiter Research summarized the results of a survey of marketing professionals, asking which website would be most important for their social marketing campaigns. MySpace sits in the middle of the pack.

MySpace Marketing Success Stories

Blockbuster UK and 7-Eleven were early entries into MySpace marketing, but they didn't make enough friends for their initiatives to become real-world successes. Here we'll take a look at some MySpace campaigns that successfully turned their friends into brand evangelists.

Roller Warehouse

A small company in California called Roller Warehouse (*http://www .myspace.com/rollerwarehouse*) succeeded in effectively marketing its online store on MySpace. In 2006, the online rollerblade skate shop created a *news ticker*—also called a *widget* or *gadget*—that

The Roller Warehouse news ticker

aggregates news from rollerskating and inline skating blogs. The ticker was designed so MySpace participants could easily embed it on their profile pages. The inspired marketing idea here is that when MySpace members embed the widget on their profile pages, they receive 5 percent off any order they place with Roller Warehouse. If rollerblading is your thing, then a news ticker on your profile not only demonstrates your affinity for the activity but also gets you a discount on all your gear.

After launching the widget, RollerWarehouse.com went from obscurity to being one of the top five search results for *rollerblades*. The result was more sales of rollerblading gear. How did the viral campaign take off? When you post a link, video, photo, or widget on your profile page, all your MySpace friends see it. Some of them add the widget to their profile pages, and in turn their friends see it and add it to their pages. And so the cycle goes. In this case, the 5 percent discount also encourages those who include the Roller

Warehouse widget on their pages to do some shopping. Currently more than a thousand Roller Warehouse tickers are running on MySpace profile pages.

Weird Al Yankovic: "White and Nerdy" on MySpace

Remember Weird Al Yankovic? The musician/satirist topped the charts in 1984 with "Eat It," a parody of the Michael Jackson song "Beat It." Weird Al was big. He sold more than 12 million albums, which was more than any comedy act in history. But his unique brand of musical parody was a flash in the pan in the '80s, and Weird Al soon disappeared from public consciousness, though he continued to make music and host his own TV show. Then Weird Al discovered MySpace (*http://www.myspace.com/weirdal*). Here's what Weird Al told CNN.com about MySpace's role in his reemergence:

> I'd kind of written off the chance of ever having another hit single, since record labels weren't really releasing commercial ones. As much as people are griping about the Internet taking sales away from artists, it's been a huge promotional tool for me.[*]

Yankovic has accumulated more than 600,000 friends since he joined MySpace in 2006. Once he realized that MySpace was a good platform for self-promotion, he began aggressively adding friends: "I used to be a little pickier. Now I just kind of click as fast as I can," he told CNN.com. MySpace was pivotal in relaunching Yankovic's career and helped to catapult the single "White and Nerdy" from his 2006 album *Straight Outta Lynwood* into the Top 40, something Yankovic hadn't achieved since 1992 with "Smells Like Nirvana."

Obama Takes the White House with the Help of Social Networks

MySpace isn't just for kids, as was definitely illustrated by President Barack Obama's masterful use of social networks like MySpace and Facebook as effective campaign tools during the 2008 US presidential election (*http://www.myspace.com/barackobama*). The viral nature of the Web makes it a perfect platform for grassroots movements, and social networks proved fertile breeding grounds for political

---

[*] "'Weird Al' Yankovic Finally Hits the Top 10," CNN.com, October 23, 2006.

enthusiasm. Not only did Obama's MySpace page provide a forum for his campaign message, but it also became a repository of online gear that supporters could use to promote the Obama campaign on their own blogs and websites. About a million friends and others visited Obama's MySpace page to get *blog badges* (support ads that can be easily embedded on any website); to sign up to receive text messages from the campaign; to obtain local organizer support tools; and, most importantly, to donate to the campaign. The Obama campaign raised more than $640 million, much of it from people who gave relatively small amounts.* While the grassroots online fundraising success fueled the campaign, David Brain, European CEO of PR giant Edelman, says it also legitimized the candidate:

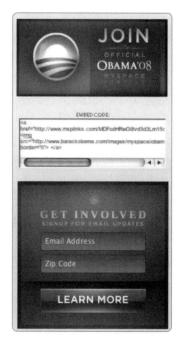

During the 2008 presidential campaign, Barack Obama used MySpace to spread campaign buzz and sign up supporters.

> I think he got an amazing legitimization from the way he raised funds—millions of people paying 5, 10, 20 dollars. A million people putting in 20 dollars carried a lot more legitimacy than 20 people putting up a million dollars.†

Catering to the MySpace Crowd

WordHampton, a mid-sized New York state PR agency, explores all possible channels when it takes on a new client. Its work with Art of Eating, a catering company, was no exception. WordHampton created MySpace and Facebook pages for the caterer (*http://www.myspace .com/artofeating*). When we spoke with account executive Lindsey

---

* OpenSecrets.org, Center for Responsive Politics, *http://www.opensecrets.org/pres08/summary .php?cid=N00009638*.

† Ann O'Dea, "New Media Plays Central Role in Obama's Success," *Business & Leadership*, December 3, 2008, *http://www.businessandleadership.com/news/article/11728/marketing/winning-with-new-media*.

Jaffe about the MySpace campaign, she described how networks like MySpace enable Art of Eating to target very specific audiences: "MySpace is a particularly desirable form of communication because it allows you to search for friends using criteria such as gender, age, geographic location, interests, and so forth. It is also one of the best ways to get your message across to the audience directly without going through gatekeepers."

WordHampton built a robust MySpace profile for Art of Eating, including background information about the company, bios of principal staff, photos from previous events, charities and community organizations the company supports, and tips on green weddings. The profile also included a "find us on Facebook" badge. Although passing visitor traffic from one social network to another (instead of to the company's website) may seem peculiar, Jaffe explains that the agency was compensating for differences in the rules around adding friends in Facebook: "We wanted to drive traffic to their business page on Facebook, as you cannot recruit 'fans' there as you can on MySpace."

WordHampton made sure the profile stayed fresh, checking it three times a week to approve new friend requests and respond to messages and comments. It's particularly active on MySpace during the high activity periods for caterers—during the summer and before Christmas. "MySpace can be time consuming," Jaffe says, "but it is a medium in which you get as much out of it as you put into it. A static page will not help your business."

And that dedication paid off. Art of Eating recently received an inquiry from a MySpace friend who was in the midst of organizing an event for 400 people. She contacted Art of Eating for a quote, and it won the job.

Banging the Drums with MySpace

The Gretsch Company makes drums and guitars. The most famous Gretsch guitars are iconic—hollow-bodied models popular with country and rockabilly legends like Chet Atkins and Elvis Presley. In 2008, the company celebrated its 125th anniversary with a contest entitled "Next Gretsch Greats," which they heavily promoted on MySpace. Unsigned bands from all over the world were encouraged to submit a song, and then MySpace users and Gretsch site visitors voted the submissions down to 10 finalists. A panel of judges chose the winning band, who then traveled to New York City to participate in a 125th anniversary concert and also receive Gretsch guitars, amplifiers, and drums.

Harkening back to MySpace's musical roots, the Gretsch Company created a profile on MySpace for the contest (*http://www.myspace.com/gretsch125th*) and added some history about the company, videos, and a widget featuring artists who play Gretsch instruments. Additionally, Gretsch regularly blogged on the profile, with company CEO Fred Gretsch writing at least one blog post a week. The company engaged in an aggressive outreach campaign, targeting bands and other music-related profiles. Aided by a $7,500 banner ad campaign on the site, the company managed to add more than 15,000 friends in five months.

Gretsch worked hard to generate the maximum amount of buzz at the outset, soliciting as many contest entrants as possible. Abby Blaylock is a partner at Jackson Spalding, the PR agency behind the campaign. She explains the strategy:

> We focused our resources on encouraging bands to enter the competition, knowing that once they had entered, we could rely on them to drive voting. Every band we could sell on the competition would be one more unpaid publicist working on Gretsch's behalf. We supplied entrants with the tools needed to do their own publicity: a stock press release they could customize for their local media; a tip sheet on how to encourage their own fans to go online and vote for their song; and an HTML "vote for our song" widget to post to their MySpace and/or other web pages. [*]

Gretsch exceeded its goal for the contest, receiving 879 entries from participating bands. During the one-month voting period, 12,661 unique registered users voted a total of 55,195 times on *http://www.Gretsch125th.com/* to select the 10 finalists. For the voting portion of the campaign, the Gretsch MySpace profile served to drive traffic to the contest site.

---

* Author interview, August 28, 2008.

The Gretsch story highlights how social media outreach can be a lot of work. Connecting with over 15,000 MySpace friends is no small feat. Abby reports, "We spent around 200 hours on MySpace outreach, which included sending friend requests, responding to friend requests, responding to messages, and creating the MySpace ad." Still, Jackson Spalding's hard work paid off in a rich vein of songs to mine and over 12,000 visitors to its contest site.

Tatango and MySpace's Network Effect

Tatango is a group SMS service that allows its users to text large groups from a mobile phone or computer. Early on, Tatango knew it wanted to target potential users in the nightlife industry—club owners, restaurant managers, and so forth. The company used a variety of marketing strategies, both on- and offline, and identified MySpace as a natural fit for its young, urban audience. Additionally, the low cost of admission appealed. In an interview, Andrew Dumont, vice president of business development at Tatango, told us, "Initially, we didn't have a very large marketing budget, so we had to find a medium we could use to contact the demographic we were targeting at a low cost, and MySpace offered this for free."

Tatango designed a straightforward MySpace profile (*http://www.myspace.com/collegetext*) in the hopes that it would drive traffic to Tatango.com. Dumont kept things "very clear, concise, and to the

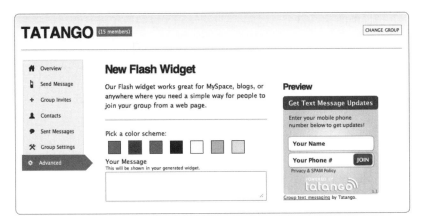

The Tatango widget is available in various colors so users can match the widget to their MySpace page.

point. Our goal was to get people to our site, and let our site take over from there, so we chose a profile picture that was eye-catching and contained our website address."[*]

Tips and Tricks for MySpace Marketers

Before traversing the wilds of MySpace, consider following these guidelines:

- Start by friending like-minded MySpacers. For example, Roller Warehouse might search for *inline skating* within the MySpace search function to find other rollerskating fans. Find your tribe on MySpace, and those users will be considerably more likely to evangelize your brand.

- Consider demographics. If you're a brick-and-mortar store selling within a particular community, friend MySpace users who live in your town. Take advantage of the thinly sliced demographic data included in the platform.

- Never send unsolicited messages to other MySpace users. You'll get tagged as a spammer.

- Stay away from corporate-speak; MySpace is a community, not a brochure.

- Be authentic and transparent. Post pictures so other MySpacers know you're for real.

- Understand MySpace before you start marketing on MySpace. Spend time hanging out to get a feel for MySpace culture and language.

- Disable comments. People spam in comments and place huge photos that take too long to load.

- Post bulletins every day if you can.

- Include a clear call to action on your profile page, whether that's a special discount for MySpace friends or just an invitation to visit your website.

---

[*] Author interview, August 21, 2008.

- Spend some time customizing your MySpace profile so it looks smart and stands apart from the mass of personal pages on the site. President Obama's profile (*http://www.myspace.com/barackobama*) is a great example of a clean, professional MySpace look. As a marketer, you may need some help from a web designer to create a good-looking profile page.

Marketing in MySpace can be a fun way to test the social networking waters. The best part is that you can have your profile up and running and start making friends in under an hour. So don't be a wallflower—get in on the action.

What's Next for MySpace?

The MySpace heyday was in 2006, when the company claimed to register half a million new users each week. That same year, MySpace was heralded as the second most popular website in the United States, second only to Yahoo!. That was pre-Facebook, of course.

We would be remiss not to point out that MySpace and Facebook are not the only social networking sites with power and pull. Bebo is popular in the United Kingdom, Google's Orkut is the most visited website in Brazil, and several other social networks in Asia boast millions of users.

But MySpace isn't going away any time soon. Its 100 million-plus users aside, MySpace is an incredibly valuable asset to the recording industry. Michael Nash, EVP of Digital Strategy and Business Development for Warner Music, said last year, "About 20% to 30% of total traffic on MySpace is music traffic. We [see] that lightning in a bottle, the social interaction around music and fans."[*] That interaction, combined with the democratic nature of the network—the Red Hot Chili Peppers have as much real estate as an unsigned polka band—will make MySpace a valuable asset for News Corporation (MySpace's current owners) for years to come.

---

[*] Ellen McGirt, "MySpace, the Sequel," *Fast Company*, August 7, 2008, *http://www.fastcompany.com/magazine/128/myspace-the-sequel.html*.

10

Where to start with Facebook? The very beginning, of course. Let's go back to February 2004 and a messy Harvard dorm room. Mark Zuckerberg is a sophomore studying psychology, but he also does a little programming on the side. He's already created some websites for his classmates. Coursematch enables students to see which other students are enrolled in their classes, and Facemash is a "hot or not" site specifically for Harvard attendees. Along with Dustin Moskovitz and Chris Hughes, Zuckerberg then launches TheFacebook.com, a social network for Harvard students. The site mimics the actual Harvard facebook, a guide distributed to freshmen that profiles students and staff. The *Harvard Crimson* covered TheFacebook.com the day after it launched and, in its article, quoted an audacious young Zuckerberg:

> "Everyone's been talking a lot about a universal face book within Harvard," Zuckerberg said. "I think it's kind of silly that it would take the University a couple of years to get around to it. I can do it better than they can, and I can do it in a week."*

TheFacebook.com catches on quickly. In the first 24 hours, 1200 students join the site. After a month, more than half of the students on campus have profiles. That summer, the founders expand the site to include other Ivy League schools. Through 2005 and early 2006, the site welcomes more and more educational institutions into the fold, including a version for high schoolers. Along the way, they drop *the* from the name, and TheFacebook.com becomes simply Facebook.

In September 2006, Zuckerberg opens the site to anybody with an email address. By the end of 2006, Facebook has more than 12 million users. The site's popularity explodes as it begins to subvert MySpace as the go-to general-purpose social network. By 2008, Facebook is so popular that, along with ABC television, it cosponsors debates in the New Hampshire primaries.

In August 2008, Zuckerberg posts to the official Facebook blog that the site recently registered its 100 millionth member. In April 2009, Zuckerberg announces the site's 200 millionth member. Users can access the site in over 40 languages.

Facebook is the elephant in the social media marketing living room. The site is enormous and daunting, and everybody's still figuring out the best ways to market within it. The number of Facebook users has more than doubled in the past six months, and the growth curve will likely remain pretty steep in the near future. A number of the features we write about in this section are very new, and predicting what's next is difficult.

* Alan J. Tabak, "Hundreds Register for New Facebook Website," *Harvard Crimson*, February 9, 2004.

Ctrl+Alt+Del *by Tim Buckley*

Profiles and the Network Effect

Much of what we've discussed earlier in the book also applies to Facebook. Your natural inclination may be to acquire as many Facebook friends as possible beyond your natural sphere of family, friends, and professional acquaintances. However, having this many friends is generally considered gauche. Besides, if you want to influence your Facebook friends, they must feel some kind of affinity to you. If you've got 4900 strangers in your list of friends, will they really care what you do?

Anatomy of a Facebook Profile

The center of the Facebook universe is the *profile*. Associated with a living, verifiably human individual (Facebook weeds out profiles for fictional characters, mascots, and the like), the profile is your personal headquarters for all your activity on the Facebook network.

In Facebook, much of your professional activity is attached to your personal profile, a reality many users don't fully grasp until they've started a profile and joined various groups. When you send an email or join a group, the recipient and other group members may have access to your profile (though you can control who sees what). Therefore, you need to be aware of how the different parts of your life may interact. We're from British Columbia, so we don't mind if you belong to the Cannabis Culture Facebook group. Your conservative boss and your pastor, however, might take offense. Understanding that Facebook can become a delicate balancing act of personal disclosures and professional pursuits is important.

Balancing these aspects of your life may limit some of the outreach activities you can do within Facebook. Using the social network, you can only invite your friends to join groups, attend events, and install applications. The good news is that this requirement is actually an effective marketing filter and a healthy limitation for the community.

A group or application has to be truly great to go viral. Groups and applications gain popularity one friend of a friend of a friend at a time. This domino effect happens because nearly all your activity inside Facebook—joining a group, becoming a fan of a page, commenting on a photo, installing an app, and so forth—is reflected in your profile and visible to your friends. Similar to Twitter, these updates trickle onto your friends' home pages and encourage them to do what you did (see a movie, buy Prada high heels, and so forth).

At last count, more than 300 million people have Facebook accounts. Chances are, you've got one too. If you don't have an account, stop reading and sign up. Get in there and mess around. Add a few friends and see what they're doing (and who they're friends with). As a late adopter, you'll be inundated with *friend requests* from your grandmother, your boss, and the kid you had a crush on in sixth grade. Grandma can probably help you with installing apps.

So what does the average Facebook account look like? That's kind of a tricky question, because Facebook is always changing. In fact, between the first and second drafts of this book, Facebook launched a major upgrade to its user profiles. As you might imagine, we're hesitant to be too precise about the constantly evolving Facebook profile. Some basic concepts are essential to the network, however:

Profile Info   This is the basic information most social networking sites ask for—everything from your birthday and current job to favorite movies and special interests. You're under no obligation to fill in every blank, but publishing some basics about who you are is considered courteous.

Status   This field is where you tell your friends what you're currently doing: "Julie is writing a book," "Darren is getting a Swedish massage," and so on. This feature is often emulated and was possibly the inspiration behind Twitter and a handful of other microblogging platforms.

News Feed   This is a stream of news and activity from your Facebook friends. If you've got a lot of friends, you'll find the News Feed is more of a torrent than a stream. The News Feed shows, in considerable detail, what your friends have been doing on Facebook. Blog posts, status updates, and newly uploaded photos and videos are all reported in the News Feed. When one of your friends breaks up with her boyfriend or girlfriend, you'll see her Relationship Status change from In a Relationship to Single.

Friends   What do all social networks have in common? Friends. Friends are the social part of networking. They may have different names (friends on LinkedIn are called *connections* and on Dogster they're called *pals*), but friends are present on every site in one form or another. If you've signed up for a few social networking sites, you've experienced the pain of adding the same 20 or 50 or 200 friends on each new service. Facebook tends to be hyperfocused on your circle of friends. Incidentally, the peculiar culture of Facebook means the connection between you and another can be pretty murky for you to become Facebook friends. You might be from the same college class of 8000 students, or perhaps you once worked for the same big company. Still, adding total strangers as friends on Facebook is considered uncool (particularly for marketers).

Networks   Facebook likes to categorize users into big groups called *networks*. These originated with Facebook's focus on schools—each college or high school had its own separate network. You could join that network only if you had a legitimate email address from that school. When Facebook opened its doors to all users, two other network types—regions and workplaces—were added. Work networks require email addresses as well, whereas no requirements exist for joining a regional network. You don't have to join a network when you sign up; the site uses networks as a means of organizing search results, privacy settings, and so on. Plus, as Facebook evolves, networks seem to be taking a back seat to friends, groups, and other taxonomies.

The Wall   Think of your Facebook Wall as that dry-erase whiteboard that used to hang on your dorm room door at the university. The wall is where your Facebook friends say hello, leave informal messages, and generally harass you publicly.

Inbox   The Inbox is Facebook's equivalent to email. This feature is exceptionally popular with Facebook users. In fact, we hear anecdotal reports of teens abandoning their email addresses for the convenience of Facebook mail and chat. Those of us who still use Microsoft Outlook can find Facebook email pretty irksome. You can receive a notification of a Facebook message in your regular email, but you need to log in to Facebook to reply to messages.

Chat   In the spring of 2008, Facebook rolled out real-time chat associated with your profile, a much-requested feature. Facebook chat is similar to many other instant messaging applications like AIM, Skype, and Google Chat. The obvious advantage on Facebook is you have an instant roster of friends with whom to converse, friends who might not have signed up for earlier IM services.

News and activity from Facebook friends

Your current status and a text box for instantly updating it

Requests and invitations that you've received

Videos and content that's allegedly popular with your Facebook friends

The home page for a typical—in this case, Darren's—Facebook profile

Now that you understand the parts of a Facebook profile, let's consider the larger ecosystem of activity in Facebook.

The Basics

Remember the Conversation Prism back in Chapter 1? In the more traditional sense, Facebook (along with MySpace and other social networking sites) is just another part of the prism. Facebook is another channel to use to connect with your customers and potential customers. In addition to an individual's profile, Facebook has events, groups, and pages.

Events

Facebook events enable you to create a central location on the social network for a particular happening. This happening can be anything from a corporate retreat to a protest march to the date your favorite band is coming to town. You can make these events private (only invitees can view the event page) or public (anyone on Facebook can view the page). Likewise, you can control who's able to RSVP for the event.

Because Facebook is the social network of the moment, make sure you include all of your events in Facebook. When you're promoting events elsewhere online, also reference them on Facebook as a way for your customers to RSVP and discuss what's going on. Facebook is almost certainly where your customers are, so follow them. Within Facebook, you can only invite your friends to events. You can, however, enable your friends to invite their friends. You can also leave the event open so that all Facebook users, regardless of their relationship to you, can join. This openness is essential if you're promoting your events on and off the Web and using the Facebook event page for RSVPs.

Speaking of RSVPs, *seeding* an event with a few reliable friends who can indicate immediately that they're attending is a good idea. Among event planners, this is common sense: Nobody wants to appear to be the only one going to a launch party. If only one or two people are displayed under Confirmed Guests, joining the event can be daunting. Ensure the event looks attractive by prepopulating some attendees. Adding photos and video—from previous events, as a preview, and so on—will also help bring your event page to life.

As with all aspects of Facebook (and, really, all forms of web marketing), be careful about inviting people to too many events. Two or three a month is about as many invitations as you want to send—any more and people will feel harassed.

Groups and Pages: Which to Use?

Traditionally (as in the past two years), groups were a focus for companies on Facebook. You started the official group for your company and encouraged your customers to join. Groups provided a natural conversational channel for communicating with customers and a clear focus for your Facebook-related activity.

Rob Cottingham, president of Social Signal, used a Facebook group to great effect as part of an initiative for BC Hydro, British Columbia's electric utility:

> We just created a Facebook group to promote the idea, which was switching off lights and nonessential electrics on a particular day. And I invited maybe a dozen friends to join. A few days later, we topped 60, and then 100, 500, and then cleared 1000 before we froze the group at around 1400 members. Once a group clears 1000 members, you can no longer send a group message to everyone.
>
> It's a testament to two things: the compelling nature of the idea and the phenomenal ease that Facebook lends to collaboration. If you're hoping to bring people together online, you could do far worse than checking out Facebook.*

This group is a great example of how you can use Facebook to assemble an affinity group for social (without the "media") marketing. Facebook groups provide an effective platform for trying to change people's views or behaviors. Facebook users often join groups that reflect their values. Their list of groups is often a badge describing what they care about—whether that's Miley Cyrus or global warming.

If you're a sizable organization, one or more groups are probably already talking about you. To choose an example at random, at the time of this writing, Facebook shows 136 groups related to Radio Shack. Some are for current or former employees, some are for Radio Shack lovers, and some are for people who strongly dislike Radio Shack. Visiting all the groups associated with your organization—pro and con—and engaging with your admirers and detractors is worthwhile. Then you can apply what you've learned elsewhere in this book.

For some organizations, Facebook has become a kind of de facto intranet. Employees use groups to connect with other employees to switch shifts, share product knowledge, complain about bosses, and so on. Particularly for companies with younger staff, this behavior

---

* Author interview, November 21, 2007.

is natural. Facebook is already their go-to online space for articulating real-world connections. Plus, they probably hate your intranet. Everybody seems to hate intranets. We mention this phenomenon because you probably want to curtail this behavior before it gets out of hand—and out of your control. Or you may want to embrace it like Serena Software did. Serena Software has a staff of 900, and the company set up a private, employees-only Facebook group to exchange documents, update corporate information, and share promotional videos.

In 2008, Facebook introduced a feature for companies called Facebook Pages. *Facebook Pages* are essentially profiles for non-humans—for example, the Toyota Prius.

Pages slowly acquired all of the same features as personal profiles, and they're the natural place to focus your corporate Facebook efforts.

A Facebook Page for the Toyota Prius

Just as you have Facebook friends associated with your profile, your page has *fans*. Companies often confront the question of whether to create a page or a group. Here's a useful way to distinguish pages and groups: Facebook Pages exist to focus attention around a business or artist, whereas groups are for promoting a common interest, cause, or hobby. The two features have a great deal in common. But here are a few notable differences:

- Groups enable you to send out invitations in bulk to your Facebook friends, so you can generate more momentum and grow your membership numbers more rapidly.

- Facebook Pages are visible to search engines, whereas most other Facebook features, including groups, are not. Although this may change, keep this in mind when developing your search engine optimization (SEO) strategy.

- Pages provide statistics for user activity; groups do not.

- Because of their name, design, and prominently featured Group Officers (those who founded and administrate the group), groups feel more social. Pages, on the other hand, offer a more formal, less conversational presence. If you choose, you can operate a page without ever disclosing your identity.

If you're starting from scratch, a page is probably easiest. If you're running a cause-oriented organization, however, such as a nonprofit or volunteer organization, a group may be a better fit. On a similar note, we're often asked a related question: "My company already has a group. Should we have a page as well?" The short answer is no. Pages and groups have far more similarities than differences, and you've probably already got a significant affinity group of users and some history around your existing group. If you really want to change, you can contact Facebook and request that they transform your group into a page. In our experience, marketers love to overthink questions like this one. Don't worry about it—the less desirable decision here is not going to destroy your Facebook strategy.

Market Passively

More than other parts of the Web, Facebook and other social networks are virtual hangouts. Their purposes vary tremendously, but more often than not, users visit Facebook with informal and playful goals in mind. They want to catch up with their friends, play their next move in Scrabble, or upload photos and videos from their vacation. Facebook is a recreation center, clubhouse, and neighborhood bar rolled into one.

Keep this in mind when engaging in the basics of Facebook marketing. We encourage our clients to market passively on Facebook. What do we mean by *market passively*? Create groups and event pages, and invite your community to join. But only invite them once or twice. And after you've built a presence on Facebook, don't constantly hound your fans or group members with messages sent via Facebook mail. Remember that, depending on your industry, you may already be connecting with these people through an email newsletter, Twitter, or your blog. You don't want to send them the same news twice (or more!).

Instead, make your Facebook page an interesting, useful place to visit. At a minimum, post compelling company and industry news that your community will definitely be interested in. One of our clients, an outdoor sporting goods company, posts short how-to videos like "how to patch a bicycle tire" or "proper care of your wooden canoe" to its Facebook page. If you run a restaurant, create a special offer that's exclusive to Facebook users and post it to your page. Maybe you run a landscaping business, and you can encourage your clients to upload photos of your work. Why not offer them 5 percent off if they post a photo? In short, think of these Facebook pages as a blog. You're inviting people to become regular visitors, not jamming media releases down their throats via Facebook mail.

Case Study: Chicken, Biscuits, and Facebook

Bojangles' Famous Chicken 'n Biscuits is a chain of more than 400 fast-food restaurants based in Charlotte, North Carolina. The company wanted to experiment with social media, so it worked with Matt Hames of Eric Mower and Associates to develop a strategy.

Matt first surveyed the landscape of existing Facebook groups related to his client. They were manifold and fervent: "Hello my name is . . . and I'm a Bojangles addict," "bojangles is more than just food," and "I Love Bojangles" were just three examples of groups with hundreds of devoted members. Clearly an untapped affinity group existed, and Bojangles' needed to join the ongoing conversation.

Starting simply, Matt created a Facebook page for the restaurant, featuring events, advertisements, photos, and links to the company website. To promote the page, he contacted the passionate administrators of the existing Facebook groups. He quickly recognized that idiosyncrasy of Facebook marketing—you often can't hide behind your corporation. "When I contact people on Facebook, I'm Matt Hames from Buffalo, New York. And Bojangles' is a southern brand. I explain why a Buffalo guy [and not someone from the South] is speaking for Bojangles'."[*]

Clearly Matt's northern roots weren't too much of a barrier to adopting the new official Bojangles' page. His original goal was to recruit 1000 fans on the page in the first six months. The campaign was far more successful, gathering more than 5000 fans in less than two months.

Bojangles' sees its Facebook fans as ardent supporters, as well as possible participants for focus groups or trial coupon campaigns. Matt Hames cautions against becoming overly focused on sales on your Facebook page. "There is a real tendency among brands, especially retail ones, to turn people into repeat customers," Matt says. "Social media is a little different and has a different kind of ROI. Instead of Return on Investment, it's more about Return on Engagement. On a purely marketing level, we're really trying to arm the really good fans with the brand's attributes so that they will spread them."

An Appetite for Fun

In May 2007, Facebook launched the *Facebook Platform*, an API (application programming interface) that enables external developers—you and me and our programming friends—to build apps for Facebook profiles and pages. *Apps* are widgets or chunks of

---

[*] Author interview, October 1, 2008.

functionality that users can add to their personal profiles. Anybody can create an app and invite friends to add it to their profiles. Apps have been created for everything—supporting causes, playing games, expressing aspirations, and so on.

According to Adonomics, a Facebook statistics site, Facebook has over 45,000 apps that are collectively used more than 35 million times a day. The top apps developed by third parties have more than a million active users. That's a lot of activity, and apps are a major focus of interaction—among friends and between users and the app builders—on Facebook.

Are these bits of functionality difficult to build? Not according to Boris Mann, Managing Director of Bootup Labs:

> It's very easy to get simple applications up and running. From there, it depends on the complexity of the applications. There are libraries and helper functions available for lots of different programming languages and platforms.[*]

Don't Be Apprehensive

So what gives a great app staying power? Jenn Lowther, social media marketer at 6S Marketing and Facebook power user, thinks three elements are key:

- "The application interacts with the user. Static applications are interesting for the first couple days. After that, the novelty wears off and the app gets deleted. Apps that have stayed on my profile for an extended period of time have an interactive quality, either with the application itself or with my friends. Good examples of these include Booze Mail, Free Gifts, and Super Wall."

- "The application is very personal or supports something you believe in. These are the Dogbook, Picture Mosaic, and Causes-style applications. I have added the Dogbook application and filled it with pics and info about my dog. I never really look at her page anymore or add new pics, but I'll never remove it either. Friend Wheel is another app that falls into this category."

[*] Author interview, November 14, 2007.

- "The application fills a need. This element is the hardest for a company to satisfy. Apps that fill a need are the ones most likely to have extended staying power. Super Wall fills the need and desire to share videos. Free Gifts allows users to save money and, at the same time, send their friends gifts."[*]

Phillip Jeffrey, a University of British Columbia graduate student researching social media and user-generated content, says the most popular applications are "visibly social." That is, they display interactions with your friends and other users on your profile. Visibly social apps also provide constant, unmistakable evidence of your popularity. They're the virtual equivalent of having flowers from your boyfriend or girlfriend on your desk.

Here are some other characteristics of popular Facebook apps:

- They're fun. Consider the current most popular apps: Super Wall, FunWall, SuperPoke, and so forth. Don't they sound SuperFun?

- They have a low usage barrier. The popular apps don't require much time to run or figure out. Sending a virtual hug to a friend is much easier than assembling a list of your favorite novels.

- They allow you to reveal yourself and your affinities. Apps like Movies and iLike enable you to talk about yourself. Who doesn't like to do that?

Facebook apps are great for building your brand's visibility, and if they're used properly, they can even act as yet another communications channel with your users. Based on the research we've done, they're not fantastic engines for driving traffic to your website. Simply put, when users are in the world of Facebook.com, they prefer to stay. They're disinclined to leave Facebook for your site, particularly if they're playing with an entertaining application.

On the other hand, we really like Facebook apps for social marketing, where you're attempting to change people's minds about something. For example, Facebook has a popular app called (Lil) Green Patch. Users tend virtual gardens and send plants or green gifts

---

[*] Author interview, December 11, 2007.

to their friends. Sponsors of the application donate to conservation groups based on the app's usage statistics. The more people use it, the more donations these environmental groups receive. Although this app by itself probably isn't going to change anybody's mind, you can let friends know your concerns about climate change and sustainability. And if they respect your opinion, you might even change a mind or two.

Working with Facebook App Developers

Most of you are probably not computer programmers, nor do you have programmers at your immediate beck and call. To create a Facebook app, you'll probably need to work with a freelance programmer or a web development agency. This may be unfamiliar territory, so here are some questions you should ask in the early stages of the development process:

Have the developers built Facebook applications before?
> This question, although it seems obvious, is also the most important one. How many apps have the programmers built? How popular are those apps? Are reviews of their apps on Facebook positive? Add a couple to your Facebook profile and try them out. Are they thoughtfully designed? Are they easy to use?

Are the developers familiar with the Facebook guidelines for application development?
> These guidelines, officially called *Platform Application Guidelines*, describe in tortuous detail what app builders can and cannot do. When you launch an app on Facebook, you're playing in somebody else's playground. If your app doesn't abide by these guidelines, you're not going to be allowed on the swing set.

How will the developers handle change requests?
> This question applies to any development process, and talking about it is important. If you need to add something to the app, how will the developers respond to and integrate that request?

Can you reuse the app's functionality elsewhere?
> Often much of the work that goes into building a Facebook app can be applied to a similar widget on another platform. For

example, you might also want to create a desktop widget with similar functionality or possibly a badge that friends can post to their blogs and websites. Ask your developer about how much of the code is reusable.

Can you help test the app?

This introduces you into the quality assurance or *QA* process as early as possible and helps ensure that you're aware of show-stopping bugs as soon as those bugs are discovered.

Can the developers help you submit the app to Facebook?

Once the application has been developed and tested, you need to follow a relatively straightforward process to submit it to Facebook's app directory. If your development team has submitted apps before, let them do it, or at least have them look over your shoulder while you do it.

Do the developers offer support, maintenance, and upgrade services?

Once your app is on Facebook, your users will almost certainly discover a bug or issue that needs to be fixed. Alternately, you may want to add features to your app. How will the developers address these requests? How much will post-release changes cost? Most importantly, how long will those changes take? Remember, the developers will have moved on to other projects, so they may be disinclined to return to an old project. Get guarantees about turnaround times for ongoing support or improvements.

And here's a bonus question for you: Do you have a clear idea of what you want your app to do? Can you write it out in less than 50 words? Answer this more specific question: What will your app do for the average Facebook user? Having a cogent vision for your app will help eliminate unneeded features, streamlining the development process and saving money.

Advertising on Facebook

We usually discourage our clients from spending a lot of money on advertising. As a colleague likes to say, "Advertising is an act of faith." Exceptions to this rule exist, though, and two of our favorites are Google AdWords and Facebook advertising. We like them both because they're pay-as-you-go, the results are extremely measurable, and the ads can be targeted. Using Facebook advertising, you can specify exactly how much money you want to spend each day and who sees your ad. More importantly, you can access detailed reports about your ad's performance.

Imagine for a moment you've started a new home business. You want to sell riding gloves to aspiring young horsewomen in the United States. Using Facebook's ad building software, you can create a simple ad that will appear in the profiles of the kind of users you specify. In this case, let's imagine we want to target female American Facebook users from ages 13 to 21 who have expressed an interest in horseback riding. Facebook enables you to show your ads only to that particular demographic. Although the ads are essentially plain old banner ads, this hypertargeting can make ad campaigns on Facebook very effective. After all, nearly every one of the young women who love horses is a potential buyer of your gloves.

Case Study: Sharpening Perception with Mystery and Social Networks

Sharp Electronics Corporation has long been an innovator in consumer electronics, but the company rarely gets the credit it deserves. From calculators in the mid-1970s to nine-foot displays, Sharp has always been a leader in LCD technology. In the hopes of cementing its expertise in the average consumer's mind, Sharp engaged advertising and marketing services firm Lowe New York.

A fun and interactive Facebook app became a critical part of Lowe's campaign to change popular perception of Sharp. The app was called Life Changing Box and accompanied a website at *http://www.lifechangingbox.com/*. The app and website began unbranded, meaning no mention of the company was made, teasing consumers with clues and the promise of winning prizes.

The app was a variation on the classic game Hot Potato. A mystery box was passed virtually among players and whoever held the box at the end of a round—lasting between 30 minutes and 8 hours—received the prize inside the box. Players could only touch a box a certain number of times each day. The prizes included large, flat-screen TVs, home theater systems, holidays, and tickets to sporting events.

Facebook's ad builder shows a hypertargeted audience of 174,820 people who might be interested in your riding gloves.

The mysterious aspect of the campaign was vital, says Matt Picheny, managing director of the Interactive division at Lowe New York. "We wanted to intrigue users and get them to look at the brand in a different way. By not telling them who the brand was but getting them to explore the many aspects of the brand, Sharp's work as a technological pioneer since the turn of the century, and the fact that the company has been leading the way in solar panels and environmental issues since the 1960s, gave people a new way to look at the brand."

In designing the application, Matt Picheny and his team at Lowe took great care to build in enticements for users to promote the game to their friends. "Why would someone want to invite someone to play the game? It could decrease your chances of winning. We added a component to the game so if you invited a friend to play, and your friend won a prize, then you would win a duplicate prize. We found this added a nice viral pick-up of the game. Those involved in the game started sending it to their friends and encouraging them to play so that their chances would increase as well."[*]

Eventually, using a robust blogger outreach and online advertising campaign, Lowe revealed that Sharp was behind the app. They announced the connection to Sharp on Facebook and replaced the stealth site with a fully branded version describing Sharp's leadership in innovation, its contributions to energy conservation, and its association with Major League Baseball.

Lowe's campaign demonstrates the value of a good mystery—everybody loves one. And we love a mystery with big prizes even more. For your next Facebook campaign, consider leaving something out—maybe even your whole brand—to tap into people's affinity for the unknown.

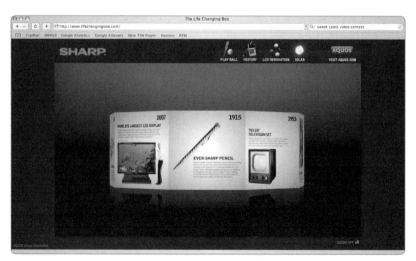

The Life Changing Box website, once its affiliation with Sharp was revealed

* Author interview, October 22, 2008.

Case Study: Self-Propelled Video on Facebook

Mountain Equipment Co-op (MEC) is one of Canada's largest outdoor equipment and clothing retailers. As a cooperative (to buy from any of its 12 stores, you must first become a member and pay a one-time $5 membership fee), it has many passionate young customers among its 2.5 million members.

Wanting to harness some of that enthusiasm for the outdoors, MEC launched its Sweet Spots video contest. MEC invited the public to submit videos of self-propelled outdoor activities—no snowmobiles or motorboats, which fits with MEC's corporate philosophy and brand. The company set up a submission and voting infrastructure on its website, enabling visitors to select their favorite videos in five categories. Participants uploaded their videos to YouTube and then submitted them on the MEC site, copying over the *embed* code that YouTube users can employ to display videos elsewhere on the Web. Then a group of judges chose the top three videos.

MEC used Facebook as one of three channels to promote the video contest. Web Marketing Manager George Weetman was wise not to rely on a single marketing channel (either online or off) for success. He explains how Facebook fit into MEC's online marketing tactic:

> This was our first year, so we restricted the marketing to our house campaigns. We dedicated real estate on our website to the contest, and it was integrated into our email marketing program throughout the year. When we had a travel promotion, we'd encourage submission in the travel category, and so forth. The Facebook page was built as a way to encourage people who were using Facebook to use that medium to promote their own videos to their friends. We're always focused in our department on both retention of existing members, and acquiring new ones. The Facebook page helped with both, I think.[*]

Members submitted over 200 videos and generated more than 10,000 votes for those videos. MEC's Facebook page for the contest ended up with more than 450 fans, and Weetman is convinced the

---

[*] Author interview, October 6, 2008.

The Facebook page for Mountain Equipment Co-op's Sweet Spots video contest

page was key to the campaign's (and the contestants') success. "In terms of votes, we found a good correlation between people who used Facebook to promote their videos, and the videos that succeeded."

Weetman already has plans for a bigger and better contest. "Next year we'll do more outreach to the YouTube community to solicit existing videos. After all, the better quality of videos submitted, the better it is for our brand. We might also look at building some custom functionality on our Facebook page to make it even easier for users to share their videos and encourage voting." MEC's campaign highlights how easy and productive it can be to integrate different online media—your website, Facebook, and YouTube—to gain maximum exposure and value from your marketing efforts.

The Future of Facebook and the Facebook of the Future

As we write this book, Facebook looks like an unstoppable juggernaut, impregnable as the preeminent social network. For the next year or three, that should hold true. The history of the social web is paved with the rubble of formerly popular websites, however. Veteran web users remember how prevalent the likes of AOL and GeoCities were in the early days of the Internet. They also remember a time when *web search* wasn't synonymous with *Google*. Facebook, too, shall fall.

But what will replace it? We'd be foolish to try to predict that with any certainty. Maybe the Facebook of the future will look more like a virtual copy of your dorm room than a web page. Or, given that mobile devices are now outselling laptops, maybe the next Facebook will live, first and foremost, on your cell phone. Who knows? In the near term, however, you can trust in Facebook's dominance.

11

VIDEO MARKETING WITH YOUTUBE AND OTHER VIDEO SHARING SITES

Has any social media site penetrated mainstream culture as rapidly and completely as YouTube? YouTube is ubiquitous. The site is referenced on the nightly news, in a Mariah Carey song, and on *Gossip Girl*. Its exploding popularity has made the term *video blog* sound as frumpily obsolete as *cyberspace* or *information superhighway*. At the time of this writing, YouTube stands with blogs and Facebook as the most omnipresent social media channels. YouTube, of course, is not alone in providing video hosting and sharing services. The Web is also home to a broad array of other video sharing sites, including Google Video, Metacafe, Dailymotion, blip.tv, Revver, and Vimeo.

Ironically, some of these other services have actually offered better features to users over the years. This is the VHS and Betamax race all over again—sometimes the best technology doesn't win. In any case, we've focused on YouTube in this chapter because it owns the lion's share of the social video market. If you find that your tribe or target market favors another tool, however, nearly everything in this chapter will still apply.

"Meteoric" fails to describe YouTube's ascent from obscurity to phenomenon. The site was founded by three ex-PayPal employees, Chad Hurley, Steve Chen, and Jawed Karim, in early 2005. In light of the earlier success of photo sharing sites, YouTube and its early competitors, Vimeo, Sharkle, ClipShack, and blip.tv, had an obvious goal: to become the Wal-Mart of online video. Before these services, distributing video online was a thorny challenge. Video files were too big to email; too many formats and associated players (who remembers RealVideo?) were available; and posting video to your website was a serious technical challenge. The Web was ready for a simpler solution.

Video sharing's emergence coincided with the evolution in hardware that allowed the average media consumer to film her own homemade movies. The price of webcam-enabled laptops declined (and continues to), and cell phones and digital cameras began to capture video as well as still images. Additionally, broadband Internet access became cheap and plentiful. After a six-month beta program, YouTube officially launched in November 2005 and practically from day one experienced extraordinary growth. A *USA Today* story reports that, by late November 2005, YouTube already had 200,000 users and was serving two million videos a day.[*] By the summer of 2006, the site was one of the most popular on the Web, delivering 100 million

---

[*] Jefferson Graham, "Video Websites Pop Up, Invite Postings," *USA Today*, November 21, 2005, *http://www.usatoday.com/tech/news/techinnovations/2005-11-21-video-websites_x.htm*.

videos with users uploading another 65,000 new videos each day.[*] On October 9, 2006, Google bought YouTube for a measly $1.65 billion. Since then, the site's astonishing growth has slowed a little, but its place in Internet history and even cultural history is assured.

Why Make YouTube a Marketing Channel?

Here's an idea that will frighten anybody over the age of 20: Young people today are as literate with video as previous generations were with text. They are, after all, the most documented generation in history. They've grown up in a world of webcams and cell phone video (not to mention omnipresent security cameras in their schools and malls). The tools to create and edit video are cheap and everywhere. Sites like YouTube and its competitors were inevitable. And, of course, YouTube's numbers are staggering. The site claims (and we believe it) to receive more than 200 million unique visitors per month, making it the sixth most visited site on the Web.[†] By one estimate, the site hosts nearly 80 million unique videos.[‡] And the average user spends nearly an hour per month on YouTube.[§]

Video is also increasingly important in search engine optimization (SEO). Search engines like Google and Yahoo! are continually integrating different media into search results pages. Instead of just seeing text summaries and links when you search for something, you'll see those summaries intermixed with video and image thumbnails. That's not by accident. Remember who owns the two most popular video sharing sites: Google. SEO experts are now focused on delivering an integrated set of results to the all-important first page of search results—and you should be, too. If videos are going to occupy, for example, 2 of the top 10 results in a search for your company's name, they'd better be videos that you own.

In social media marketing, videos tend to work in one of two ways. More commonly, they're an asset of a larger campaign in

---

[*] "YouTube Serves Up 100 Million Videos a Day Online," *USA Today*, July 16, 2006, *http://www .usatoday.com/tech/news/2006-07-16-youtube-views_x.htm?*.

[†] YouTube Advertising Programs, YouTube, *http://www.youtube.com/t/advertising*.

[‡] "YouTube Statistics," Digital Ethnography, Kansas State University, March 18, 2008, *http:// mediatedcultures.net/ksudigg/?p=163*.

[§] Emily Steel, "YouTube to Start Selling Ads in Videos," *Wall Street Journal*, August 22, 2007, *http:// online.wsj.com/article/SB118773972468004675.html*.

Beware of Big Promises

More than any other social media channel, many black hats and shysters will promise you YouTube glory and millions of views. Like unscrupulous search engine optimization companies, they may use unethical or downright nefarious tactics to get your video more attention. Considerations of honesty and your reputation aside, the viewers they promise probably aren't as targeted as you'd like. These shysters are likely to sacrifice factors like demographics and target markets in the pursuit of big returns. Be sure to research such agencies thoroughly if they haven't been referred by a trusted colleague.

---

which you're using YouTube (or its competitors) as one of several communications channels. In other cases, the video itself is the focus of your marketing efforts. As opposed to being a marketing medium, the video is the end result—the thing you want to talk about. We've seen companies become a little distracted by the awesome video they created. Instead of thinking, "Let's tell the world about our great product" or "Let's rally citizens to our cause," they start obsessing about "Let's get more people to watch our bitchin' video!" This chapter isn't about making you a YouTube star, so we focus on the former scenario: video as part of a larger campaign. And if your ultimate goal is a lot of YouTube views, you might want to reevaluate your strategy. Keep your eye on the big picture.

Setting Your Expectations and Measuring Results

Marketing is a marathon, not a sprint. A successful campaign is usually the result of a hundred correct decisions and actions. Remembering this is especially important when creating and promoting a YouTube video. We all look enviously upon those corporate success stories in which a particular video garners hundreds of thousands of views. That's the exception, not the rule. When you start, set modest goals for your YouTube videos. Approach YouTube with a similar philosophy to writing a corporate blog. Build an audience for your YouTube offerings over time. You may strike viral video gold with your first attempt, but success is likelier to come after your fifteenth video than after your first. How can you measure success on YouTube? We touch on this topic in Chapter 6, but the issue is worth revisiting here. Here's a list of potential metrics to track on YouTube:

- Number of views

- Number of times the video has been rated

- Number of times the video has been marked as a favorite

- Number of comments associated with the video

- Number of video responses to the video

- Number of websites and blogs linking to and embedding the video

The *number of views* is the default measure—the Nielsen rating of this decade—but we encourage you to keep these other metrics in mind. The number of comments, for example, can reflect a deeper level of engagement from your viewers. If you're spending a lot of resources on a video-based campaign, consider using a tool like TubeMogul or Vidmetrix; these services enable you to upload videos to and track results across multiple video sharing sites and monitor how your videos are being spread and linked to across the rest of the Web.

Don't forget to check out YouTube Insight, YouTube's built-in statistics package for your videos. Insight not only provides basics like view count and information about where the video is viewed (on YouTube.com, external sites, and so forth), but also offers demographic information about who is viewing and commenting on your video. Take the age and gender stats with a grain of salt, however, as they're based only on those viewers who are logged in to YouTube accounts. If three-quarters of your video views happen outside of YouTube.com, then these statistics aren't particularly useful. Finally, Insight offers Hot Spots, a kind of interactive chart that, according to YouTube, shows:

> . . . the ups-and-downs of viewership at each moment in your video, compared to videos of similar length. The higher the graph, the hotter your video: fewer viewers are leaving your

video and they may also be rewinding to watch that point in the video again. Understanding which parts of your video your audience likes enables you to make better content.[*]

It's easy to become a little obsessed with Hot Spots, editing and reediting your videos to maximize the amount of time that line stays above "Average." Don't overemphasize this—or any—metric. For example, every video we've seen is hotter near the start than at the end.

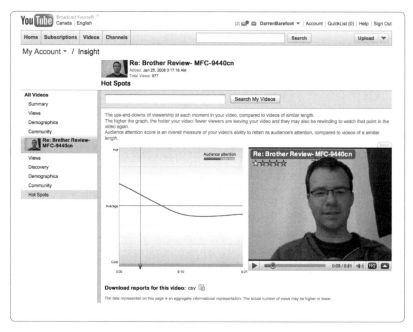

An example of YouTube's Hot Spots report

What Makes a Popular YouTube Video?

Let's be honest—producing a successful YouTube video isn't all that different from creating a great television ad or show. Ideally, you need an enticing, original video that captures and holds the viewer's attention and cuts through the morass of distractions. If you've got any experience producing video or working with ad agencies, then you're a step ahead of most marketers when it comes to YouTube. We obviously can't offer you a complete video production guide in

---

[*] Tracy Chan and Kenny Stoltz, "Step into the Spotlight with YouTube Insight," Official Google Blog, *http://googleblog.blogspot.com/2009/05/step-into-spotlight-with-youtube.html.*

a single chapter. We can, however, highlight the characteristics that make for successful videos or performers in the world of YouTube:

Recent and topical

Videos that trade on trends in pop culture or politics can generate a great deal of attention. Did you notice how quickly the producers of *Saturday Night Live* recruited Tina Fey to do impressions of Sarah Palin? The window for satirizing or otherwise exploiting events in the public imagination is usually short, and the advantage often goes to those who are quickest off the mark. That said, this approach can also work for a longer-term news story. Amber Lee Ettinger, better known as Obama Girl, is the star of a series of videos supporting then-Senator Obama's run for the Oval Office. Her video, "I Got a Crush . . . on Obama" shot to popularity in June 2007, in the early days of Obama's campaign.

Sex

In ancient Rome and on YouTube—sex sells. If you've ever browsed the most popular YouTube videos for a given week or month, you'll notice a prevalence of busty, scantily clad women in the thumbnail previews. Until recently, YouTube displayed a preview image based on what was shown at three precise points in a video (25 percent, 50 percent, and 75 percent). The user who uploaded the video could select which of these three images to display. Savvy video creators would ensure the mathematical middle of their videos featured an enticing image, either through careful editing or through baldly inserting a photo of a girl in a bikini. The video was then more attractive to the casual YouTube viewer (or to half of them anyway). This was in direct violation of YouTube's Community Guidelines, but the rule was rarely enforced; the trick no longer works, as YouTube recently changed the algorithm that chooses the thumbnail preview images.[*] Nonetheless, YouTube's Most Popular page will always feature a lot of provocatively named videos highlighting hot or hunky young things.

---

[*] Erick Schonfeld, "YouTube Cracks Down On Sexy, Spammy Videos And Ning Closes Its Red Light District," TechCrunch, December 2, 2008, *http://www.techcrunch.com/2008/12/02/youtube-cracks-down-on-sexy-spammy-videos/*.

Your Message Should Reflect the Medium

We recently helped a client—an environmental advocacy group—spread the word about a campaign. The group had built a variety of social media assets before we became involved. Among these was a two-minute video it had created and uploaded on YouTube. Though they were amateur video editors, the staff had put the suite of free tools available on the average Apple computer—iMovie, Garage Band, iPhoto, and so forth—to good effect. The video featured evocative photos of endangered animals and pristine wilderness that swooped in and out of the frame. The group's message and call to action were clearly articulated in scrolling text and narration. The video looked like a professional (if banal) public service announcement and received very little attention on YouTube.

We recommended that, in addition to the PSA, the group recruit a few young, attractive members of its staff or volunteers to make videos of their own. These videos would be straightforward talking-head videos in which the presenter, speaking directly to the camera, would simply and directly articulate the group's cause and call to action. This is an example of how that old Marshall McLuhan chestnut, "The medium is the message," still applies to new media and the Web. The direct personal monologue facing the camera is the de facto staging of a YouTube video. Just as you adopt local customs when visiting a foreign land, try acting like the natives on YouTube.

If you follow this advice, you'll be in excellent company. Increasingly, you can spot the head-and-shoulders direct address style of YouTube in music videos and film. And performers have, en masse, adopted the body language of the medium. When the group released its recent album, the two lead singers of Barenaked Ladies recorded videos of themselves playing acoustic guitars and singing in their bathroom and posted them to a YouTube competitor, Revver.com. Likewise, Alanis Morissette released an amusing and very low-budget parody video of the Black Eyed Peas hit "My Humps." In both cases, very famous rock stars co-opted the cultural practices and aesthetics of YouTube. Keep this strategy in mind before you commission a $500,000 ad for your YouTube campaign. Your intern may have better luck with a curtain and a webcam.

Unexpected

Many successful videos promise you one kind of video but show you another. They draw on a classic storytelling technique— *the reversal*. Most blooper videos work on this premise. You're watching a heartwarming wedding ceremony that's taking place poolside at a fancy resort. The bride and groom look happy and carefree. The best man steps forward to hand the ring to the groom. He trips on some bunting and sends the bride and pastor head first into the deep end. Another example is Ghyslain "The Star Wars Kid" Raza. He predates YouTube, but he became famous—his video has allegedly been viewed nearly a billion times[*]—because viewers responded to the unexpected, private joy with which he wielded his mock lightsaber. Also, who hasn't pretended to be Luke Skywalker or Indiana Jones or Lionel Richie (not Darren, certainly) in the solitude of his bedroom? We don't, however, expect that exclusive performance to go public. When it does—and when it reveals something unexpected—viral video marketing nirvana beckons.

Originality

Being unexpected is, of course, just one way to be original. The notion of originality goes to the question of whether you have something worth talking about. Even if you don't, original takes on conventional ideas abound. Consider the runaway success of Blendtec's video series, "Will It Blend?" With over 35 million views and an associated website at *http://www.willitblend.com/*, the company hardly needs an introduction, but in case you haven't seen the videos, they offer a simple premise: Will Blendtec's blender be able to mulch, mutilate, or liquefy a particular object? Blendtec's cheerful founder Tom Dickson indulges the kitchen fantasies of a six-year-old. In each short video, he gleefully drops whole avocados (pit included), Nike sneakers, and even an iPhone into his company's blender and speculates about the outcome. The answer to the question, "Will it blend?" is, inevitably, "Yes." Dickson has also built a loyal audience because he frequently accepts viewer suggestions for new items to mince. Of course, if Mr. Dickson wants to top himself, he might produce some YouTube outtakes, where he unsuccessfully tries to blend, say, hubcaps or weapons-grade plutonium. After all, no one expects

---

[*] "Star Wars Kid Is Top Viral Video," BBC News, November 27, 2006, *http://news.bbc.co.uk/1/hi/entertainment/6187554.stm.*

a blender to be invulnerable, and the outtakes might prove to be an ingenious twist on an original idea.

Extraordinary skill

We love to watch remarkable accomplishments in all their forms. On YouTube, the documentation of crazy feats is another reliably popular style of video. Totally sick skateboard or parkour videos are one thing, but the quirkily astonishing achievements are the ones that get views in the millions. A kid, seated on his bed, plays a note-perfect rendition of Pachelbel's Canon on his electric guitar. An ethnically diverse set of young men—aided by silk boxers for reduced friction—do effortless back flips into their jeans. Combine this level of practiced skill with humor and a charismatic performer and you get one of the most popular YouTube videos of all time, Judson Laipply's "Evolution of Dance." As a marketer, you're probably thinking, "I can't do anything really well, and I don't have time to practice." Don't be too quick to decide; you may be able to apply skills acquired in an unrelated hobby or pastime. Maybe you show terriers in your spare time. Can you train them to leap through an obstacle course of your company's products, whether those products are tractor tires or toasters? Or maybe you can knit faster than anybody in your family. What about a time-lapse video of you manically crafting a company sweater?

Meta-YouTube

How many songs do you know about the life of a musician? Or books about writers? Or movies set among the backlots of Hollywood? One rote formula for blogging success is to write endless posts on "how to blog" or "how to get more readers for your blog." In short, using a medium to talk about that medium is very common. The same is true on YouTube. Videos that trade on a community's tribalisms—its leaders, practices, or in-jokes— can be successful. Consider, for example, the video for "Pork and Beans" by punk-lite band Weezer. The video features a rogue's gallery of YouTube stars and is entirely about the customs of the website's users. In fact, if you're not at least a casual YouTube user, the video is largely meaningless. Nonetheless, Weezer's video has nearly 20 million views to date. Be careful, though. This tactic can go horribly wrong if you're not sufficiently immersed in the culture of YouTube natives. We're not big fans of this approach because your message can often get entirely lost in the gimmick.

Brevity

Keep it short. Though rare exceptions exist, nearly every really popular video is less than 5 or 6 minutes long. Many are less than 2 minutes, which is probably a good duration to aim for. If you absolutely must make a 25-minute video, consider breaking it up into 8 or 10 *webisodes*. And, of course, ask yourself why you need 25 minutes to say what you want to say. Some of the exceptions to the brevity rule include videos of President Obama's speeches during the 2008 election; these sometimes exceeded the hour mark. As with most of social media marketing, however, less is usually more on YouTube.

Funny Beats Pretty

The previous section discusses seven qualities that tend to make videos popular. Here are two factors that, maybe to your surprise, don't matter: quality and the visibility of a company's involvement. After giving up control, the aspect of social media that companies are least comfortable with is its apparent amateurism. Companies often launch corporate blogs with a lot of editorial oversight, ensuring blog posts are reviewed for content and style. As a result, the blogs tend to describe new vice president appointments and office openings and are incredibly dull to read. Many companies make the same sort of mistakes when producing videos for the Web. They've either never marketed using video or have only created television ads and corporate videos. A better model for YouTube is the home video.

The reality is that social media, including blogging, works best when it's a little messy around the edges. After all, social media is a medium founded by and for amateurs. Browse through the most popular YouTube videos for the last month. Aside from the professionally shot music videos on YouTube's Most Popular list, consider how many look like they were shot in somebody's bedroom. The videos look that way because, of course, they *were* shot in somebody's

> ### Learning Isn't Always Funny
>
> Let's put all of these creative strategies for popular videos aside for a moment. Don't disregard YouTube's potential as a great instructional medium. Whether you're selling floor tiles or chocolate chips, you may have to teach your customers how to use your products. Consider creating short, informal explanatory videos for your products or services. Maybe you can create a series that guides the customer from being an out-of-the-box noobie to an advanced user. Home Depot does a great job of this on its YouTube channel (*http://www.youtube.com/homedepot*). The company offers more than a hundred videos that explain a specific home repair or improvement activity in less than 10 minutes. These videos coincide with Home Depot's strong do-it-yourself-but-we'll-help brand aesthetic and probably convert some customers from rival stores.

bedroom. So if you pay $50,000 to produce a slick video with professional actors and sharp editing, don't be surprised if the YouTube community gives it the cold shoulder. Though your video might still be a raging success, polishing that video doesn't improve your odds. Here's a truism about popularity on the Web that's as old as the first Photoshop contest on Fark.com: Funny beats pretty every time.

The Wisdom of Stealth Videos

The *stealth* or *guerilla* viral video is now a staple of corporate involvement on YouTube. These videos appear to be produced by an individual, not a company—they don't feature any obvious corporate endorsement. The really successful ones—backed by (sometimes shady) marketing and SEO firms—get hundreds of thousands or even millions of views. Eventually, because of careful investigation by viewers or a corporate media release, a company reveals that it created the video. Sometimes the company changes the video's name or description in order to more directly associate it with the brand being promoted. If everything goes as planned, the company and its marketing firm take a bunch of media interviews and the video gets even more attention. Here are a few examples of this phenomenon:

"Cellphone Popcorn"   Some kids point their ringing cell phones at popcorn kernels and the radiation that the phones allegedly give off causes the kernels to pop. The ad, made with a little computer graphics post-production, actually belongs to Bluetooth headset retailer Cardo Systems.

"Bike Hero"   A real-world remake of the popular game *Guitar Hero* shot from the seat of a mountain bike. The video is actually a promotion for *Guitar Hero: World Tour*. Notably, this video only makes sense if you've played Guitar Hero. If you're under 40, you probably have.

"Guy Catches Glasses with Face"   An agile young man manages to catch his sunglasses on his face, time after time. You guessed it—the video is a viral campaign for Ray-Ban.

We've got to be honest here: We're often puzzled by this tactic. You only hear about the runaway successes. For every video that captivates millions of viewers, hundreds or thousands of anonymous brand-backed videos have earned a mighty 614 views. The hot-guys-jump-into-Levis is the home run. Most of these videos don't make it to first base. Of course, this is true of *all* YouTube videos. If you want to conceal the origin of your video, however, you're restricted in how you can promote it. Crucially, you can't use your established relationships—with your customer base, affinity groups, media, bloggers, and so forth—to kick start the video's promotion. Your marketing tactics have to be as anonymous as the video itself, and you may find that seriously hamstrings your work. Of course you can always return to your core audience once the video has been unveiled for what it is, but only if the video is a big success. If your video only has 874 views and one comment that reads, "Wherez the LOLZ?" you're going to look pretty lame. And your loyal followers are going to wonder why you didn't give them first crack. Additionally, if you want a video to remain anonymous for any length of time, you have to establish and maintain that anonymity. Swearing your staff to secrecy is one thing; concealing any tracks you leave in promoting the video is more difficult. The Internet is full of amateur sleuths with too much time on their hands.

When these stealth videos are successful, the creators usually enjoy three tangible benefits: earned coverage from the mainstream media and the blogosphere, more visitors to their website, and users who subscribe to their YouTube channel. These rewards are fleeting. As we keep emphasizing, your revelation will only gain media attention if the video has already earned a huge viewership. As a PR strategy, the stealth viral video seems like a poor wager.

Most of the time, after the big reveal, companies add links or annotations declaring that they're behind the video. These additions have the added benefit of driving traffic toward the website associated with the campaign (often a campaign-specific microsite). That traffic, of course, only represents a fraction of those viewers who watched the video after the reveal. Say, for example, you launched a successful stealth video that earned a million views. You unveil the true origin of the video, and it receives another 500,000 views over the next year. Maybe you enjoy a 1 percent click-through rate—5,000 visitors—from the link added to your video's description. Of course, you missed out entirely on the first million viewers. If they don't revisit your video page or learn the truth elsewhere, these viewers may never know that you're the hip corporation behind that super-cool viral video. This leads to the essential question: How many viewers would you have received if you'd been up front and honest about your video's origins? If you would have gotten more than 500,000 viewers, then you're better off just owning your video, without subterfuge.

Your Latest Picture

You might think that if you enjoy great success with your first video, you've got it made. You've got an instant, loyal audience who will return for each subsequent video. As they say in Hollywood, you're only as good as your latest picture. Domino's ran a five-video campaign featuring a 16-year-old girl wigging out because when her father bought her a new car, he chose the wrong color. The rest of the videos feature her talking to her webcam about the incident. Only in the fourth video is the Domino's connection exposed. Consider the viewership a month after the campaign began: The initial video had 351,000 views, and the fourth video had 9,790 views.[*] For every 100 people who saw the first video, less than 3 viewed the last video.

---

[*] Steve Hall, "Domino's Rips Off CarMax Campaign with YouTube Video Series," Adrants, January 25, 2007, *http://www.adrants.com/2007/01/dominos-rips-off-carmax-campaign-with-you.php*.

As you can see, instant fame is no assurance of ongoing success. We generally agree with video marketer Dan Ackerman Greenberg, who argues against the timed release of videos:

> If we have multiple videos, we post all of them at once. If someone sees our first video and is so intrigued that they want to watch more, why would we make them wait until we post the next one? We give them everything up front. If a user wants to watch all five of our videos right now, there's a much better chance that we'll be able to persuade them to click through to our website.[*]

This tactic is more of a guideline than a hard-and-fast rule and applies specifically to time-limited campaigns like Domino's. If you're in it for the long haul and producing an ongoing series of videos (such as "Will It Blend?"), then you're obviously going to release the videos on a regular schedule.

How much does transparency in YouTube videos matter? This question is a hard one to answer. We recommend you err on the side of truthfulness. In addition to the issues we've already described, viewer backlash can occur. In the YouTube community, you'll find a diversity of views about the issue of brand-backed sneaky videos. On the other hand, we've heard from YouTube viewers who say, "If it's a cool video, then it doesn't matter who makes it." Here's a good rule of thumb: People generally don't like to be deceived. And that's what you're doing when you claim the "Bike Hero" video was, in fact, made by some guy in Fort Wayne, Indiana.

Marketing with YouTube Videos

You've created a YouTube account and a channel. You've produced one or more clever, original, and brief videos that might become stout Louisville Sluggers in your marketing bat bag. Now what? Before we continue, recall two recommendations from earlier in this chapter: See your videos as part of a larger marketing strategy, and set reasonable expectations. Now let's turn to what you can do with your freshly hosted YouTube video and how to get it seen.

---

[*] Dan Ackerman Greenberg, "The Secret Strategies Behind Many 'Viral' Videos," TechCrunch, November 22, 2007, *http://www.techcrunch.com/2007/11/22/the-secret-strategies-behind-many-viral-videos.*

Set the Stage

As with your profile on any social media site, take time to customize your YouTube account and channel. Take advantage of all the ways in which you can personalize your space: uploading a photo, tweaking the colors, and so forth. As a general rule, we recommend picking an account name that reflects, directly or indirectly, your organization or brand. If you plan to feature your videos on your corporate blog and your blog has a clever name, then you might use the same name for your YouTube account.

Keep in mind that your username becomes part of your YouTube URL. For example, Save the Children UK's username is, aptly, *savethechildrenuk*. That makes the organization's YouTube web address *http://www.youtube.com/user/savethechildrenuk*. If you want to share your URL, you can safely shorten it by removing the *user* part, making the previous address simply *http://www.youtube.com/savethechildrenuk*.

Save the Children UK has created a good-looking, complete YouTube channel.

Pick the Right Title

Increasingly, people navigate the Web using search. Instead of typing *www.ESPN.com* into their address bar, they simply search for *ESPN*. As we mentioned previously, video is increasingly important to SEO, so consider the title of your video carefully. Make the title descriptive and evocative without being hysterical. A common practice on YouTube and other video sharing sites is for video creators to write melodramatic or exaggerated titles and descriptions for their videos. They also may add totally irrelevant terms to the title and description ("sex!", "Lindsay Lohan!", and so forth). This tactic is a very obvious bid to obtain more views. Resist these temptations. For example, imagine you're the VP of Marketing for ACME Locks. You've produced a video demonstrating how indestructible your padlocks are. In the video, your lock is exposed to increasing levels of kinetic force—a hammer, a crowbar, a handgun, and so on. Here are some good titles:

- How Much Abuse Can This ACME Lock Withstand?

- We Smash, Trash, and Shoot a Padlock—Will It Survive?

- Harold Shoots a Lock

  On the other hand, here are some ill-advised titles:

- Paris Hilton Fondles a Lock—You've Gotta See This!

- ACME Lock Marketing Video #18

- woot!!! r locks r best!

Describe and Lead with a Link

Write an accurate, keyword-rich description for each of your videos. As elsewhere, try to avoid using boilerplate marketing text or anything that feels like advertorial copy. Simply faithfully describe what happens in the video. If you want to drive YouTube viewers to your website (and why wouldn't you?), we recommend beginning the description with the complete (sometimes called *fully resolved*) web address. That means including the *http://* at the beginning. If you've got a long URL as a landing page (say, more than 25 characters), your web designer or site manager can set up a *redirect* with a shorter URL. Here's an example of a good description:

> *http://www.acmelocks.com/*—In this video, ACME Locks Quality Assurance Manager Harold Druken tests our new padlock for durability. He starts with a hammer, then tries a crowbar, and finally shoots it with a 9mm handgun. The results may surprise you! Oh, and don't try this at home.

Categorize and Tag Responsibly

In addition to titles and descriptions, you can assign a category and tags to a video when you upload it. Like many social media sites (we're looking at you, Digg), the categories seem limited and a bit baffling. Just choose the one that fits best—we don't think this is a particularly important bit of metadata. You should write your tags wisely, however. Don't be deceptive in applying tags to your video, but do try to be as exhaustive as possible. Consider synonyms for your targeted keywords and industry terms. Be as specific as possible. You'll find applying a core group of relevant tags to all of your videos worthwhile (they may then show up under Related Videos on your video's pages) along with some additional tags specific to each video.

Play Nice with Others

As with the other social media channels we've discussed, becoming a member of the YouTube community is advisable. Create a complete and personalized YouTube profile. Watch other users' videos and provide feedback through commenting, rating the videos, and marking them as favorites. Record a few video responses for YouTube users who might have an affinity for your video—those who live in the same city or share an interest or work in the same industry. Just as bloggers monitor their blogs' statistics, YouTube users notice when you participate in this fashion. Just as you do on MySpace and Facebook, add YouTube users as friends. This friend group will come in handy when you want to spread the word about a new video.

Join Groups

If a group exists in the YouTube community for your industry or interest, join it. You can upload your videos to the group and

Fans engage with one another through the Celine Dion YouTube group.

interact with other members. If no group exists, you may want to launch and promote a group. Obviously creating and maintaining a YouTube group takes time and effort, so you'll want to gauge the relative importance of the video channel in your web marketing work.

Curate with Playlists

YouTube enables you to assemble videos—your own and others'—into playlists of related content. To do so, you click **Playlists** and select the playlist to which you'd like to add the video. By creating a useful playlist for your industry or cause, you act as a DJ or museum curator. If you create compelling playlists on specific topics or themes, they benefit the larger community and, if popular, get others' videos more views. Additionally, YouTube tends to include playlists in search results on the site, so be sure to use keyword-rich titles and descriptions for your playlists. Assuming it's appropriate,

Ninety Percent Less Moron

Speaking of community, we need to warn you about YouTube comments. As you may be aware, YouTube commenters seem to have the language skills and sense of humor of a dimwitted eleven-year-old. We're not sure why, but it endangers our faith in humanity. YouTube recently implemented an Audio Preview button, which encourages users to listen to their freshly composed comment before clicking Post Comment. If you're a Firefox user, we encourage you to install the YouTube Comment Snob browser plug-in. This plug-in automatically hides YouTube comments that abuse basic rules of spelling, grammar, and punctuation. You'll enjoy a YouTube with 90 percent less moron. If you've got videos on YouTube, feel free to take the advice we provide elsewhere in this book and delete any comments that don't meaningfully contribute to the conversation. On YouTube, that may very well be most of them.

you can always include your own videos in your playlists. Just be sure your first priority is to deliver value to the person browsing the playlist. Include new or unpopular videos; a playlist won't be of much interest to the average user if she has already seen 9 out of 10 of the videos.

Include Videos in Pitches

Be sure to link to those other channels in your emailed pitches and on your website. In particular, embed your videos or YouTube channel widget on your social media resource page and in posts on your organization's blog. For lots of busy social media creators, a quick post featuring your video in their blog or Twitter stream may be an enticing alternative to a longer post about your product or cause.

Feature Videos in Other Communication Channels

Depending on the focus of your videos, promoting them to your existing customers or constituency may be appropriate. For example, feature your videos in your company email newsletter or invite readers to "Look for us on YouTube" in offline advertising.

Annotate Your Videos

In mid-2008, YouTube added the Video Annotations feature. This feature enables you to overlay text, graphics, and sundry other effects to a video. YouTube users are still experimenting with how to implement annotations without annoying their viewers. Some common annotations we've seen so far include simple calls to action ("Subscribe to our channel") or references to other videos. Currently, you can only link to other YouTube videos, not to external sites. If you're publishing a connected series of videos, you might want to add a message near the end of each one that reads, "Click here to watch the next video in this series." We expect these post-production features to continue to expand on YouTube and other video sharing sites, so keep an eye out.

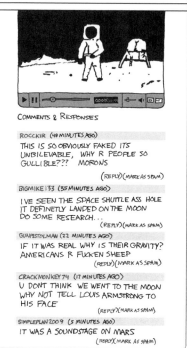

xkcd *creator Randall Munroe offers some insight into YouTube commenters.*

Case Study: Elastic Path Makes E-commerce Platforms Fun—No, Really

In 2007, we worked with e-commerce platform vendor Elastic Path to devise a viral marketing campaign that would bring new visitors to the company's blog. By their nature, e-commerce platforms don't often capture people's imaginations.

What does? Funny videos on YouTube, of course.

We built a meme. We devised, developed, and promoted a series of seven YouTube videos called "The Crazy, Messed Up World of Ecommerce" (*http://www.getelastic.com/crazy-ecommerce/*). The videos asked the question, "What if shopping offline were as cruel and difficult as buying online?" The videos were all under two minutes, and we intentionally shot and edited them to feel a little hokey and rough around the edges. As mentioned previously in this chapter,

What's in a Meme?

A *meme* is a virally transmitted unit of cultural information. Memes are everywhere, and have existed throughout human history. Catchphrases, melodies, icons, inventions, and fashions are typical memes. A chain-letter is a meme, as is the idea of a meme itself.

The most important thing about a meme, and the only way it can survive, is that it's compelling enough to pass on. No one wants to retell a bad joke, and nobody gets a tuneless song stuck playing relentlessly in their head after they hear it. Memes thrive because they're worth talking about.

The Internet is a natural habitat for memes. Why? Because the Web has evolved into the world's biggest, fastest information exchange. Concepts can emerge, evolve, permeate, and perish in days or weeks. The growing popularity of blogs, social networks, and other frequently updated sites, combined with email and synchronous communications channels like instant messaging and Twitter, means that a compelling idea can reach hundreds of thousands of people within hours.

the social web is notoriously intolerant of anything that feels too slick or corporate. The videos we created are almost entirely free of a marketing message; they just feature Elastic Path's logo at the end of each short video. We did cast a professional actress, but she played opposite an extroverted VP from the company. The inclusion of an Elastic Path staff member ensured companywide buy-in and enthusiasm for the project.

After uploading the videos to YouTube and a couple of other popular video sharing services, we pitched them to Internet retailers, e-commerce and web marketing bloggers, and industry journalists. Elastic Path also showed the series at industry trade shows and events. By being creative with the content and using a popular medium to deliver the message, Elastic Path's videos have been viewed more than 40,000 times. These aren't lonelygirl15 numbers, but don't forget to consider the bigger picture of how a social media marketing project can impact your organziation. Former vice president of innovation at Elastic Path, Jason Billingsley, points out how the YouTube project extended past the videos themselves. "The blog got more popular in the search engines, which brought in more traffic, and more people saw the videos, which generated more links, which generated higher rankings in the search engines, and the cycle continued." Using "The Crazy, Messed Up World" project as a springboard, Elastic Path increased the number of subscribers to its blog from 100 to about 2000 in seven months.[*]

YouTube Killed the Video Star

As with every social media channel, you'll find that YouTube gets more rewarding as you spend more time within the community, engaging with your viewers and learning the ways of the new world that is YouTube Nation. Start small, set humble goals, and split your energies equally between creating a great original video and promoting it to your tribe and the larger Internet community. Even if you never achieve success on a "Will It Blend?" scale, you'll enjoy some search engine optimization benefits and an increase in visitors to your website over the long term.

---

[*] Danny Bradbury, "Web Techniques to Build Market Buzz," *Financial Post*, December 22, 2008, *http://www.financialpost.com/story.html?id=1103282*.

12

THE TWITTER REVOLUTION

In January 2009, a US Airways jet crash-landed in the Hudson River. Because of the pilot's heroic actions, the plane made a surprisingly gentle landing and all passengers and crew survived. The Hudson is a busy waterway, and the first boat—a passenger ferry—arrived on the scene four minutes after the crash. Janis Krums was on that ferry and snapped what's become an iconic photo of the incident with his iPhone. He posted the photo to the popular microblogging service Twitter, and within minutes, the photo had spread among thousands (and then hundreds of thousands) of Twitter users and then out to the mass media. Krums's photo was just the latest in a series of examples of how microblogging—sometimes called *micromedia*—is making the Web more and more real-time. From celebrity spottings to the Iranian protests around the 2009 elections, Twitter has developed into the go-to service for instant updates to the Web from the real world.

Microblogging is the most recent form of social media to gain mainstream media attention. Introduced and popularized by Twitter in mid-2006, *microblogging* refers to the posting of very short messages to the Web—in Twitter's case, postings no longer than 140 characters in length. These messages may be reports from the real world, random musings on your day, questions to friends, or links to useful or amusing webby stuff. Each Twitter user sends their own mix of *tweets*, or short messages, to the service. As with all social media channels, a number of microblogging services exist, but Twitter is by far the largest and most popular. Reliable statistics are hard to come by and are typically immediately out of date, but you can safely assume that by the time this book is in your hands, Twitter will have tens of millions of users.

From Broadcast to Conversation

Twitter was initially conceived as a one-way broadcast channel. Like the Facebook status update, you used Twitter to tell your friends what you were doing right now. Evan Williams, co-founder of Twitter, describes how the service has evolved since its early days:

> We didn't anticipate the many, many other uses that would evolve from this very simple system. . . . You send one message and it goes out to everybody, and you receive the messages you're interested in. One of the many ways that users shaped the evolution of Twitter was by inventing a way to reply to a specific person or a specific message. . . . We didn't build it into the system until it already became popular with users, and then we made it easier.[*]

---

[*] Evan Williams, "Evan Williams on Listening to Twitter Users," talk presented at TED Conference, February 2009, *http://www.ted.com/talks/evan_williams_on_listening_to_twitter_users.html.*

These days, Twitter seems more like an ongoing cocktail party. Many people still use it exclusively to answer the question "What are you doing?" but many more see Twitter as a kind of ongoing public conversation. The discussions are as varied as those you might find at a backyard BBQ or in a doctor's waiting room. Thanks to Twitter's mobile-friendly format, the average Twitter feed also feels very much in-the-now. Users may be tweeting from the front row of a concert or from the operating room.

Duane Storey tweets about his impending surgery.

Just like popular blogs, though, Twitter tends to revert to the broadcast model when a user has thousands or millions of followers. We can all follow Ashton Kutcher's tweets about how much he loves his famous wife. Even if he wanted to, however, he can't keep up with his many followers' daily routines. He may reply to the occasional inquiry, but these one-to-many interactions don't scale particularly well. On the other hand, if you're part of an organization with many followers, you can distribute the work among several marketing or customer support staff, applying the same many-to-many model that you use for the firehose of phone calls or email messages.

Twitter users can publish using many different avenues, including text messaging from cell phones, instant messaging clients, email, desktop software, or simplest of all, via the website itself. And, in turn, they can receive other users' updates on these devices. Like a traditional blog, these short messages appear as a kind of river, with the most recent postings at the top. Twitter users *follow* one another's messages: Each user has a public *follower* and *following* count. Think of Twitter more as a service or utility than simply a website (see "Tweeting Beyond the Browser" on page 226). Like the water flowing in and out of your home, you can use Twitter in many different ways.

As with the US Airways jet crash, the real-time nature of Twitter has also made it an exceptional tool for discovering timely information. The moment a news story breaks, tweets start flowing. The story might be as banal as a local power outage or as exceptional as the election protests in the streets of Tehran. In either case, Twitter users are often the first people to learn about breaking news when it happens. Not surprisingly, as we write this chapter, CNN's Breaking News Twitter account (*http://twitter.com/cnnbrk*) is the fourth most popular one, behind Ashton Kutcher (that's the power of early adoption for you), Ellen DeGeneres, and Britney Spears.

Twitter tracks emerging topics that display as real-time Trending Topics in the sidebar of your Twitter page and on the search page (*http://search.twitter.com/*). Glancing over these topics provides up-to-the-minute insights into the hottest topics in the Twittersphere. Just like any real-time, crowdsourced content, you should be a little skeptical of this information at first. For example, when reports began emerging about Michael Jackson's death, different Twitter feeds—whether newspapers, gossip blogs, or plain old folks—reported that the King of Pop had been in an accident, was in a coma, or had passed away. Although content creators are always seeking the freshest possible news, be sure you're acting on correct information. Put on your critical thinking cap. Just because information is fresh doesn't mean it's accurate.

Getting Started with Twitter

Just as with the other social media channels discussed in this book, start by setting up a profile. Setting up a profile on Twitter is much simpler than on Facebook or MySpace.

The first and most important decision you'll make is choosing your account name. That will determine your Twitter URL and how people will refer to you, as in *http://www.twitter.com/<youraccountname>* and *@youraccountname*. Brevity is important

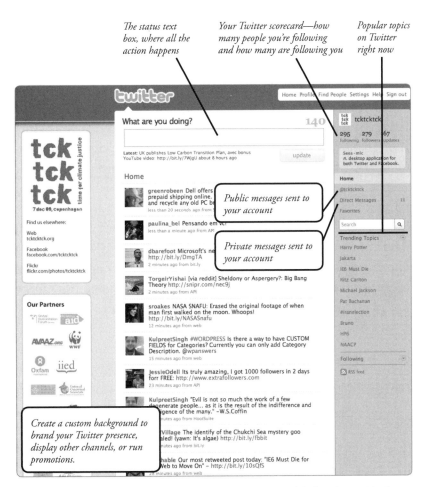

The status text box, where all the action happens

Your Twitter scorecard—how many people you're following and how many are following you

Popular topics on Twitter right now

Public messages sent to your account

Private messages sent to your account

Create a custom background to brand your Twitter presence, display other channels, or run promotions.

The anatomy of a typical Twitter account. Note how you can modify the colors and background to match your brand.

because other Twitter users will include your account name when they want to send a public or private message to you specifically. We recommend sticking close to the name of your brand or organization. Keep it as short, simple, and punctuation-free as possible. Since there are already millions of Twitter accounts, your preferred account name may no longer be available. Consider some variation, such as adding *HQ* or *dotcom* to the end of your name. If you're really unsatisfied with the options available, you may have recourse. At the time of writing, Twitter is experimenting with offering *verified accounts*. Thus far, these are "well-known artists, athletes, actors, public officials, and public agencies" whose identities Twitter has confirmed through a manual verification process. We imagine that Twitter will expand this service to include registered trademark holders, companies, and nonprofit organizations that (for a price) want to wrest an account away from an imposter.

After selecting your name, you have to complete a bio in 160 characters or less. Focus on clarity and facts here. Be humble. Make sure your grandmother and your ten-year-old could read it and understand what you're about. We like the bio for the organic retailer @Wholefoods: "Fresh organic tweets from Whole Foods Market HQ in Austin, TX."

Finally, you'll upload an avatar or small image for your account. Remember that Twitter users will be viewing it as a 48-pixel-wide square, so keep the avatar neat and tidy. The best approach is to use your logo if it's simple enough or part of your logo if it's more complicated. In other words, if you're McDonald's, just use the golden arches.

Know Your DMs from Your Hash Tags

For any social media tool or web-based community, a certain amount of jargon and lingo insinuates itself into the way people communicate. Twitter is no exception. Here are some of the odd terms applied to the Twitter microcosm:

@   Used to reply to or send a message publicly to a particular person. For example, you might tweet, "@dbarefoot That link you posted was totally lame."

Block   To prevent another Twitter user from following you. The blocked user won't be able to add you, and your updates won't appear on his profile page.

Direct message (DM)   A private message sent to another Twitter user. Unless the user has changed her default settings, the user is notified of this message via email. You can send private messages just as you do tweets, appending a *D* or *DM* before the user's name and the message; for example, "d aplusk I've got a crush on you."

Fail Whale   When Twitter is down, you'll see an illustration of a jovial whale being airlifted by eight birds. This was a fairly common occurrence in late 2007 and early 2008, when Twitter was struggling to scale with its rapid growth. You may encounter it occasionally now or hear about it in passing tweets.

Followers   The number of people who subscribe to your Twitter feed. They see your tweets in their activity stream. This number is public and thus a very obvious and oft-debated measure of a Twitter user's influence.

Hash tag   A hash mark (#) placed in front a word or phrase indicates that it references a specific topic, often an event. Hash marks also signify certain "inside baseball" Twitter traditions or games. For example, posting a list of Twitter users who you like on Friday and tagging the tweet with *#followfriday* has become a tradition. As Twitter's search engine and filtering software improves, we suspect hash tags will go out of style.

Retweet   When another Twitter user reposts a message that you originally posted, it's called a *retweet*. Retweets work like votes for a particular tweet, and they're how one-way messages go viral on the site. Retweeters often use the abbreviation *RT*, or simply *via*, to attribute others; for example, "RT @dbarefoot Why does Quentin Tarantino retain the sensibility of a 10-year-old boy?"

Shortened URLS   Because space is at a premium on Twitter, users often use URL shorteners to turn a long web address into a very short one. For example, the URL *http://en.wikipedia.org/wiki/Saint_Pierre_and_Miquelon_national_football_team* could be shortened to *http://bit.ly/stpierre*. Popular services include TinyURL.com, tr.im, and bit.ly.

Tweet   A message of 140 characters or less posted to Twitter. Also, *tweet* is a verb meaning to post to Twitter.

Tweetup   A variation on "meet up" (and the site Meetup.com), a *tweetup* refers to a group of Twitter users gathering offline.

Tweeting Beyond the Browser

The creators of Twitter chose 140 characters as the length limit for each message because that number was close to the 160 characters permitted for sending an SMS or text message from a mobile device (the extra 20 characters leave room for a username). We can actually credit this decision with creating a lot of Twitter's popularity. In many cases, users respond positively when you ask them for specific responses, such as "Tell us what you're doing right now in 140 characters or less."

This critical early decision helped Twitter rapidly become a service as much as a website. Twitter is a kind of microblogging infrastructure that users can interact with in a variety of different ways. According to a recent HubSpot survey,[*] less than half of all Twitter users read and post tweets through the traditional website. Another 21 percent use desktop applications, and 18 percent tweet using their cell phones or other mobile devices.

If they're not using the web interface at Twitter.com, then what tools are Twitter users employing? A variety of desktop applications are available that you can use to read and update your Twitter account. Three popular options are TweetDeck (*http://tweetdeck.com/*), twhirl (*http://www.twhirl.org/*), and Twitterrific (*http://iconfactory.com/software/twitterrific*). In all three cases, you can download and install the software on your computer. You then connect with your Twitter account (or accounts—TweetDeck supports multiple accounts) by entering your username and password, and you can read and post tweets from your desktop instead of inside a browser.

Many of these tools extend or enhance Twitter's basic functionality as well. For example, TweetDeck enables you to organize your Twitter followers into discrete groups. This feature comes in handy if you want to pay more attention to the tweets of, say, key customers or partners. Likewise, you can find an ecosystem of applications for using Twitter from your iPhone, BlackBerry, or other mobile device. Popular options include Tweetie (*http://www.atebits.com/tweetie-iphone/*), Echofon (*http://echofon.com/*), and

---

[*] Mike Volpe, "New Data on Top Twitter Applications and Usage," HubSpot's Inbound Internet Marketing Blog, February 27, 2009, *http://blog.hubspot.com/blog/tabid/6307/bid/4584/New-Data-on-Top-Twitter-Applications-and-Usage.aspx*.

TwitterBerry (*http://www.orangatame.com/products/twitterberry/*). Lastly, all sorts of efforts are being made to implement Twitter in other popular applications. For example, TwInbox (*http://www.techhit .com/TwInbox/twitter_plugin_outlook.html*) enables you to tweet from Microsoft Outlook. You can learn more about applications that extend Twitter's functionality beyond the browser by visiting *http://twitter.com/downloads*.

Although this section is called "Tweeting Beyond the Browser," you can also find dozens of other websites that enable you to post to Twitter. URL shorteners like tr.im or bit.ly interact with your Twitter account, and photo sharing sites like TwitPic.com and Flickr recently launched Twitter integration. Tools like CoTweet (*http://cotweet .com/*) or HootSuite (*http://hootsuite.com/*) offer a layer of business management functionality on top of Twitter. If you have multiple Twitter accounts or multiple people managing your account, you may find that a service like CoTweet helps you keep tabs on all the activity.

Tweeting for Fun and Profit

How can organizations use Twitter? Start by accepting Twitter as another online communications channel. Most likely your customers are already on Twitter, conversing about your brand. Let's start with a lesson in Twitter monitoring. Twitter offers a robust real-time search engine at *http://search.twitter.com/*. Go to that web address, enter your company's name, and click **Search**. The results provide an up-to-the-second snapshot of what people are tweeting about your organization. Assuming the flow of references isn't too plentiful, consider subscribing to an RSS feed for this search by clicking **Feed for This Query**. If you're trying to monitor multiple keywords, such as different products or your competitors, simply search again and add another feed to your feed reader. You can also use desktop tools such as TweetDeck to help monitor real-time searches for your brands. (We discussed these tools in the previous section, "Tweeting Beyond the Browser.") Carefully monitoring Twitter in this way can help you to head off controversy before it spirals out of control. The "Motrin moms" episode described in Chapter 8 offers a classic example of what you want to avoid.

NOTE *If your product or company uses a common name, you can get a lot of irrelevant results in this list. Just as Google allows you to refine your search, Twitter Search lets you exclude tweets based on keywords by using the minus sign (–). So if you're interested in No Starch Press but don't want to hear about the latest dieting craze, you might search for* nostarch no starch –diet –vegetables –atkins.

Companies use Twitter for the same reasons they write corporate blogs or, before that, email newsletters: to engage with customers, provide technical support, promote special offers, and so forth. And the same rule applies: Keep your followers happy by delivering value. *Value* can mean special discounts, contests, and early announcements of sales. But value also refers to being a contributing member of this online community. As with other social media channels, you should talk mostly about things other than yourself. Provide useful and entertaining links to stuff that your customers will be interested in. If you're a television producer, point your followers to stories about your stars and other shows that you think they might like. Tease them with tidbits of news about upcoming episodes. If you own a corner store, tweet about what's happening in the neighborhood around you. Alert your followers to the fire alarm down the street, the weekend block party, and the new drycleaner that just opened. These approaches bolster the value of your Twitter activity in the eyes of your followers and encourage them to pay more attention when you do occasionally tweet company news or a special offer.

Carnival Cruise Lines, for example, uses Twitter to distribute company news and promote sales and events. Tony Hsieh, CEO of the online shoes and accessories store Zappos.com, has an exceptionally popular Twitter feed. Part of his success is in the utter normalcy of his posts. He behaves not like the CEO of a company that Amazon bought for $847 million but like your everyday Twitter user. He tweets about his new haircut, posts photos of his cat, and occasionally replies to other Twitter users. On occasion, he also announces short-term Zappos sales that are exclusive to his followers. For that reason alone, if you're a Twitter user and a Zappos customer, you'd naturally follow Tony's tweets. Hsieh's enthusiasm for the tool has encouraged Zappos staff to join as well. In fact, the company maintains a sort of portal page at *http://twitter.zappos.com/* that lists all of the Zappos employees on Twitter and shows their latest tweets. At the time of this writing, almost 500 employees have Twitter accounts. Zappos has a legendary culture of customer service—they famously test the loyalty of all new employees by offering them $2000 to leave the company after their first week. So we aren't surprised that the company has embraced Twitter as another means of unfiltered, immediate customer interaction.

Zappos CEO Tony Hsieh replies to a question about why he spends so much time on Twitter.

Don't shy away from offering special pricing, coupons, or other deals to your Twitter followers. Dell, the computer vendor, has successfully promoted special offers to its Twitter community. In particular, Dell uses an account called @DellOutlet to promote the sales of refurbished or used Dell products at discount prices. A Dell spokeswoman talks about the company's success with this new channel:

> I started tweeting more regularly and doing more Twitter-exclusive offers, which created more buzz and helped us to grow our follower base (we're now over 600,000). Our followers responded by re-tweeting @DellOutlet messages to their followers, and our numbers rose even more.
>
> We've surpassed $2 million in revenue in terms of Dell Outlet sales, but we're also seeing that it's driving interest in new product as well. We're seeing people come from @DellOutlet on Twitter into the Dell.com/outlet site, and then ultimately

decide to purchase a new system from elsewhere on Dell.com. If we factor those new system purchases that come from @DellOutlet, we've actually eclipsed $3 million in overall sales.*

As of this writing, the @DellOutlet account has over 1.3 million followers. For a company the size of Dell, $3 million is just a tiny fraction of its annual revenue. Naturally, a sales channel for cheap computer parts would be an early Twitter success story. Geeks are the first adopters of tools like Twitter, and they love a cheap PC or monitor. Yet @DellOutlet also provides evidence that you can increase your bottom line by tweeting.

Other organizations use Twitter as a medium for running contests and giveaways. In fact, in these early days of Twitter adoption, contests are an effective means of increasing the number of followers in your organization. For example, photographer and author Scott Bourne ran a contest where he offered a camera to one new follower on Twitter over a specific period of time. He added over 1000 followers in the first 24 hours after his announcement. Contests aren't particularly new or innovative, but they are a proven way to engage with customers and potential customers on this new channel.

Another way to deliver value is to treat Twitter as a public, time-sensitive customer support channel. Once you start monitoring Twitter, you may notice that your customers are publishing questions, concerns, and complaints about your organization. If you don't have a Twitter presence, how can you ensure that customers receive answers in a correct and timely fashion? If you can make Twitter an easy and painless way for your customers to ask for help, you're more likely to earn their trust.

Twitter also manifested itself as an effective crisis communication tool during the California wildfires in the fall of 2007. KPBS is a San Diego radio station that was briefly knocked off the air due to the wildfire threat. The staff used Twitter, along with custom Google Maps they created, to distribute brief reports about evacuations and updates on the fire's scale.

---

* @StefanieAtDell, "@DellOutlet Surpasses $2 Million on Twitter," June 11, 2009, *http://en.community.dell.com/blogs/direct2dell/archive/2009/06/11/delloutlet-surpasses-2-million-on-twitter.aspx*.

Don't ignore the possibility of creating an original gimmick around Twitter. People have gotten very creative with real-world objects that "talk" to Twitter's API. For instance, @PiMPY3WASH is the washing machine that tweets when it's finished a load. @kickbee is a high-tech belt expectant mothers can wear that tweets when their babies kick. @GusAndPenny is a cat door that publishes tweets (and associated photos) each time a cat uses it. And @mytoaster—well, you can guess what it tweets about. These feeds are all pretty whimsical, but the Web loves whimsy. The cat door, for example, has nearly 1500 Twitter followers. More importantly, if you search the Web for *Twitter cat door*, you'll find many articles and blog posts about this wacky endeavor. Can you apply a similar approach inside your organization? If you work at an automobile plant, maybe you can publish a tweet every time a new car comes off the assembly line. Or maybe you own a tanning salon, and your tanning beds can tweet every time a client turns a little more orange.

Case Study: Insta-Fundraising with Twitter

David Armano is a designer and communicator in Chicago. He has run the popular marketing blog Logic+Emotion for several years, and at the time of this story had about 8000 followers on Twitter. Armano and his wife took in a family friend, Daniela, who was divorcing an abusive husband and desperate for a place where she and her three children could live. Using the social media tools at his disposal, Armano reached out to his online communities through his blog and Twitter account:

> Here's what we are asking. Right now, Belinda and I are opening our home, but it's tight as we have no basement. We've committed to giving as much as we can spare, diverting funds from other places. I'm asking if you could think about doing the same. Or at the very least, helping get the word out about this. We are looking to raise 5k for Daniela and her family. Enough so that she doesn't have to worry about a deposit or rent for a while.[*]

He used a service called ChipIn that enables anybody to collect donated funds through PayPal. ChipIn provided a widget that he displayed on his website and could share with others. His tribe of followers swung into action, and in a matter of a couple of days, they had collectively raised nearly $17,000 for Daniela and her family. A story like this highlights the power of crowdsourcing, but also the importance of wielding trust and influence in online communities. Armano wouldn't have been able to raise nearly as much money if he only had 800 followers and if he hadn't earned a degree of trust from his tribe through years of being a good online citizen.

Five years ago, Darren ran a similar ad hoc campaign for sending flowers to gay couples standing in line at San Francisco's City Hall waiting to get married. Called "Flowers for Al and Don," the campaign raised about $14,000 from nearly 900 donors. The difference was that the word was mostly spread through blogs, and the money was raised in about ten days. The fact that Armano executed a similar project in less than two days highlights just how much faster the Web has become.

Individuals and nonprofit groups continue to experiment with Twitter as a means of focusing attention and opening people's wallets. Twestival, for example, is an annual, hyperlocal fundraising event that happens in 200 cities across the globe, organized on Twitter.

---

[*] David Armano, "Please Help Us Help Daniela's Family," Logic+Emotion, January 6, 2009, *http://darmano.typepad.com/logic_emotion/2009/01/pleas-help-us-help-daniellas-family.html*.

Counting Clicks from Twitter

Web marketers take a great interest in *click-through rates*. Usually expressed as a percentage, this number indicates what fraction of web users will click something—an ad on a search results page, the Buy Now button, and so forth. Higher click-through rates mean greater success. If you increase your click-through rate for your online store from 1 percent to 2 percent, you've just doubled your sales.

So what click-through rate can you expect from links you share on Twitter? We couldn't find any conclusive research on the subject, so we ran our own semiscientific survey. We asked 150 Twitter users to report on their click-through rates. When all the numbers were in, we found the average rate was 1.7 percent. That means if you have 1000 followers, 17 of them will click a link you share. A clear relationship exists between total number of followers and click-through rate. The more followers you have, the lower your click-through rate becomes. For those respondents with more than 5000 followers, the click-through rate is a mere 0.8 percent. For those with less than 5000 followers, the rate is 3.5 percent. For those with less than 1000 followers, the rate is 6.2 percent.

What does this mean for marketers? A click-through rate of 1.7 percent is a pretty decent outcome. Although lower than the average for email newsletters in most industries, the rate outperforms the vast majority of online advertising stats that we've seen.

Ten Ways to Be a Jerk on Twitter

As with any communications channel, you can behave acceptably or you can behave in a way that identifies you as clueless or downright wicked. Avoid these ten Twitter sins, and you'll stay on the right side of the microblogging mob:

Automatically send direct messages to greet each new follower.

Some Twitter users set up a service like TweetLater to send auto-responses to new followers. The response usually goes something like, "Thanks for following—please visit my site." Receiving these is no fun—these messages are a bit like calling a customer service line and never actually speaking to a human. They're impersonal and often include a blatant attempt to sell something.

Use Twitter as an "everything aggregator."

We're not fans of Twitter users who use third-party services to republish every Facebook status update, name of the song they're listening to, or link to new blog posts to Twitter. Twitter already has a lot of noise, so people don't appreciate you contributing to it with aggregated feeds from other social media channels. Highlighting a blog post or tweeting about your love for a particular Lily Allen song is okay occasionally, but refrain from oversharing. If somebody wants to read your blog, they'll subscribe to its RSS feed or visit it regularly.

Repost your tweets to your Facebook page or blog.

Just as you shouldn't republish all of your other social media channels to Twitter, you should refrain from reposting your tweets on those channels. Tools are available that enable you to publish your tweets to your Facebook profile and aggregate a day's or week's worth of tweets on your blog. We discourage this behavior. Drawing connections between your channels with links that read "Follow us on Twitter" or "Check out our Facebook page" is okay; pushing the same message on your tribe through multiple channels isn't.

Constantly veer off topic.

If you run a seaplane company and have a Twitter feed, why are people following you? To receive discounts, industry and corporate news, and the occasional pretty sunset photo from the cockpit. They probably don't want to hear what you thought of *Transformers 2*. Be informal and conversational, but try to focus on your industry or cause in one way or another. This rule is analogous to a conversation you might have with a clerk in a shoe store. You talk about the weather, but sooner or later you get down to loafers. If you have the itch to share your private life, consider an official account for your brand and a separate one associated with your real name.

Conduct lengthy private conversations in public.

Don't exchange 20 or 30 messages with a colleague about a topic that isn't relevant to at least a portion of your followers. That's what direct messages (or email or chat) are for. This behavior is the equivalent of engaging in a loud conversation over dinner about something that none of the other diners care about or can contribute to.

Ignore context.

This is a corollary of the previous sin: Avoid tweets that are just "*@twitteruser* Thanks!" or "This is awesome! *http://someurl.com.*" If you want to thank someone, do it using a direct message, and if you're sharing links, add a description of what people will find when they click through. This is doubly true because Twitter users often use URL shorteners like TinyURL.com or bit.ly, so the URL doesn't offer any clues to the linked page.

Deploy the spam bots.

By this stage of the book we shouldn't have to tell you that any behavior that has the slightest whiff of spam is very bad news. A recent example is including Twitter's Trending Topics keywords in totally irrelevant messages. The European furniture chain Habitat got in trouble in June 2009 for including words like *Iran* and *Mousavi* in tweets that had nothing to do with the election protests in Iran. For example, one message read "#MOUSAVI Join the database for free to win a £1,000 gift card."* That kind of flagrant spam didn't sit very well with Habitat's followers. The story was covered by the BBC and the *Guardian* newspaper, among others, and the humbled company had to issue an apology.

HabitatUK: #MOUSAVI Join the database for free to win a £1000 gift card http://bit.ly/2wPLO (expand) ? Now!!
4 days ago from web · Reply · View Tweet

HabitatUK: #TRUE BLOOD Join the database for free to win a £1000 gift card http://bit.ly/2wPLO (expand) ? Now!!
4 days ago from web · Reply · View Tweet

HabitatUK: #KOBE Join the database for free to win a £1000 gift card http://bit.ly/2wPLO (expand) ? Now!!
4 days ago from web · Reply · View Tweet

HabitatUK: #AT&T Join the database for free to win a £1000 gift card http://bit.ly/2wPLO (expand) ? Now!!
4 days ago from web · Reply · View Tweet

Some of the tweets where Habitat abused Trending Topics keywords like Mousavi *or* Kobe. *Screenshot courtesy of Tiphereth Gloria.*

* "Habitat Sorry for Iran Tweeting," BBC News, June 24, 2009, *http://news.bbc.co.uk/2/hi/uk_news/8116869.stm.*

Tweet too much.

If you're following 50 people, you expect to see a reasonable distribution of tweets from each of the people you're following. That actually never happens—20 percent of people do 80 percent of the tweeting. Even if you're one of those 20 percent, show some restraint and don't pile up 8 or 10 tweets in a row. Nobody likes a blabbermouth. If you have that much to say, get thee to thy corporate blog.

Obsess about your follower count.

Twitter is an extremely informal medium. People will follow you or unfollow you for reasons way beyond your ability to understand, so don't sweat it. Yes, you want your follower count to grow, but let it happen organically. Focus on quality interactions with your followers, not the quantity that you have. Counting your Valentine's Day cards in high school wasn't cool or healthy, and it still isn't.

Ignore @ replies.

When a message starts with *@yourcompany*, you had better pay attention. This type of message is as important as a phone call to your store or an email message sent to your customer support team. We discuss the various ways you can monitor Twitter for such replies elsewhere in this chapter, but the simplest way is to keep a close eye on *http://twitter.com/#replies* once you're logged in to your Twitter account. You can also subscribe to an RSS feed of your username in your feed reader, if you only occasionally log in.

Remember, of course, that rules are meant to be broken. Twitter etiquette will continue to emerge and evolve, so we can offer few hard and fast decrees within this channel. Discover what works best for you. If you're worried that you're tweeting too much, ask your followers. They'll be very happy to let you know how you're doing.

Beyond the Twitterdome

Is Twitter a broadcast channel, a new form of instant messaging, or just another online time waster? We're not quite sure, but we can see its influence in recent changes made to sites like Facebook and Google. Twitter is yet another example of the Web becoming more real-time, more about right now. This trend coincides with the increasing number of people using the Web through mobile devices. These days our cell phones are more like computers that allow us to make phone calls. How long will Twitter remain on top? We give it another few years. Eventually—just like all the tools in this book—some other service will emerge as the Next Big Thing. Foursquare, for example, is a location-based social network that geeks and other early adopters are excited about. For now, though, get on board the Twitter rocket and enjoy its meteoric rise.

13

THE POWER OF CROWDS:
UNDERSTANDING AND PARTICIPATING IN
ONLINE COMMUNITIES

We've talked a lot about direct outreach and pitching because these are the nuts and bolts of any social media relations campaign. But there are other ways to get noticed online. Crowds are gathering all the time on the Web, and they're often working together toward a particular goal like presenting the best news, bookmarking and annotating websites, penning reviews, or even writing encyclopedia articles. You can think about these crowds in a few ways. Forrester Research characterizes them as *collectors*:[*] they organize content for themselves and others using RSS, news feeds, tags, and voting systems on social news sites. Another way to depict the crowd is as *curators*. Just as a gallery owner selects paintings with a goal of creating an exhibition of compelling work, web curators sift through and filter information to bring the best content to their online audiences. In this chapter, we'll show you how these crowd-based sites work and how you can participate in them to build your brand.

Social News and the Wisdom of Crowds

In Chapter 1, we discussed the rise of citizen journalism as evidence of the Web's democratizing effect on information. Today, crowd-powered social news websites permeate the Web. Digg and reddit are two of the most popular sites that crowdsource news. That means anyone—including you—can submit an article to these websites. Users submit, tag, and vote and comment on articles, with the most popular stories bubbling to the top and reaching the greatest number of people. These sites work in slightly different ways, but their workflows follow these basic principles:

1. A user submits a story and enters the relevant URL, a description, and a category that best describes the story.

2. Other users see this story. If they like it (or if their friends encourage them to), they vote it up. On Digg, the most popular of these sites, this is known as *digging* a story. See Chapter 4 for step-by-step instructions on how to do this.

3. The most popular stories appear on these websites' highly trafficked front pages, and receive thousands of visitors.

User-submitted news and member voting are the critical and unique features of social news websites; they're what differentiate social news from traditional media, where journalists and editors are gatekeepers. While some news sites employ human editors to

---

[*] Charlene Li with Josh Befnoff, Remy Fiorentiono, and Sarah Glass, "Social Technographics: Mapping Participation in Activities Forms the Foundation of a Social Strategy," Forrester.com, April 19, 2007, *http://www.forrester.com/Research/Document/Excerpt/0,7211,42057,00.html*.

determine the value and thus the visibility of submitted stories, most social news websites make their members the content curators.

Why Marketers Should Care About Social News

Simply put, social news sites can send torrents of traffic to your website. If you average 500 visitors a day, then welcoming 10,000 or more new folks through your digital front door in just a few hours is exhilarating. In fact, getting dugg has become a kind of brass ring for the online marketing industry. The following diagram shows a classic pattern for a website that reaches the front page of Digg. The illustration shows the launch of RobotReplay for our client, Nitobi.

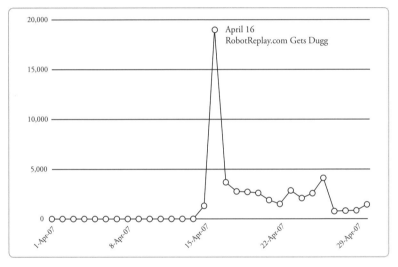

A classic example of the Digg effect for the RobotReplay launch

Here's the catch: Visitors from social news sites—particularly in those first few hours—tend to be transients who spend little time on your website before moving on to the next shiny bauble. Not all visitors are created equal; visitors become users and customers at radically different rates. For example, one traffic source may be as much as 30 or 50 times more valuable than another. In our experience, visitors coming from social news sites convert at a low rate of about 1 percent. Still, even if just 1 percent of visitors from social news sites subscribe to your organization's blog, that could add up to 200 (or if you're very lucky, 500) new subscribers in a single day.

This kind of marketing has another upside. The best long-term result of the Digg effect is that many users of these services are social media creators. If they find your news compelling, they may blog about it on their own site, post it to their Facebook profile, or bookmark it on their social bookmarking site of choice. We often aim for this outcome.

Using Social News to Build Buzz

Unfortunately, simply submitting your article to these social sites isn't enough to pull in a massive audience. The good news is that you can act to improve your chances of hitting the social news jackpot. Search the Web and you'll find plenty of articles on how to "game" social news sites, most often by paying a dodgy service to skew votes using nefarious methods. We can't discourage you from this approach strongly enough. Not only will your story immediately get buried by legitimate users, but going this route will also tarnish your organization's name and pretty much ensure that no other stories from your company's web address ever get promoted on that site. It's the kiss of death! Sites like StumbleUpon and Yahoo! Buzz are also efficient at filtering out lame, planted, or paid-for stories. If your news isn't remarkable to these sites' users, no amount of trickery, money, or prayer is going to help.

Here's what you *can* do. Your first plan of attack should be to generate mind-blowingly entertaining content that will make the masses laugh, cry, and be inspired all at the same time. Yep, this is a tall order. If you use social news services for any length of time, however, you'll get to know their constituencies. You'll start to see recurring themes among the popular stories. Studying these can help you to frame your own content appropriately. Here are some strategies that seem to consistently resonate with social news communities. Following these guidelines can help move your stories up the ranks and closer to the front page.

- **Write a top 10 (or 20 or 53) list.** Social news readers seem to love lists and often promote them.

- **Share stories about technology innovation.** As we've mentioned, social media early adopters tend to be techies, so these news sites are often geek-heavy. Industry-specific tech wars, such as Apple versus Windows, can be great fodder on technical sites like Slashdot.

- **Teach something.** Tutorials and advice are popular; for example, we've seen front-page stories on Digg about "How to take photographs in direct sunlight" and "Fifty scientifically proven ways to be persuasive."

- **Be political.** Hot or politically charged news stories typically attract attention. A colleague of ours at DeSmogBlog (*http://www .desmogblog.com/*) has been successful getting DeSmogBlog stories on the Digg front page over the years. Aside from writing quality content (which always helps), he harnesses the environmental movement's political and social will. Digging a DeSmogBlog story isn't just a vote for DeSmogBlog; you're making a political statement, propelling the community to take action and click the Digg button.

- **Be controversial.** Controversial findings from scientific studies or polling results often initiate heated debate.

- **Post anything cute and cuddly.** Why is it that we can't resist stupid pet tricks, sneezing pandas, and other amusing memes?

By reading your social news sites of choice diligently, you'll get a clear understanding of which stories are popular. Keep that firmly in mind when creating content to post on social news communities.

Your next plan of attack is to become a regular on your social news sites of choice—Digg, Sphinn, kirtsy, Yahoo! Buzz, or others. These member-driven news sites can be as community oriented as Facebook. They are active, social spaces where members interact and build relationships. Remember Muhammad Saleem back in Chapter 4? He's the Digg guru with heaps of credibility, or cred, in that community. One of the reasons he thinks Digg is so great is because, "by participating over the years I have built a fairly close group of friends." Just as in blogger outreach, you need to build relationships and a good reputation in these communities.

To get active on these sites, sign up for your account with your real name, not a wacky handle like *catlady34*. Then complete your profile and begin using the services regularly. Add your colleagues as friends on these sites. Vote for and comment on stories that appeal to you. Once you've become a user of the service, you can occasionally submit stories related to your organization and industry. If they're of interest to the site's user base, your stories will gain traction. Many of these sites have a sharing functionality (Digg calls this a *shout*) that allows you to broadcast a story to your friends on the service. Shouts are an effective way to give your submitted news story an initial boost and attract some attention. The members who enjoy your content will promote it and, in the process, send more visitors to your website. Here are some basic principles for becoming a trusted content creator on social news sites:

- Create and nurture your social news accounts. Like many other social networking sites, you build credibility and reputation by using the site regularly and responsibly.

- Make friends within the community. Many prolific members check out their friends' articles and favorites every day. They vote up those articles to help initiate the viral effect.

- Tag your content with the right keywords. If your blog post, photo, or video delivers on your keyword's promise, visitors are more likely to stick around. Think of it this way: If you're in the mood for a romantic comedy but come to find out you've rented a horror flick, you'll probably give the rental a pass. Do your best to ensure that your content matches visitors' expectations.

Making friends and gaining cred on social news sites is a tall order that requires another dose of authenticity and transparency. You can submit news about your latest product release or post your top recipe ideas for cooking with your brand's maple syrup. But to demonstrate that you're a valuable member of the community, not just a marketing flack, those submissions should represent a small percentage of your activity on social news sites. The rules of engagement on social news sites echo our guidelines for new influencer outreach. Whether you're wooing a single influencer or attempting to charm an entire community, a compelling, highly targeted, and honestly presented story can get the crowd on your side and garner some attention for you and your organization.

Social Bookmarking and Crowdsourced Curation

Crowdsourcing isn't just for breaking news. In fact, the success of social media as a whole relies on the crowd to gather and archive a potpourri of information collectively so the very best online content rises to the top where the rest of us can find it. Here's a primer on how social bookmarking works and why it's become such a crowd pleaser.

A Social Bookmarking Primer

The Internet has more than 15 billion web pages—that's a lot of content to keep track of. How many times have you found a useful resource only to navigate away from the page and then never be able to find it again? That's why web browsers come equipped with a bookmark menu feature that lets you easily save and organize web pages in the same way you do files on your hard drive. But this system has drawbacks. First, these bookmarks are stored on your local computer. That means you can't access the pages you've marked at work from your home computer or from your laptop when you're on the road. Similarly, the folder tree system used to file these bookmarks can become complex and convoluted, in part because the variety of topics searched for on the Web don't always fit into neat folder categories. Here's where social bookmarking comes in.

Social bookmarking doesn't use a web browser; it uses a website. The earliest and most popular of these services is Delicious, but others include Furl, BlinkList, and Google Bookmarks. The benefits of moving your bookmarks from your browser to a website are threefold. First, by using one of these social bookmarking websites, you can access your bookmarked links from any computer that has an Internet connection. Second, you can organize and categorize bookmarks with keywords using the intuitive tagging method we discuss in "Tag, You're It" on page 248. You can even annotate a bookmark, adding a short note so you remember why you found the site relevant in the first place or to provide commentary that others will appreciate. Third, you can share your bookmarks with colleagues, customers, and journalists, and also check out what other people are bookmarking.

Find Your Niche

Digg, StumbleUpon, and reddit are the largest and most popular social news sites, but there are many, many more. Most important to the marketer are a growing number of websites that cover niche industries and categories. Identifying the niche social news websites in your industry and focusing your efforts there is more valuable than trying to get noticed in a place where your tribe doesn't hang out. If you run a winery, then 500 oenophiles from Cork'd or OpenBottles will be far more valuable than 15,000 Digg users. The number of niche news sites is expanding at an astonishing rate. Here is a selective snapshot of some of the most popular social news sites:[*]

AutoSpies Covers automotive news, car reviews, photos from car shows, and so on.

Digg The largest and most popular social news site on the Web. Though Digg tends to have a technology slant, the site covers all topics, including politics, entertainment, technology, and general news.

Fark Fark is one of the oldest social news sites on the Web. The site aggregates unusual news and other items from various websites, submitted every day by more than 2000 readers. Unlike some of these other sites, editors decide which submissions to post, though readers can comment on stories. Fark is a catch-all for off-beat sports, business, tech, Hollywood, politics, and music news.

Hacker News Covers any news hackers might like. Or, as expressed in the Hacker News Guidelines, "anything that gratifies one's intellectual curiosity."

kirtsy A general news site with a focus on fashion, entertainment, and design. Has a large female user base.

MetaFilter A community blog that allows users to ask each other questions and discuss topics of interest. Human editors moderate topics and discussions on this site.

Mixx A more mainstream (less techie) Digg with all the typical categories, including business, entertainment, sports, and life.

Newsvine A community-driven site of news stories and opinions. Users have their own blogs, and they can write articles and vote and comment on other users' articles.

[*] "50 Social News Websites: A List of General and Niche Social Media Communities," Dosh Dosh, January 10, 2008, *http://www.doshdosh.com/list-of-social-media-news-websites/*.

NowPublic   A participatory news network focused on citizen journalism. Each user has an individual profile page where he can upload video, images, and news stories.

reddit   A popular social news site that covers a variety of topics, including computer programming, science, politics, and business.

Slashdot   Primarily a techie news site, but it also covers books, games, politics, and entertainment. Slashdot differs from reddit and Digg in that editors, not the crowd, decide which submitted stories get published on the site.

Small Business Brief   A niche social news site focusing on small business news.

Sphinn   A site for interactive marketers (like you!).

StumbleUpon   A social network and browser toolbar that allows users to surf the Internet for highly rated web content.

Teenwag   Like Digg, but focusing on celebrity gossip.

Tip'd   A social media site for finance, investing, and business topics.

Yahoo! Buzz   Similar to Digg, readers can publish their own news stories and vote up stories they like. Categories include business, entertainment, health, sports, and travel. The content on this site is considerably more mainstream than what appears on Digg, reddit, or Slashdot.

New, niche news sites are coming online every month. You may be surprised to discover that an active community is already covering your industry.

The interesting thing about Delicious, Furl, and BlinkList is that unless you choose to make your bookmarks private, anyone can see them. That's why it's called social bookmarking, after all! Let's say you're planning a holiday in Panama with four friends. Your Internet research may turn up hotel deals, sightseeing tours, travel articles, restaurant reviews, and some stunning photos from the Caribbean coast. You bookmark these links on Delicious or another social bookmarking website with the tag *panamatrip* for future reference. Surely your travel companions would benefit from seeing your bookmarks? Since they're public, you can simply tell your friends to search for your *panamatrip* tags in Delicious to view all the great information you've discovered. Your colleagues can start

Tag, You're It

Almost as soon as you delve into any form of social media—whether blogging, photo sharing, or social bookmarking—you'll encounter the concept of tagging.

A *tag* is a relevant keyword or phrase assigned to a website, computer file, digital image, or online bookmark. We use tags to create meaning for ourselves on the Web. Once you start working with social media services, you'll get the hang of tagging quickly. New users, however, do seem to have difficulty comprehending one essential tag-related concept: You can make them up. You don't have to follow any rules, and you can apply any tag you want to any piece of information. For example, a Flickr user might describe this photo with *Malta, blue sky, car, Morris Minor*. Or he might tag it with *pretty, I love convertibles, got lost*.

How would you tag this photo?

Thanks to tags, your bookmarks and news stories will be more findable on the Web—for you and for your communities.

Tagging is a critical concept for marketers. If you tag content well, you'll attract quality visitors. For instance, you can certainly tag this photo with the phrase *got lost*. But if you're an antique car dealer, that tag won't help your target audience of classic car enthusiasts find you via search. If you tag the photo with phrases that accurately identify the car and its features, the niche group of buyers looking for a sky blue Morris Minor convertible will locate you much more easily. Whether you're tagging photos, videos, or articles submitted to social news sites, keep your marketing goals and your target audience in mind.

bookmarking, too, adding their finds to Delicious so all your travel research can be accessed from the same place.

There's more to social bookmarking, however. You and your friends aren't the only ones who've tagged interesting information about Panama. Many other Delicious users are employing similar tags. For instance, new and relevant materials are likely organized by the keyword *Panama*. By using a social bookmarking site, your online research becomes collaborative, and you can benefit from the wisdom of crowds to improve your own research efforts.

How Marketers Can Benefit from Social Bookmarking

Why are social bookmarking sites useful for marketers? Like so many social media tools, social bookmarking sites keep track of popular items. Like social news sites, Delicious promotes the most popular bookmarks on its home page. You can also search popular tags from the home page. As we write this chapter, *software*, *web design*, *programming*, and *web 2.0* are some top tags on the site. These tags reveal that in the second half of 2009 most Delicious users are still technology folks. See, you're ahead of the curve! If you want your website to gain visibility inside social bookmarking communities, try prominently displaying book-marking buttons on your site. These buttons, also called *widgets*, pop up corresponding social media services so users can immediately bookmark, vote up, or even tweet content directly from your website. With a single click, visitors can share your content with their friends and followers without even leaving your website or blog.

Getting attention from social bookmarking communities can help bring a few more visitors to your website, but that's just one market-ing reason to use these tools. We also find them useful for market research.

Here are some sharing widgets you can add to blog posts, web pages, videos, and other content you create and publish on your website. By clicking the Delicious button, for instance, readers immediately save your content as a bookmark in their Delicious account. Visitors can also use these sharing button widgets to post your content to their Facebook profile or submit it to social news sites like Yahoo! Buzz and StumbleUpon, all in one easy step.

Because social bookmarkers tag links with their own descriptive keywords, you can browse and search on these keywords to see how others describe and categorize your products. How do they talk about your competition? What are the online resources your site's visitors value most? Let's say you run *http://www.couchsurfing.org/*, a website that makes it easy for travelers to meet locals when they travel. CouchSurfing has been a popular link under the *travel* tag on Delicious—at the time of this writing, more than 8000 users have bookmarked the site. Tags that describe this site include *social*, *community*, *free*, and *culture*. These descriptors tell you how others perceive the service. You can then drill down to see which users have bookmarked *http://www.couchsurfing.org/* and take a peek at other sites they've bookmarked. This tells you a little more about your target audience. To strike a chord with this particular audience, you'll want to go easy on the corporate-speak. Instead, write copy that employs some of the adjectives the crowd is already using to describe you in their bookmarking metadata.

Just like nurturing relationships on social news sites, building up a network of friends on social bookmarking sites can help you garner more attention for your cause, your product, or your service. But that's not all. You'll be surprised how useful your network can be as a filter, or curator, for information that jibes with your interests. After a time, friends on social bookmarking and social news sites become human filters who help you to find and organize information from the Web.

Surprisingly, media and blogger relations also take place inside social bookmarking communities. In 2005, popular PR blogger Steve Rubel famously asked readers to pitch him exclusively via Delicious. Overwhelmed by the amount of reader email he received, Rubel instructed PR types to pitch him in Delicious by tagging their websites with *micropersuasion*—the name of Rubel's blog at the time—and to include a short pitch in the extended entry section.[*] This was a radical move in 2005, but other sites have followed suit. For example, *http://www.lifehack.org/* asks readers to submit their

---

[*] Steve Rubel, "Pitch.Me Del.icio.usly," Micropersuasion, March 7, 2005, *http://www.micropersuasion.com/2005/03/pitchme_delicio.html*.

products for review via Delicious by tagging their websites with *for:lifehack*. Search Delicious for the tag *for:lifehack* and see which companies have followed these instructions. If you're responsible for media or blogger relations in your organization, we suggest setting up a Delicious account and getting used to the idea of submitting content to journalists and bloggers this way.

We've seen social bookmarking bolster visitor numbers, so every marketer should explore this tool. Even more important, by becoming a collector, a curator, or just one of the crowd on sites like Delicious, you'll come to appreciate that sharing and collaborating online with friends and strangers is one of the key benefits of social media and is a much-appreciated, value-added service your organization can offer others.

Should You Build Your Own Social Network?

Companies sometimes look around at all of this social networking activity and think they want a piece of the action—they want to play host to the masses gathering around a particular industry. So

---

Search Engine Optimization and the Long View

Participating in social news and bookmarking communities has another positive side effect in terms of search engine optimization (SEO). When you submit stories to Yahoo! Buzz, or a similar social news site, each link from your submission back to your website increases the number of inbound links to your site. Over time, these links add significant long-term value because the number of inbound links determines where search engines rank your site in their results. Search engines read each of these inbound links as a vote of confidence for your website. After all, no one links to dismal site content, right? Additionally, if popular websites—like Digg—link to your website, those links are weighted more heavily than links from less popular websites. This is also why getting covered on popular blogs is so crucial; incoming links from Huffington Post, Gawker, or Treehugger can go a long way toward raising your website's rank in search engine results.

If your goal is to be on the first page of Google results—and it should be—then incoming links count. By submitting content to these communities, you bolster that number. Plus, you better your chances of others seeing your content and linking to your website from their own sites—a practice aptly called *link love*.

---

they hire a crack team of web designers and developers, spend six figures, and build themselves a made-to-order social network. But is this the right move? Unless you're a major player with a great deal of mindshare in your industry, we don't think so. Neither does web marketer Monique Trottier, who's built her fair share of complex websites and social networks. In an interview, she tells us why:

> We're already busy connecting, networking, and being social in other digital spaces. Why should we move? The reason has to be incredibly compelling. Companies starting their own social networks neglect to realize that the hard sell is not about who has the better feature set, but whether the network is worthwhile enough for members to change platforms and solicit their friends to change also. Social networks exist because we want to be where our friends are, not because we've found yet another place to hang out online.[*]

In 2007, the early days of social networking, the Anheuser-Busch brewing company launched Bud.TV, an online entertainment network targeting young men with short- and long-format bawdy comedy, sports, and drama videos. Despite a rumored $30 million budget, Bud.TV failed to draw enough visitors to make the project a worthwhile marketing venture, and the site was shut down in early 2009. Although speculation has been rife as to why Bud.TV failed, we chalk much of it up to a basic miscalculation: Bud.TV failed to go to the crowd and instead forced viewers to come to it. Original programming created for Bud.TV wasn't portable. Viewers had to sign up for a Bud.TV account; they couldn't see the videos on YouTube or easily pass them to their friends in an email. Bud.TV wasn't designed to be viral. Though the site made efforts not to overwhelm consumers with Budweiser ad content, the URL—*www.Bud.TV*—may have been enough to turn off potential viewers, fearing they'd be inundated by Budweiser advertisements disguised as video content. With a torrent of marketing messages already filling our inboxes, commercials playing at the start of movies, and ads sweeping across our favorite websites, we're less inclined than ever to sign up for branded entertainment and social networks.

---

[*] Author interviews, November 2007 and February 2009.

Indigo Books & Music is Canada's biggest book retailer. Indigo runs its own branded social network as part of its online web presence. The online community features all the bells and whistles you'd expect from a robust social network—friends, groups and clubs to join, reviews, blogs, and so forth. But they've struggled to create a thriving community like Amazon's. Trottier speculates on why Amazon has such a lead on Indigo, even in Canada:

> Aside from early bird advantage, Amazon created an open API (application programming interface) for certain services. This means software developers can freely use the API to create infinite ways to integrate Amazon bibliographic feeds and searches into platforms.

This integration has been a clever move. By encouraging software developers to use Amazon's API freely, the company benefits from the innovative third-party applications and websites built on its API—and from the marketing buzz and sales generated by these sites. Here are some examples:

- LibraryThing (*http://www.librarything.com/*) uses Amazon data to generate a library-quality digital catalog of your personal book library that you can share with others.

- Goodreads (*http://www.goodreads.com/*) is a book lover's social network with more than 2 million members. Members recommend books, compare the titles they're reading, and track the books they've read. Goodreads uses the Amazon API to generate accurate book data, covers, and more.

- Zoomii (*http://www.zoomii.com/*) brings the real-world bookstore experience online by displaying Amazon's most popular titles just as they would appear on the shelves of your favorite bookstore. Zoomii updates book data via Amazon's API, and when Zoomii refers a sale to Amazon, it gets a cut.

Amazon's API aside, Trottier believes Indigo's real problem is that its social network doesn't satisfactorily answer these questions: Is it worthwhile to post my content here? Are my friends already here or am I stuck in a dead zone? Why would I move from Amazon to

Zoomii's real-world rendering of Amazon's best-selling titles. Click a book cover for publisher and author info or to purchase the book.

Indigo and leave my friend group behind? Before you begin day-dreaming about your own branded social network, be sure you've got solid answers to these difficult questions.

What About Wikipedia?

When discussing social networks and collaborative websites, we'd be remiss to gloss over Wikipedia. Wikipedia is, of course, the world's collaboratively written encyclopedia. Its size is extraordinary: 13 million articles in more than 260 languages, nearly 3 million articles in English, almost 10 million registered users, and about 65 million visitors each month.[*] Millions visit Wikipedia every day. Wikipedia is a trusted source of information. It wields remarkable authority, often features prominently in search results, and can send considerable traffic to your website. You may have noticed that Wikipedia

---

[*] "About Wikipedia," Wikipedia, *http://en.wikipedia.org/wiki/Wikipedia:About#Technical_attributes*.

articles often appear as top search results for keywords relating to your business. Wikipedia is constantly being linked to by bloggers. Heck, a number of this book's citations are from the site. For some of our clients, Wikipedia consistently ranks in the top five among referrers—sites that send them visitors. Increasingly, having a Wikipedia entry validates a business's reputation.

We regularly hear from companies who grumble that they don't have a Wikipedia entry and deserve one. Or they have an entry, but the entry is inaccurate and out of date or not complimentary enough for their taste. Or they think their website is worthy of links from Wikipedia pages covering topics in their industry.

Making your mark in Wikipedia is a worthwhile endeavor, but navigating through the collaborative, heavily policed encyclopedia can be tricky. Here are some guidelines to ensure that editors looking out for self-aggrandizing submissions don't delete your entry:

- You should not, under any circumstances, write an entry for your own company. You'll be discovered, the entry will be deleted, and you'll have to wait longer for a legitimate entry to be written. When junior marketers are tasked with contributing to social media channels, they sometimes make the mistake of adding self-promotional content to Wikipedia. Be sure your colleagues know how to interact on Wikipedia before all their hard work gets deleted—or worse.

- You can request an article. This is the appropriate way to notify Wikipedia editors that you think your topic merits an article.

- Your topic must satisfy Wikipedia's notability guidelines. Notability is a core tenet of the encyclopedia, so spend the time needed to understand the rationales behind it completely. You can find these guidelines at *http://en.wikipedia.org/wiki/Wikipedia:Notability.*

- If an article about your organization exists in Wikipedia, do not edit it. This rule has only a few exceptions: You can delete obvious wiki vandalism, correct inaccurate facts, and remove out-of-date information. You should, however, be prepared to support any change with confirmable, reliable third-party sources.

- If you'd like to make changes beyond the scope of the exceptions—for example, if you want to add a reference—you can post requests on the article's Discussion page or connect with the article's most active editors. This approach applies to any article that you or your company has an interest in and is particularly important if you're trying to add your website as a linked reference or source.

For Wikipedia to work, the entries must be as unbiased as possible. If we could all write our own entries, Wikipedia would read like a bunch of advertisements.

Remember Charlene Li from Chapter 8? She's the author of the social media book *Groundswell* and wrote the blogging policy we feature in that chapter. Here she shares some top tips for interacting successfully on Wikipedia:[*]

Q: Links from Wikipedia can drive a lot of traffic to a website. When is it appropriate to include links to your own site in Wikipedia articles?

A: You should never edit articles you're associated with—that includes Wikipedia articles about your organization, its staff, the competition, or your industry. The Golden Rule applies to Wikipedia, too. Would you want your competitors to add their links to articles? In most cases, if your company has a Wikipedia article, the article should already include at least one link to your company's site.

Q: How can you be a good citizen on Wikipedia?

A: First off, be transparent with the account name you choose. Use your own name or that of your company's. Then edit some articles that interest you to build up experience and demonstrate that you understand how the online encyclopedia works. Your basic objective on Wikipedia is to improve every article you touch.

---

* Author interview, conducted March 2009.

Q: Why do so many turf wars and nerd fights occur on Wikipedia?

A: People get really spun up about Wikipedia because they can't control it. The best that you can hope for is neutrality—for Wikipedia to represent the truth accurately. If an article about your company achieves that, be happy.

Don't underestimate the role Wikipedia can play in building your company's online reputation and driving visitors to your website. But to make Wikipedia work for you, you've got to play by its rules.

NOTE   *Just in case you're still tempted to edit your own company's Wikipedia entry, remember that tools like WikiScanner (http:// wikiscanner.virgil.gr/) can trace users via their IP addresses and identify the authors of individual entries or edits.*

Photo Sharing with Flickr

Just like Digg and Delicious, Flickr has a passionate user base of millions who gather on the site to contribute, curate, and promote each others' photography. Flickr is the much-loved photo sharing website that almost every blogger uses to host photos online and share them with friends. In addition to individual profiles, thousands of groups exist on Flickr that share photos and converse about specific topics, from photos of Sydney beaches to pictures of peaches.

But Flickr isn't just for bloggers. We think every organization should have an account because Flickr provides yet another place on the Web to display your content and link it back to your website. Remember the ThoughtFarmer social media resource page from Chapter 2? ThoughtFarmer puts all kinds of images on its Flickr page—trade show snapshots, product screenshots, even photographs of marketing outreach materials. Thanks to some nifty embed code available for Flickr-hosted images, bloggers and site publishers can easily add your photos to their own websites. Self-serve access to your images via Flickr encourages publishers to grab screenshots, product photos, or your CEO's mug shot and add those pictures to their stories.

Embed code, seen under "Grab the HTML," makes it easy for bloggers and publishers to add your photos to their sites.

But Flickr isn't just an image archive; the site can play a leading role in outreach. We've hosted some effective photo contests on Flickr. For DeSmogBlog's "Greenest Photo Ever Contest," we invited photographers to submit their greenest photo to our Flickr photo group for a chance to win a new digital camera. We looked for Flickr users with active accounts and for those who were already members of Flickr nature or environmental photography groups. We then notified those groups from inside the Flickr community about the contest. We chose five finalists from hundreds of entries and invited the public to vote on DeSmogBlog's website for the winner.

Why host the contest on Flickr? Social media marketing works best when you go to the content creators, instead of trying to drag them back to your own site and through a complex submission process. We went to where photographers hang out online and held the contest in their familiar forum. Eventually, we brought the focus back to DeSmogBlog for the final voting process. And when we did, we brought some first-time DeSmogBlog visitors with us. Before you launch a contest using Flickr, be sure to check the small print on Flickr's contest guidelines at *http://www.flickr.com/guidelines.gne.*

For the right cause, the Flickr community can be rallied to support your charity, event, or product. In 2007, Oxfam America ran a campaign that called on coffee industry leaders to sign an agreement that would benefit Ethiopian coffee farmers. They promoted the cause on Flickr with the "Starbucks Flickr petition," asking supporters to upload photos of themselves holding a sign that read, "I support Ethiopian farmers." More recently, thousands of photos of the 2009 protests in Iran have appeared on Flickr. The photos shared online have provided the international community with a more complete picture of the protests, especially when world media wasn't able to obtain and share the same kinds of images.

NOTE   *Although Flickr is the most popular photo sharing site on the Web, other sites are out there. Competitors include Zooomr, SmugMug, and Photobucket.*

Stand Out in Your Crowd

Blogger outreach will likely be the backbone of most of your social media marketing campaigns, but don't overlook these other channels. Take two actions from this chapter. First, make it easy for your crowd to share your content with their audiences. That can be as easy as adding sharing widgets to your website or blog or enabling public ratings and reviews of your products on your website. Second, become a content curator. As a marketer of cruise holidays, vacuum cleaners, or environmental sustainability, you're presumably a subject-matter expert and have a lot to offer by participating as a human filter in your industry. By annotating and bookmarking interesting industry news on Delicious and submitting it to social news sites, you provide a valuable service to your crowd. As an added bonus, earning cred and a good online reputation as a collector or curator in these communities can soften the ground when the time comes to launch your own social media outreach campaign.

AFTERWORD

The cheeky title of this book emphasizes how much of marketing on the Web is about building relationships. Successful marketing is about making friends as much as anything else. After all, it's far easier to convince a friend to support your cause or buy your product than it is a stranger.

Here are three lessons to take with you on your relationship-building journey. We think they're lessons for both marketing and life. First, be original. Being ordinary will get you nowhere. As Seth Godin says, "Safe is risky and risky is safe." Next, listen first. It's unlikely you'll make a misstep if you've spent time learning from the conversations happening around you. Never stop listening, and you'll be ready to respond to opportunities and put out brushfires before they become infernos. Finally, be yourself. Humans have an exceptional nose for the disingenuous and the deceptive. Behave in a genuine and authentic manner, and you'll receive that same treatment in return. Shakespeare has some age-old advice on being genuine:

> To thine own self be true,
> And it must follow, as the night the day,
> Thou canst not then be false to any man.

We emphasize this philosophy at this book's end because, while the social media tools will change at a rapid pace, the underlying principles we discuss throughout the book will hold. Over time, Facebook and Twitter will go the way of Friendster and ICQ. But if you grasp the central tenets of being a genuine, responsible, and effective marketer online, you'll easily adapt to the ever-changing social media landscape and make important friendships along the way.

RECOMMENDED READING

Books

Bernoff, Jeff, and Charlene Li. *Groundswell: Winning in a World Transformed by Social Technologies*. Boston, MA: Harvard Business School Press, 2008.

Brogan, Chris, and Julien Smith. *Trust Agents: Using the Web to Build Influence, Improve Reputation, and Earn Trust*. Hoboken, NJ: John Wiley & Sons, 2009.

Fox, Vanessa. *Marketing in the Age of Google: Your Online Strategy IS Your Business Strategy*. New York, NY: Wiley, 2010.

Gardner, Susannah, and Shane Birley. *Blogging for Dummies*. New York, NY: For Dummies, 2008.

Godin, Seth. *Purple Cow: Transform Your Business by Being Remarkable*. New York, NY: Portfolio, 2003.

Godin, Seth. *Tribes: We Need You to Lead Us*. New York, NY: Portfolio, 2008.

Goodstein, Anastasia. *Totally Wired: What Teens and Tweens Are Really Doing Online*. New York, NY: Saint Martin's Griffin, 2007.

Israel, Shel. *Twitterville: How Businesses Can Thrive in the New Global Neighborhoods*. New York, NY: Portfolio, 2009.

Kaushik, Avinash. *Web Analytics: An Hour a Day*. Indianapolis, IN: Sybex, 2007.

Levine, Rick, and Christopher Locke, and Doc Searls, and David Weinberger. *The Cluetrain Manifesto: The End of Business as Usual*. Cambridge, MA: Basic Books, 2000. Find the book online at *http://www.cluetrain.com/book/*.

Shirky, Clay. *Here Comes Everybody: The Power of Organizing Without Organizations*. New York, NY: Penguin Group, 2008.

Solis, Brian. *Putting the Public Back in Public Relations: How Social Media Is Reinventing the Aging Business of PR*. Upper Saddle River, NJ: FT Press, 2009.

Weinberger, David. *Everything Is Miscellaneous: The Power of the New Digital Disorder*. New York, NY: Times Books, 2007.

Blogs and Websites

Copyblogger, *http://www.copyblogger.com/*

Nine By Blue, *http://www.ninebyblue.com/blog/*

Conversation Agent, *http://www.conversationagent.com/*

MarketingProfs, *http://www.marketingprofs.com/*

Mashable: The Social Media Guide, *http://mashable.com/*

OneDegree.ca, *http://www.onedegree.ca/*

Web Strategy, *http://www.web-strategist.com/blog/*

The Steve Rubel Lifestream, *http://www.steverubel.com/*

SEOMozBlog, *http://www.seomoz.org/blog/*

INDEX

NUMBERS

6S Marketing, 184–185
7-Eleven, 162
60 Minutes, 6

A

AAConversation blog, 141–142
advertising. *See* pitching products;
      social media marketing
AdWords, 187
aggregation, 26–28
alerts, 106
Alexa Toolbar, 56–57, 58
Allen, Lily, 156
alternate reality marketing, 88–91
Amateur Gourmet blog, 48
Amazon API, 253
Amazon.com, 253–254
American Airlines, 140–142
America Online (AOL), 193
analysts, 32
Anderson, Chris, 119
Anheuser-Busch, 252
anonymity, 66
AOL (America Online), 193
apologies, 138, 143–144, 145
Apple Dashboard, 163
apps, 183–187. *See also* widgets
Archives, Internet, 70–71,
      121–122, 135
Armano, David, 231–232
Armstrong, Heather, 81
Art of Eating, 165–166
astroturfing, 72–73
Atom, 25
Audio Preview button, 214

authenticity, 10–11, 67–68
Autoblog, 48
AutoSpies, 246
avatars, 224

B

b5media, 49
BackType, 103
Banjo, Shelly, 68
banner ads, 167, 188
BBSs (bulletin board systems), 1–2
BC Hydro, 179
Beacon program, 138
Bebo, 170
"Bike Hero" video, 207
Billingsley, Jason, 216–217
bit.ly URL shortener, 227, 235
BlackBerry devices, 226
Blaylock, Abby, 167
BlendTec, 203–204
BlinkList, 245, 247
blip.tv, 196
Blockbuster UK, 162
blog badges, 165
Blog Council, 150
Blogger, 3, 30, 61
bloggers
    appraising, 50–58
    backlash from, 118–120
    bribing, 96–97
    contacting, 67–68
    corporate, 30–31
    embargoes, 70
    ethics, 151
    frequency of posts, 60, 69
    honesty, 72–73

bloggers, *continued*
  influential, 74–77
  inviting to review products, 81–82
  vs. journalists, 67–70
  misinformed, 136
  no response from, 116
  outreach campaigns and, 91–93
  personal, 48, 49
  probloggers, 48–49, 70
  reputation, 70–71
  social media masters, 74–77
  subject matter, 69
blogger's code of ethics, 151
blogging
  policies, 148–151
  from press box, 91
  software for, 30
blogging services, 3, 61. *See also specific*
    services
Bloglines, 25
blogosphere, 103
BlogPulse, 56
blog-related tools, 49–58
blogrolls, 42, 58–59
blogs. *See also* corporate blogs; websites
  adding photos to, 257–259
  anecdotal evidence, 58–60
  authority, 56
  character, 36–37
  comments. *See* comments
  comparing, 49, 50–58
  as crisis management tool, 142
  design of, 61
  early years, 3
  ego feeds, 42
  examples of, 19
  finding with Google, 51–52, 64
  flame wars, 37
  links to. *See* links
  location of, 34–35
  lurkers, 34
  measuring success of, 52–53,
      99–114, 128
  netiquette, 63–78

  news, 6
  number of views, 103
  offsite, 35
  personal, 48, 49
  popularity of, 49–54, 60–61
  ranking. *See* rankings
  references from, 103
  RSS feeds. *See* RSS feeds
  searching for content in, 107
  sidebar content, 60
  skins, 61
  small vs. large, 50
  social media services, 61
  spam, 108–109
  spreadsheets, 52–53
  subscribers to, 57, 104
  topical, 48–49
  types of, 48–49
blog swarms, 134–135
blooper videos, 202–203
Bojangles' Famous Chicken 'n Biscuits,
    182–183
Bollwitt, Rebecca, 59
bookmarks, 245–249. *See also* social
    bookmarking
books, reference, 19
Bootup Labs, 184
Booze Mail, 184
boyd, danah, 158–159
Bradburn, Jen, 145
Brain, David, 165
Bray, Tim, 71
bribes, 96–97
broadcast media model, 5
brochure websites, 38
Bud.TV, 252
bulletin board systems (BBSs), 1–2
bulletins, 169
Burger King video, 144–145
burning RSS feeds, 104
Bush, George, 6
business blogs. *See* corporate blogs
businesses. *See* corporations
Butler University, 152

C

Calgary, City of, 103
California wildfires, 230
Campaign for Real Beauty, 124
Camtasia Studio, 41
Captain's Blog, 36
Capulet.com, 85
Capulet Communications, 119
Cardo Systems, 207
Carey, Mariah, 195
Carnival Cruise Lines, 117, 228
cause-oriented organizations, 8–9,
        181, 184, 259
CC (Creative Commons), 40, 41
"Cell Phone Popcorn" video, 206–207
cell phones
    capturing photos/video with,
        196, 197
    Facebook on, 193
    iPhone, 84, 219, 226
    popularity of, 193, 196
    Twitter on, 226–227
Center for Risk Communication, 132
channels, social media, 11–13
character blogs, 36–37
charities, Internet, 8–9
Chen, Steve, 196
chicklet, 57
Chic Knits, 51
ChipIn service, 232
citizen journalism, 5–6
City of Calgary, 103
clarity, 68
click-through rates, 233
ClipShack, 196
collaboration, 7–9
    authenticity, 10–11
    crowdsourcing history, 8
    online philanthropy, 8–9
    overview, 7–8
    scope, 10
    Wikipedia, 9
collectors, 240. *See also* crowds
Comcast sleeping technician, 133–134
comic pitches, 87–88
comic shops, 92

comments. *See also* feedback; reviews
    benefits/risks, 120–122
    blogs, 5
    considerations, 34
    fake, 73
    guidelines, 111–113
    on MySpace, 169
    negative, 121–122, 136–139
    number of, 60, 102–103
    overreacting to, 136
    pitches in, 84–85
    responding to, 111–113
    on stories, 244
    tracking, 102–103
    YouTube, 214
communities, 239–259. *See also*
        crowds; *and specific*
        communities
    bookmarking, 245–249
    closed, 10
    finding, 47–61
    niche, 7
    number of, 10
    online, 123
    outreach campaigns, 82–97
companies. *See* corporations
company blogs. *See* corporate blogs
Compete Toolbar, 57
competitors, 17, 19, 64, 73, 129
connections, 2, 60, 69, 175, 234. *See*
        also friends
Consumer Packaged Goods (CPG)
        blog, 145
contests/giveaways, 191–193, 230
contributions, 102–103
controversy, 243
Conversation Prism, 12–13, 65,
        142, 177
conversations
    Facebook. *See* Facebook
    MySpace. *See* MySpace
    private, 234–235
    sponsored, 96–97
    as success measurement, 102–103
    Twitter. *See* Twitter
Cork'd, 246

corporate bloggers, 30–31
corporate blogs, 28–37. *See also* blogs
   advantages of, 28–33
   analyzing, 64–65
   blogging don'ts, 35–37
   blogging software for, 30
   considerations, 49, 126–127
   creation of, 29–30
   damage control, deploying, 32
   for departmental
      communication, 32
   described, 48
   examples of, 36
   flame wars, 37
   how often to blog, 33
   improving customer relationships
      via, 31–33
   increasing staff profile, 32
   location of, 34–35
   objectives, 30, 31–33
   obtaining customer feedback,
      32, 34
   policies, 148–151
   recruiting new employees, 32
   soft launch of, 29–30
   subject matter, 33
   for technical support, 32
corporate-speak, 169
corporations
   competitors, 17, 19, 64, 73, 129
   reputation, 70–71
   success metrics, 52–53,
      99–114, 128
   use of Facebook, 178–193
   use of Twitter, 227–231
Cottingham, Rob, 179
CoTweet tool, 227
CouchSurfing, 250
Coursematch, 171
Covello, Dr. Vincent, 132, 135, 139
CPG (Consumer Packaged Goods)
      blog, 145
"The Crazy, Messed Up World"
      campaign, 215–216
Creative Commons (CC), 40, 41
creativity, democratizing effect on, 10

crisis communications, 139–140, 230
crisis management, 131–153
crisis management team, 147
crowds, 239–259. *See also*
      communities
   as collectors, 240
   overview, 239–240
   social bookmarking and, 245–251
   social news, 240–244
   standing out in, 259
   wisdom of, 240–244
crowdsourced curation, 245–251
crowdsourcing, 8, 245
CrunchGear, 50
Ctrl+Alt+Del, 173
customer feedback. *See* comments;
      feedback
customers
   engagement, 120–121
   finding online, 16–17
   getting to know, 100–105
   importance of honesty, 10–11,
      72–73, 127
   improving relationships with, 16,
      31–33
   inviting to events, 178
   notifying of sales/deals, 117,
      228–230
   online presence of, 10
   potential, 100–101, 117, 124, 230
   rejection by, 121–122
   unhappy, 136–147
   using photos of, 41
   visits to brick-and-mortar stores, 17
customer support, 221, 230, 236

D

Dailymotion, 196
damage control, 32, 131–153
Dashboard, 163
DCI Group, 73
DeGeneres, Ellen, 222
Delicious, 12, 104, 245, 249–251
Dell Computers, 36, 229–230
@DellOutlet, 229–230
democracy, 4

demographics, 169
DeSmogBlog, 93–94, 163, 243, 258
developers, 186–187
Dial2Do.com, 125
Dickson, Tom, 203–204
Digg, 6, 65–66, 75–76, 240–247
Digg effect, 126
"digging" stories, 75, 240, 243
digital press junket, 91–92
Direct2Dell blogs, 36
direct messages (DMs), 224
discussion forums, 107
discussions, 5
DMs (direct messages), 224
Doctorow, Cory, 71
Dogbook, 184
Dooce blog, 48, 81
Dove Campaign for Real Beauty, 124
Drudge Report, 6
Drupal, 30
Dumont, Andrew, 168–169
Dunn, Chris, 2

E

Echofon, 226
e-commerce platforms, 215–217
Edelman PR, 165
ego feeds, 42
Elastic Path, 86–87, 215–217
elevator pitch, 39–40
email
    advertising via, 82, 85–86
    follow-up, 97
    pitches via, 82, 85–86
    popularity of, 82
    spam, 71, 82–83
employees
    as industry experts, 32
    participation in social networks,
        179–180
    recruiting via corporate blogs, 32
    showcasing via corporate blogs, 32
encyclopedia, online, 9
Engadget blog, 80, 134
Eric Mower and Associates, 182–183
etiquette, Internet, 63–78

etiquette cheat sheet, 77–78
Ettinger, Amber Lee, 201
events
    Facebook, 178
    searching for, 107
"Evolution of Dance" video, 204

F

Facebook, 171–193
    activity, 102
    advertising on, 182–183, 187–188
    applications for, 183–193
    basics, 177–183
    case studies, 182–183, 188–193
    on cell phones, 193
    chat feature, 176–177
    corporate use of, 178–193
    early years, 171–172
    employee participation in, 179–180
    events, 178
    fans, 181–183
    fictional/nonhuman profiles, 37
    friends, 67, 102, 173–179
    future of, 193
    groups, 178–183
    Inbox, 176
    networks, 176
    News Feed, 175
    Pages, 180–181
    popularity of, 12, 172
    profiles, 174–177
    promotions on, 72
    reposting tweets to, 234
    status, 175, 177
    Wall, 176
Facemash, 171
fail whale, 125, 225
FAQs (Frequently Asked Questions),
    146, 147
Fark.com, 206, 246
FastLane Blog, 34, 151
feedback. See also comments; reviews
    advantages of, 32
    managing, 34
    negative, 121–122, 136–139
    overreacting to, 136

FeedBurner, 57, 104
Fey, Tina, 201
finding content, 107
Finkelstein, Brian, 133–134
flame wars, 37
Flanagan, Mike, 140–141
Flash, 38
Flickr
    charity support, 259
    Creative Commons, 40
    DeSmogBlog, 93
    early years, 120–121
    Library of Congress images, 8
    MOO printing and, 81–82
    photo sharing with, 257–259
    success of, 12, 120
    tags, 248
    Twitter and, 227
Flickr Blog, 36
Flickr contest, 258
"Flowers for Al and Don"
        campaign, 232
focus groups, 151–152
followers, 102, 221–222, 225–236
Foremski, Matt, 11
Forrester Research, 149
Foursquare, 237
Fox, Vanessa, 58
Free Gifts, 184, 185
FreeRepublic.com, 6
Frequently Asked Questions (FAQs),
        146, 147
FriendFeed, 26–27, 59, 61, 108
friends. *See also* connections
    on blogrolls, 59
    Facebook, 67, 102, 173–179
    making, 67
    MySpace, 160, 169
    on social bookmarking sites, 250
    Twitter, 67
    viewing photos, 121
    YouTube, 212
Friendster, 156
Friend Wheel, 184

fundraising
    Obama campaign, 164–165
    with Twitter, 231–233
FunWall, 185
Furl, 245, 247

G

gadgets, 162–164
Game Neverending, 120–121
Gawker, 50
General Motors (GM), 34
GeoCities, 2, 193
Gillmor, Dan, 22
Gizmodo, 80
GM (General Motors), 34
GM FastLane Blog, 151
Gnip, 77
Godin, Seth, 101–102
Goodreads, 253
Google
    AdWords, 108, 187
    Alerts, 106, 118
    Analytics, 102, 105, 128
    Blog Search, 52, 56
    Bookmarks, 245
    Docs, 12
    FeedBurner, 104
    Local Business Center, 16–17
    Maps, 17
    Orkut, 170
    PageRank, 53–55
    Reader, 25
    searches
        caching system and, 121–122
        finding blogs with, 51–52, 64
    Trends, 54–55
    Video, 196
Gore, Al, 73
Gossip Girl, 195
grassroots support, 73
Greenberg, Dan Ackerman, 209
Green Patch app, 185–186
Gretsch Company, 166–168

groups
    on Facebook, 178–183
    focus, 151–152
    YouTube, 212–213
guerilla videos, 206–208
Guitar Hero, 207
"Guy Catches Glasses with Face"
    video, 207

H

Habitat spam incident, 235
Hacker News, 246
Hames, Matt, 182–183
Hand Maiden Fine Yarn, 127–128
Harvard Law School, 150
hash tag, 225
headlines, 43–44
Heffernan, Virginia, 11
Hijinx Comics, 92
home video, 205–206
honesty, 10–11, 72–73, 77, 209
HootSuit tool, 227
Hot Spots, 199–200
Hsieh, Tony, 228–229
Huffington Post, 6
Hughes, Chris, 171–172
Hurley, Chad, 196
Huyse, Kami Watson, 92–93
hyperlinks. *See* links
hyperlocal, 2
hypertargeting, 188

I

IceRocket, 56
images. *See also* photos
    archives of, 8
    embedding, 43, 45
    for news releases, 45
    in pitches, 81
    RSS feeds, 24
    sharing, 227, 257–259
incentives, 81–82
Indigo Books & Music, 253–254
industry bloggers. *See* corporate
    bloggers

industry experts, 32
instructional videos, 206
Internet. *See also* websites
    archives, 70–71, 121–122, 135
    democratic effect of, 4–7
    etiquette, 63–78
    longevity of online records, 70,
        121–122, 135
    as marketing tool, 16
    ubiquity of, 10
Internet Archive, 70–71,
    121–122, 135
Internet charities, 8–9
Internet insta-crisis, 133–134
Internet memes, 215, 216
IP addresses, 73
iPhone, 84, 219, 226
Iranian election protests, 222, 259
Itzkoff, Dave, 157

J

Jackson, Michael, 222
Jackson Spalding PR agency, 167–168
Jaffe, Lindsey, 165–166
Jensen, Pam, 2
JetBlue Airlines, 145
Jonathan's Blog, 36
Joomla, 30
Joseph, Kingsley, 109–111
journalists, 32, 67–70

K

Karim, Jawed, 196
keywords. *See also* tagging
    ads on, 146
    news releases, 43–44
    photos, 107
    in tags, 244, 248–250
    videos, 107, 212
Kirkpatrick, Marshall, 76–77
kirtsy, 243, 246
Kiva site, 8–9
Knit Witch blog, 51
KPBS station, 230
Krums, Janis, 219–220

Kryptonite Locks, 134–135
Kutcher, Ashton, 221, 222

L

Laipply, Judson, 204
landing pages, 146, 211–212
Last.fm site, 61
Li, Charlene, 149, 151, 256
Library of Congress, 8
LibraryThing, 253
Life Changing Box, 188–190
Lifehacker.com, 119
lifestreams, 27
Lil Green Patch app, 185–186
Lincoln Fry blog, 36
link love, 251
linkrolls, 42–43
links
    blogrolls, 42, 58–59
    blogs, 72
    importance of, 68, 69, 251
    incoming, 102
    PDF downloads, 40
    pitching products, 81
    tracking links to website, 19,
        51, 102
    video, 211–212
    between websites, 38–39
LiveJournal, 3, 160
Logic+Emotion blog, 231–232
lonelygirl15, 11, 216
Lowe New York, 188–190
Lowther, Jenn, 184–185
Ludicorp, 120–121
lululemon, 127
lurkers, 34
Lynn, Christopher, 45–46

M

Mackey, John, 73
mad cow disease, 132
Ma.gnolia, 112–113
mainstream media, 4–5
Major League Baseball, 190
Mann, Boris, 184

Marcoullier, Eric, 77
marketing. *See also* pitching products;
        social media marketing
    dashboard, 100
    goals, 15
    messages, 69
    research, 32
mashups, 7, 92, 94
mashups, RSS, 27–28
Mason, Margaret, 74–75
massively multiplayer online role-
        playing game (MMORPG),
        120–121
McDonald's, 36
McLuhan, Marshall, 202
McNeil Consumer Healthcare,
        142–144
MEC (Mountain Equipment Co-op),
        35, 191–193
media. *See also* social media
    broadcast, 5
    mainstream, 4–5
    micromedia, 220
    multimedia, 40
    one-to-many model, 5
    traditional, 4
media junket, 91–92
meet ups, 225
memes, 215, 216
Metacafe, 196
metadata, 109, 212
MetaFilter, 246
meta-YouTube, 204–205
metrics, 52–53, 99–114, 128
microblogging, 83, 175, 219–220. *See
        also* Twitter
micromedia, 220
Microsoft, 121, 148
    FrontPage, 2
    Outlook, 227
Mighty Goods, 74–75
Milligan, Andrew, 68
Miniwatts Marketing Group, 124
Miss604.com, 59
Mixx, 246

MMORPG (massively multiplayer online role-playing game), 120–121
mobile devices. *See also* cell phones
  Facebook on, 193
  popularity of, 193
  Twitter on, 226–227
MOO printing company, 81–82
Moosetopia blog, 36
Moose Tracks ice cream, 36
Morissette, Alanis, 202
Moskovitz, Dustin, 171–172
Motrin apology, 142–144, 146, 152
Mountain Equipment Co-op (MEC), 35, 191–193
MovableType, 30, 61
multimedia, 40
Munroe, Randall, 215
MySpace, 108, 155–170
MySpace Records, 156–157

N

namespace, 152
Nash, Michael, 170
NBA.com, 27–28
Neeleman, David, 145
nerd fights, 37
netiquette, 63–78
Netvibes, 25
Newmarch, Paul, 103
news. *See also* social news; stories
  citizen journalism, 5–6
  forums, 6
  independent news sites, 6
  mainstream media, 4–5
  participatory sites, 6
  releases, 43–46
  RSS feeds, 22–28
  ticker, 162–164
  TV, 4–5
  user-submitted, 240–241
News Corporation, 158, 170
NewsGator, 25
newspapers, 4–5
Newsvine site, 6, 246

niche communities, 7
Nielsen BuzzMetrics, 56
Nitobi, 241
NowPublic site, 6, 247

O

Obama, Barack, 164, 170
Obama campaign, 164–165
Obama Girl, 201
The Office, 36
OhmyNews site, 6
one-to-many media model, 5
online
  adversaries, 136
  archives, 70–71, 121–122, 135
  communities. *See* communities; crowds
  encyclopedia, 9
  identities
    reputation, 70–71
    sockpuppets, 73
    usernames, 66
  marketing map, 100–101, 104
  media page, 39
  philanthropy, 8–9
  PR campaigns, 99–114
  visibility, 15
OpenBottles, 246
OPML file, 59
  Opus Hotel's Blog, 36
originality, 203–204
Orkut, 170
Owyang, Jeremiah, 100
Oxfam America, 259

P

pagecasts, 59
Pageflakes, 59
PageRank Checker, 54
Palin, Sarah, 201
PayPerPost, 96
PDF downloads, 40
people, objectives, strategy, technology (POST), 100–101

personal blogs, 48, 49
personal profiles, 159–160
philanthropy, online, 8–9
Photobucket, 259
photos. *See also* images
    adding to blogs, 257–259
    finding, 107
    keywords, 107
    product, 40
    sharing on Twitter, 227
    sharing via Flickr, 257–259
Picheny, Matt, 189–190
Picture Mosaic, 184
pitching products, 79–97. *See also*
    social media marketing
    in comic form, 87–88
    in comments area, 84–85
    following up, 97
    getting noticed, 93–94
    incentives, 81–82
    including videos, 214
    links, 81
    tactics for, 85–91
    tips for, 80–82
    via Twitter, 83–84
    via YouTube, 86–87
    what not to do, 94–97
Platform Application Guidelines, 186
playlists, YouTube, 213–214
podcasts
    considerations, 126–127
    finding, 107
    number of downloads, 103
policies, blogging, 148–151
political stories, 243
popularity
    blogs, 49–50, 53–54, 60–61
    Google PageRank, 53–54
    subjective indications of, 60–61
Popurls.com, 26, 27
"Pork and Beans" video, 204–205
POST (people, objectives, strategy,
    technology), 100–101
posts. *See* comments
presidential election, 164–165

press
    box, blogging from, 91
    junket, 91–92
    kits, 39
    releases, 43–46, 139
prewritten scripts, 147
print advertising, 128
proactive approach, 126–127
probloggers, 48–49, 70
products
    advertising for. *See* social media
        marketing
    contests/giveaways, 191–193, 230
    coupons for, 183, 229
    demo, 126
    photos of, 40
    pitching. *See* pitching products
    recalls, 145
    reviews of. *See* reviews
    on sale, 228–229
profiles, Facebook, 174–177
programmers, 186–187

Q

QA Labs, 35
QA Podcast, 35
Quantcast rating service, 57

R

Radian6, 111
Radio Shack, 179
Regalado, Antonio, 72–73
rankings. *See also* search engine
    optimization
    blogs, 50–57
    Google PageRank, 53–54
    improving, 242–243
    links and, 50
    PageRank Checker, 54
    search engines and, 74, 251
Rapleaf, 159
RateMyProfessors.com, 122
Rather, Dan, 6
Ray-Ban campaign, 207
Raza, Ghyslain, 203

ReadWriteWeb, 76–77
Really Simple Syndication (RSS),
    22–28
RealVideo, 196
recalls, product, 145
reddit site, 6, 246, 247
redirects, 211–212
reference books, 19
Reiss, Spencer, 161
relationships, long-term, 117–118
reputation, 70–71
research, market, 32
retweets, 225
ReviewMe, 96
reviews. *See also* comments; feedback
    benefits of, 17, 68
    cultivating, 68, 81–82, 96–97
    longevity of, 121–122, 135
    negative, 121–122, 136–139
    paying for, 96–97
    positive, 17, 122
    responding to, 137–139
    ReviewMe, 96
Revver, 196
risk communication, 132–133
risks, 115–129
RobotReplay launch, 241
Rodwell, Lisa, 82
Roller Warehouse, 162–164
RSS (Really Simple Syndication),
    22–28
RSS aggregators. *See* RSS readers
RSS feeds, 22–28
    advantages of, 22
    aggregation, 26–28
    basics, 22–23
    burning, 104
    corporate news feeds, 42
    filtering, 27–28
    monitoring blog mentions, 106
    subscribing to, 24, 106
    Twitter Search, 227–228
RSS mashups, 27–28
RSS readers, 24–25, 28, 106
RSS subscribers, 57, 104
Rubel, Steve, 20, 36, 250

S

Saleem, Muhammad, 75–76, 243
sales, as metric, 16
Saturday Night Live, 201
Save the Children UK, 210
Schrute, Dwight, 36
Schweber, Arieanna, 49
Sci-Fi Channel, 91–92
Scoble, Robert, 121
scope, 10
ScreenFlow, 41
scripts, prewritten, 147
scrutinizers, 138
search engine optimization (SEO).
    See SEO
search engines
    crisis communications and, 181
    Google. *See* Google
    optimization. *See* SEO
    rankings. *See* rankings
    Technorati, 55–56
    Twitter, 227–228
    Yahoo!, 197
search results pages, 145–146
search tools, 107–108
SeaWorld San Antonio, 92–93
Second Life, 120–121
"seeding" events, 178
self-propelled video, 191–193
SEO (search engine optimization)
    blogs and, 34–35
    Facebook and, 181
    long view of, 251
    overview, 51
    video and, 197
SEODigger tool, 108
Serena Software, 180
sex, 201
sharing
    photos on blogs, 257–259
    photos via Flickr, 257–259
sharing, *continued*
    photos via Twitter, 227
    videos, 196
    widgets, 249
Sharkle, 196

Sharp Electronics Corporation, 188–190
Shirky, Clay, 5
shouts, Digg, 244
Sieling, Todd, 112–113
skins, blog, 61
Slashdot, 247
Slashdotting, 126
Small Business Brief, 247
SMS service, 168, 226
SmugMug, 259
social bookmarking
  basics, 245–249
  crowdsourced curation and, 245–251
  as indicator of success, 104, 251
  for marketing, 249–251
  online tools for, 111, 112, 247, 249
  sharing bookmarks, 245
  widgets for, 44–45
social media. *See also* media
  campaigns, 151–153
  crisis management, 131–153
  democratic aspect of, 4–7
  five fundamentals of, 4–11
  getting ready for, 21–46
  news releases, 43–46
  overview, 1–20
  pitfalls, 148–153
  preparing website for, 37–43
  success metrics, 52–53, 99–114, 128
  tagging, 212, 244, 245, 247–249
  vs. traditional media, 4
social media channels
  monitoring, 106–111
  overview, 11–13
Social Media Firehose, 109–111
social media marketing. *See also* pitching products
  alternate reality, 88–91
  banner ads, 167, 188
  benefits of, 14–15
  considerations, 16–17
  conventional tools, 39–40

via email, 82, 85–86
via Facebook, 182–183, 187–188
getting started with, 18–19
goals, 15
keywords. *See* keywords
lack of control in, 120
long-term relationships, 117–118
management buy-in, 18–19
marketing dashboard, 100
marketing goals, 15
marketing messages, 69
market research, 32
motivating colleagues, 19
no response, 116
overview, 13–16
peer pressure, 19
print, 128
proactive approach, 126–127
resources for, 17
risks of, 115–129
on search results pages, 145–146
social bookmarking and, 249–251
social media resource page, 39
staying engaged, 122–123
success metrics, 18, 52–53, 99–114, 128
tagging. *See* tagging
time investment in, 18
too much success, 125–126
via video. *See* video marketing
viral, 13–14, 161–162
word-of-mouth, 13–14
via YouTube, 197–217
social media masters, 74–77
social media resource page, 39, 42–43
social media spammers, 71–72
social media tools, 10, 105–111
social network activity, 102
social networks. *See also specific social networks*
  build-your-own, 251–254
  making friends, 67
  monitoring blog mentions, 108
  rise of, 3–4
social news, 240–251, 259. *See also* news; stories

social news sites
  becoming trusted contributor on,
    242–244
  bookmarking and, 259
  building buzz, 242–244
  effect on marketing, 241–242
  freedom of, 6
  listed, 246–247
  niche, 246–247
  popularity of, 241
  RSS feeds. *See* RSS feeds
  search engine optimization
    and, 251
  stories. *See* stories
  top 10 lists, 242
  visitors from, 241–242
  voting principle, 28
  wisdom of crowds, 240–244
Social Signal, 179
sockpuppeting, 72–73
Solis, Brian, 12, 13
spam blogs, 108–109
spam bots, 235
spammers
  email, 71, 82–83
  MySpace, 169
  social media, 71–72
  Twitter, 235
Spears, Britney, 222
Sphinn, 243, 247
spin, 69–70
sponsored conversations, 96–97
spreadsheets, 52–53
SpyFu tool, 108
Stars and Stinkers campaign, 94, 163
"Star Wars Kid," 203
stealth videos, 206–208
Storey, Duane, 221
stories
  buried, 65, 242
  commenting on, 244
  controversial, 243
  cute and cuddly subject matter, 243
  "digging," 75, 240, 243
  guidelines for, 242–243
  political, 243

popular, 65, 240
technology innovation, 242–243
tutorials, 243
user-submitted, 240–241
voting for, 240–244
StumbleUpon, 78, 104, 242, 246, 247
subscribers, 57, 104
success metrics, 52–53, 99–114, 128
Sumo Lounge International, 68
Sun Microsystems, 36, 149–150
SuperPoke, 185
Super Wall, 184, 185
Sweet Spots video contest, 191–193
Syfy channel, 91–92
syndication, 22

T

tagging. *See also* keywords
  social media, 212, 244, 245,
    247–249
  videos, 212
  websites, 250–251
Tatango, 168–169
TechCrunch, 125, 126
technical support, 32
technology innovation stories,
  242–243
Technorati, 55–56
Techrigy, 111
Teenwag, 247
ThoughtFarmer, 88–91, 257
TinyURL, 235
Tip'd, 247
Tocci, Donna, 134–135
topical blogs, 48–49
Toyota Prius Facebook page, 180
traditional media, 4
traffic spikes, 126
transparency, 10–11, 67–68, 209
Trapani, Gina, 119
Tribe.com, 156
tr.im URL shortener, 227
TripAdvisor, 136–138
trolls/trolling, 136
Trottier, Monique, 252, 253

TubeMogul, 199
Tubetastic campaign, 89–91
tutorials, 243
TV news, 4–5
TweetDeck, 226, 227
Tweetie, 226
TweetLater service, 233
tweets, 220, 224–236
tweetups, 225
twhirl, 226
TwInbox, 227
TwitPic.com, 227
Twitter, 219–237
    account name, 222–224
    avatar, 224
    bio, 224
    blocking users, 224
    breaking news and, 222
    Carnival Cruise Lines, 117
    on cell phones, 226–227
    click-through rates, 233
    considerations, 3, 61
    contests/giveaways on, 230
    corporate presence on, 227–231
    creating gimmicks around, 231
    as crisis communication tool, 230
    customer support via, 230
    direct messages, 224
    fail whale, 125, 225
    followers, 102, 221–222, 225–236
    friends, 67
    getting started with, 222–227
    hash tag, 225
    importance of context, 235
    insta-fundraising with, 231–233
    overview, 219–222
    pitching via, 83–84
    popularity of, 220
    private conversations and, 234–235
    providing value, 228–231
    reposting tweets to Facebook, 234
    sharing photos on, 227
    sins, 233–236
    spam bots and, 235
    status text box, 223, 231
    staying on topic, 234
    terminology, 224–225
    Trending Topics, 222, 235
    tweets, 220, 224–236
    unacceptable behavior on, 233–236
TwitterBerry, 227
TwitterFone, 125–126
Twitterrific, 226
Twitter Search, 227–228
Tylenol, 132

U

Universal Resource Locators (URLs),
    38–39, 68
The Unofficial Apple Blog, 48
Upcoming.org, 12, 102, 116
URLs (Universal Resource Locators),
    38–39, 68
URL shorteners, 225, 227, 235
US Airways, 219–220
US presidential election, 164–165
Usenet, 2
usernames, 66, 210, 226, 236
users, anonymous, 66

V

Vancity credit union, 35
Video Annotations feature, 214–215
video blogs, 195
video marketing, 195–217. *See also*
    videos; YouTube
    advantages of, 197–198
    articulating message, 201
    challenges, 198
    element of surprise, 202–203
    humor, 205–206
    links, 211–212
    measuring results, 198–200
    originality, 203–204
    overview, 195–197
    pitches, 86–87
    showcasing extraordinary skills, 204
    tips for successful videos, 200–206
    video sharing sites, 196

video responses, 212
videos
    annotating, 214–215
    "Bike Hero," 207
    blooper, 202–203
    brevity, 204–205
    Burger King, 144–145
    categories, 212
    "Cell Phone Popcorn," 206–207
    featuring in other venues, 214
    finding, 107
    guerilla, 206–208
    "Guy Catches Glasses with
        Face," 207
    home, 205–206
    honesty in, 209
    Hot Spots, 199–200
    humor, 205–206
    including in pitches, 214
    instant fame vs. ongoing success,
        208–209
    instructional, 206
    keywords, 107, 212
    links, 211–212
    marketing with. *See* video
        marketing
    news releases, 45
    number of views, 103, 199
    originality, 203–204
    recent/topical, 201
    self-propelled, 191–193
    stealth, 206–208
    tagging, 212
    titles, 211
    transparency in, 209
    viral, 203, 206–209
    webisodes, 205
    "Will It Blend?", 203, 209, 217
    YouTube. *See* YouTube
Vidmetrix, 199
Vimeo, 196
viral marketing, 13–14, 161–162
viral videos, 203, 206–209
visitors, website, 101–106
voting principle, 28

W

Ward, Brad J., 152
Warner Music, 170
Washington Capitals, 91
Web 2.0, 3, 4, 26, 28
web analytics, 102, 105–106
Weber Shandwick PR agency,
    140–141
webisodes, 205
web marketing. *See* marketing
web monitoring, 106–111
websites. *See also* blogs; Internet
    brochure, 38
    early years, 2–3
    landing pages, 146, 211–212
    links. *See* links
    popularity of, 51
    preparing for social media, 37–43
    ranking. *See* rankings
    redirects, 211–212
    RSS feeds. *See* RSS feeds
    tagging, 250–251
    visitors to, 101–106
Webtrends, 102
Weetman, George, 191–193
Weezer, 204–205
Whole Foods, 73, 224
whuffie, 71
widgets, 57, 162–164, 249.
        See also apps
wiki pages (wikis), 9, 102–103, 108
Wikipedia
    Charlene Li on, 256–257
    contributions, 102–103
    described, 9
    editing, 255–256
    guidelines for, 255–256
    importance of, 257
    interacting with, 256–257
    nerd fights, 257
    notability, 255
    overview, 254–257
    popularity of, 254–255
    size of, 254
    spam and, 72
    turf wars, 257

Wild Oats, 73
Williams, Evan, 220
"Will It Blend?" video, 203, 209, 217
Wired magazine, 119
wire services, 45–46
WordHampton PR agency, 165–166
word-of-mouth marketing, 13–14
WordPress, 30, 61
World Wide Web, 2–3

X

Xanga, 156
xkcd, 215

Y

Yahoo! Buzz, 242, 243, 247
Yahoo! Pipes, 28, 109
Yahoo! search engine, 197
Yankovic, "Weird Al," 164
Yarn Harlot, 51
YouTube. *See also* video; video
    marketing
  annotating video, 214–215
  Audio Preview button, 214
  comments, 214
  considerations, 41

customizing account, 210
early years, 196–197
friends, 212
groups, 212–213
marketing via, 197–217
membership, 212
meta-YouTube, 204–205
pitches via, 86–87
playlists, 213–214
popularity of, 12, 195–197
RSS feeds, 26
Sweet Spots video contest, 191–193
tips for successful videos, 200–206
username, 210
video responses, 212
video titles, 211
YouTube Comment Snob plug-in, 214
YouTube Insight, 199

Z

Zappos, 228–229
Zeller, Tom, 11
Zoomii, 253
Zooomr, 259
Zuckerberg, Mark, 138, 171–172

Friends With Benefits is set in Adobe Garamond Pro. It was printed and bound at Malloy Incorporated in Ann Arbor, Michigan. The paper is Glatfelter Spring Forge 60# Smooth Eggshell, which is certified by the Sustainable Forestry Initiative (SFI).

Visit *http://www.nostarch.com/friends_benefits.htm* for updates, errata, and other information.

ABOUT THE AUTHORS

Darren Barefoot and Julie Szabo are the co-founders of Capulet Communications, a marketing agency based in Vancouver, BC, Canada. Since 2003, Capulet has been helping companies—from startups to national retailers—understand and engage with today's and tomorrow's Web.

Darren is a writer, marketer, technologist, and professional speaker. He speaks regularly about marketing and Web 2.0, and has been quoted as an expert on social media on the CBC, BBC, in *Wired*, the *Wall Street Journal*, and dozens of other magazines, and TV and radio programs. Julie has worked as a writer, marketer, and publicist for all kinds of companies—from Vancouver's largest live theater to Ireland's smallest startups. Darren and Julie are co-founders of Northern Voice, a personal social media conference held in Vancouver, BC.

Darren and Julie love to travel and live abroad. They've operated Capulet Communications from three continents over the last six years. In fact, *Friends With Benefits* was written in six countries. They are also married. To each other.